Virgin  rock yearbook 94/95

Virgin rock yearbook 94/95

Carlsberg

edited by **tony horkins**

Virgin

First published in Great Britain in 1994 by
Virgin Books
an imprint of Virgin Publishing Ltd
332 Ladbroke Grove
London W10 5AH

A catalogue record for this book is available from the
British Library

ISBN 0 86369 823 9

Produced by **Cooling Brown**
9-11 High Street
Hampton, Middlesex TW12 2SA
for Virgin Publishing Ltd

Editor: Tony Horkins
Editorial Manager: James Harrison
Design: Arthur Brown
Concept design: Mark Norton at 4i, Sue Rawkins
Picture Research: Jenny Kirby, Sharon Mew
Computer make-up: Peter Cooling
Production: Rupert Wheeler
Colour reproduction: Wellmak Ltd, Hong Kong

Printed and bound in Great Britain
by BPC Paulton Books Limited

for Virgin Publishing
Publisher: Philip Dodd
Editor: Carolyn Price

Contributors:
The Year In Review: Nick Duerden
Critics' A-Z: Tom Doyle
Off The Record: Graeme Kay
Listings: Lisa Blakebrough
Acts/Genres of the year: Phil Alexander,
Tom Doyle, Jim Irvin, Cliff Jones, Graeme Kay,
Paul Lester, John Masouri, Andrew Mueller,
Caitlin Moran, Sylvia Patterson, Andy Pemberton,
Peter Paphides, Chris Roberts, David Sinclair,
Paul Trynka and Jon Wilde

Virgin 1215 presenters:
Nick Abbot, Jonathan Coleman, Graham Dene,
Gary Davies, Gary King, Wendy Lloyd,
Richard Skinner, NJ Williams, Russ Williams

**special thanks to Howard Pearce for
supplying the birth dates**

the photographers:
Aki / Retna 22
Andy Cameron 70
Andrew Catlin 21bl
D-Clarke / Retna 15b
Danny Clinche 9t
Gavin Evans 57
Dean Freeman 25b
Steve Gullick 19br
Jon Hall 2
Michael Halsbad 11t
Liam Hill / Retna 23bl
Steve Jennings 28t
Lisa Johnson 56
Youri Lenquette 47b
Kip Lott 58
Michael Malfer / Retna 28b
Ari Marcopoulos 29b
Michael Melia / Retna 7, 27bl
Tony Mottram / Retna 15t, 30
Frank Noon
Dennis O'Regan 32, 42
Petshop Boys Partnership 13t
Valerie Phillips
Neil Preston / Retna 8
Michael Putland / Retna 10, 27br
Alan Reck 68
Bill Reitzell 61t/b
Retna 20
M. Rosenburg 46
Steve Schapiro 60
Tom Sheehan 11b, 13b
Ed Sirrs / Retna 16
Pennie Smith 48
Amelia Stein 40
Stephen Sweet 6
David Titlow / Retna 18
Lawrence Watson 36
Kevin Westenberg 9b, 34, 69t
Zanna 35b
Fingus Costello & Jon Hall
(Carlsberg Festivals feature)

the record labels:
4AD
A & M Records
Arista
Atlantic
Carlton
Chrysalis
Circa Records
Columbia
Eastwest
EMI Records
Epic
Food
Geffen
Greensleeves Records
Hut
Imago
Island
London
Maverick
MCA
Motown
Music For Nations
Mute
Nude
Parlophone
Phonogram
Polygram Video
Polydor
RCA
Reprise
SBK Records
Silvertone Records
Sire
UK Records
Virgin Records
Vision Video Ltd
Warner Bros
Warner Home Video
WEA

Front cover (clockwise from top left): Crowded House, Cranberries,
Bjork, Blur / Back cover (clockwise from top left): Phoenix Festival,
Tori Amos, Primal Scream

contents
contents contents contents contents contents

SECTION 1

the year in review 6
a look at the year in music
news, views and comments
month-by-month

SECTION 2

acts of the year 32
blur 34
cranberries 36
pink floyd 38
bjork 40
crowded house 42
paul weller 44
tori amos 46
primal scream 48

carlsberg festivals 50

the year in... 54
rock 54
heavy rock 56
country 58
blues 60
indie 62
dance 64
pop 66
reggae 68

SECTION 3

**on the record:
the critics' a-z 70**
a year's worth of album
releases... and what the
critics thought

off the record: 92
books, video, film, tv, awards

SECTION 4

charting the year 102
UK and US album and singles
positions

inside information 130
fully revised industry reference

record companies & labels 130
music publishers 132
artist management 134
music solicitors 135
publicists & pluggers/
  ticket agencies/
  cassette duplication 136
newspapers & magazines/
  trade & professional
  organisations 137
venues 138
london venues 139
recording studios 140
rehearsal studios 142
pa & equipment hire 143

It's only been 12 months, but this year's Virgin Carlsberg Rock Yearbook catalogues an overwhelming amount of change. Just one year has seen them come (Oasis, Blur, Cranberries), return (Floyd, Stones, Weller) and, sadly, go (Nirvana, Wonder Stuff, the original Suede). And this 94/95 edition keeps track of all the highs and lows: *the critics' A-Z* revisits the reviews of every major LP release from September 93 to August 94; *the year in review* re-tells the headline stories of every month; and the country's best rock writers – and Virgin 1215 djs – offer their opinions on the acts and styles that have shaped the year.

For fact freaks, there's a year of US and UK singles and album charts, a completely revised, indispensable, reference section, as well as a trip through the long hot summer of festivals.

So sit back and enjoy the rock and roll year, Virgin style. Twelve months never sounded so interesting...

tony horkins
(editor)

snippets

Mojo magazine is launched, initially a 10 issues a year magazine "for anyone who loves rock'n'roll". **Bob Dylan** and **John Lennon** adorn the cover, Dylan smoking, Lennon clapping, and the magazine itself doing a bit of both.

The Rolling Stones are rumoured to be writing and rehearsing new material in a farm house in Dublin. Why a farm house? They want to capture a "fucking-around" spirit, and where better than a farm house...?

"One of my favourite memories is driving through New York in a white limousine. It was like Jim'll Fix It." Radiohead's Thom on the sweet stuff of success.

"The age of consent thing has never stopped me from having sex with other people - since I was 13. Why should I have to wait until I'm 21 to have sex? It's complete discrimination." **Suede**'s drummer Simon Gilbert on the age of consent for gay men.

Jamiroquai, Stevie Wonder with a lighter hue, plays a special show in Denmark, in protest of whale culling. It is estimated that up to 1500 whales are slaughtered by the Danish government each year.

Frankie Goes To Hollywood experience some kind of comeback as WEA release their entire back catalogue, Greatest Hits and everything, starting with *Relax*, which this time Radio One deign to play.

US 3 ride high in the charts with the seductive *Cantaloop*, a song which has everyone craving for drumsticks, as the original version also features on the latest Kentucky Fried Chicken ad.

Meat Loaf begins his reign atop the UK album chart with the monster *Bat Out Of Hell II - Back Into Hell*. And stays there. And stays there.

Pearl Jam grace the cover of *Melody Maker*, with the magazine pondering: "Can Eddie Vedder save the world?" The answer lies somewhere in the negative. Probably.

"Rape me, my friend, rape me again/Waste me, taste me, my friend." **Nirvana**'s *Rape Me* comes under criticism for its contentious lyrics.

The Wonder Stuff release what will become their fourth and final studio album in *Construction For The Modern Idiot*. Singer Miles wears T-shirt emblazoned with the legend *Idiot*, which some people find perfectly appropriate.

"I think any kinda quick success of the kind we had is inevitably bound to provoke some degree of contempt or hostility. I end up having a lot of difficulties with it myself." **Pearl Jam**'s Eddie Vedder on the many vagaries of success.

October**Diary**

1 Nirvana's *In Utero* surprises no-one by crashing in at Number One in the LP charts.

★

4 Alice In Chains, second division grunge stars, play a stomping live show in an attempt to win promotion into the big league.

★

The Mission begin a week of live dates all around London proving, much to many people's dismay, that goths are alive and, um, well.

★

Kate Bush pirouettes back into national consciousness with her new album, *The Red Shoes*, her first recorded work since 1990.

★

7 The Lemonheads, fronted by top slacker 'babe' Evan Dando, begin a national tour to coincide with the release of their new LP, *Come On Feel The Lemonheads*. Soul Asylum, fronted by another top slacker 'babe' Dave Pirner, support on four dates.

★

Spin Doctors fever! The New York band, having sold several million copies of their *Pocket Full Of Kryptonite* album worldwide, play three sold-out nights at the Brixton Academy.

★

9 Virgin 1215 gets exclusive first radioplay of Counting Crows' *Omaha* ("recorded in the living room of our big house in LA" as the CD blurb goes.)

11 The Other Two, aka New Order's Stephen and Gillian, release three formats and seven mixes of their single *Selfish*.

★

Spiritualized, hypnotic, drug-addled trance experts, release their new single, *Electric Mainline*, a hypnotic, drug-addled trance thing.

★

18 *Vs*, Pearl Jam's second album, is released, and in America becomes the fastest selling album of all time.

★

Crowded House, with a little help from mega producer Youth, release their new album, *Together Alone*, their most accomplished work to date.

★

18 PJ Harvey release a mini-album of demos, titled *Four Track Demos*. It proves to be her most abrasive and compelling work to date.

★

25 Morrissey, a name now synonymous with controversy, releases his new single *The More You Ignore Me, The Closer I Get*.

★

27 Soul Asylum, whose star is now shining very brightly indeed, play a sold-out show at London's Astoria. Singer Dave Pirner, who is dating Winona Ryder and never washes his hair, becomes an unlikely sex symbol.

▼ *Soul Asylum*

13th Paul Simon (1941) • 14th Cliff Richard (1940). Justin Hayward (1946) • 18th Chuck Berry (1926) • 21st Julian Cope (1957) • 31st Johnny Marr (1963)

November

Pearl Jam – Vs

Right now, Pearl Jam are America's biggest band. They've shifted more records than Nirvana, sold more concert tickets than Madonna, and won more MTV awards than anyone else. To call them famous, successful and absolutely bloody huge is to undersell them greatly. And their reaction? They hate the pressure and look this close to cracking under the strain. And so they release Vs, an album with a sheep's face on the cover. Go figure ...

album of the month

"This is a raw, festering fucking wound of an album, a brilliant, relentless passion play. It's all we hoped for and one hell of a lot more than many suspected Pearl Jam capable of." **Melody Maker**

"Whether *Vs* will prove a transitional platter, a peephole on a band in the throes of re-invention, or a half-hearted experiment to diss their critics, the fact remains that it's not a great record." **NME**

"The bravely diverse unformulaic follow-up to the mega-unit shifting *Ten* sees Eddie and co displaying a softer musical side. Veddy good." **Sky**

"A monster of an album - the kind that sets standards and spawns imitators for years to come." **Billboard**

"One day you'll be able to put together the band of your choice by computer without leaving the comfort of your own bedroom. Until that time, however, we'll have to make do with Pearl Jam, whose seriousness and talent allow them to be almost any band of your choice so long as they're a mixture of Led Zeppelin and REM." **Time Out**

"After such a classic album debut, most other new bands would not have been able to get their second effort to meet the same standards. Pearl Jam have done it. Buy this album – it really grows on you." **Hot Press**

"This is the problem with grunge. After two years it's all starting to sound samey. Perhaps when it's all over, Pearl Jam will appreciate that they come across much better on their winsome acoustic numbers. The new REM maybe." **Sunday Telegraph**

"Even the awkward moments here signal creative growth – occasional misfires are part of the process. If Pearl Jam continue like this, they probably won't burn out or fade away." **Details**

"Pearl Jam are explosive. Few American bands have arrived more clearly talented than this one did with *Ten*; and *Vs* tops even that debut." **Rolling Stone**

"The follow-up album that will keep their peers looking on in open-mouthed awe." **Kerrang!**

LIVE

At Orb gigs, the strobe lighting is as much a hallucinogenic as the drugs. At Orb gigs, everything you know is wrong. And at Orb gigs, nothing is as it seems. "As The Orb journey further into the fourth dimension, several members of the audience enter the fifth," *Melody Maker* noted, continuing that "... for the first 30 minutes, there is no semblance of a groove. Self-indulgent? Abso-fucking-lutely. The best bands always are." *NME*, however, found it all a little too abstract. "There's no ambience, no rave, no trance, no dance, no higher planes and, ultimately, no point."

Birthdays: 5th Art Garfunkel (1941), Bryan Adams (1959) • 7th Joni Mitchell (1943) • 8th Bonnie Raitt (1949) • 12th Neil Young (1945) • 18th Kim Wilde (1960), Joe Walsh (1947) •

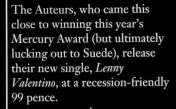

snippets

New Order headline the Reading Festival amid rumours that this is to be their last ever performance before bowing out for good. The band neither confirm or deny this, either before, during or after the show.

Pet Shop Boys bounce back with *Very*, a new album ensconced in a Lego-like CD case. "The first PSB album with an alarming built-in capability to hug its listener to death," say *Vox*. ▶

It's now five years since the **Stone Roses** released their classic, legendary, ace etc, debut album and *Mojo*, for one, commemorate the occasion. Tony Wilson, Factory Records' founder, says "Great bands are great bands. I don't think The Roses have lost it; that's their way."

Bob Mould, not so fresh from an ear-splitting tour with his band **Sugar**, is said to be working on a children's book and album as "therapy".

Kate Bush, a woman who makes a full-length film to accompany the release of her album, *The Red Shoes*, stars in it, dances in it and directs it, informs us straight-faced that she "never wanted to be famous".

Courtney Love rubs shoulders with Sinead O'Connor and offers her a quick feed of her baby Frances Bean's milk. Sinead, however, declines politely.

The Spin Doctors show no sign of slowing down, their album now topping four

million sales. The Great British Public love 'em, the critics, however, aren't quite so keen. "There is something, frankly, Not Quite Right About Them," decide *Mojo*.

William S Burroughs, infamous author of *Naked Lunch*, teams up with **Disposable Heroes Of Hiphoprisy** for their new concept album.

"I've still not learnt to master that Mariah Carey dog-whistle." The UK's own Mariah Carey, **Lisa Stansfield**, with claws drawn.

Chief **Lemonhead**, Evan Dando, comes under increasing pressure as his fame increases. He drinks, he drops out, he drugs up. Plenty. "I've been feeling strange..." he admits.

Michael Jackson has his multi-million-dollar sponsorship deal with Pepsi Cola cancelled in the light of child abuse allegations made against him last month.

1 Elastica, fronted by the girlfriend of Blur's Damon, Justine Frishman, release their debut single, *Stutter*, a song about brewers' droop, to ecstatic reviews.

★

Red House Painters release their third album, eponymously- titled, proving that you can carve a career out of musical miserabilism.

★

2 Brian Wilson gives a rare TV interview, reminiscing about his experiences with a Theremin - the very first electronic synthesiser.

★

Christy Moore, second only to Van The Man in the godlike stakes in Irish rockin' stroll, begins the first of three nights at the Royal Albert Hall, bodhran in hand.

★

13 Aussie grave-robbing carries on apace, this time with the Australian Doors, who add yet more live dates due, apparently, to exceptional public demand.

★

15 Suede, the cream of the milk-cart in '93, release *Love And Poison*, a live video capturing the band in full swaggering effect at London's Brixton Academy. ▼

The Auteurs, who came this close to winning this year's Mercury Award (but ultimately lucking out to Suede), release their new single, *Lenny Valentino*, at a recession-friendly 99 pence.

★

Tom Waits, the Charles Bukowski of the music world, releases what is widely regarded as the devilishly good *The Black Rider*.

★

Eurythmics, no longer a musical item, have a mammoth live album out today. 22 tracks recorded around the world, lots of Annie, lots of Dave, lots of applause.

★

The nation strolls down Reminiscence Avenue as all seven Smiths albums are re-issued. A light that never goes out, evidently.

★

22 Bjork brings half of New York to a standstill as she films the video to *Big Time Sensuality* on the city's streets.

★

"The Beavis And Butthead Experience" becomes frightening reality in the shape of a compilation album. Contributions from Red Hot Chili Peppers, Run DMC and Nirvana, who give us *I Hate Myself And I Want To Die*.

★

The Charlatans' Tim Burgess and St Etienne's Sarah Cracknell entwine bodies and souls for an indie Xmas single, *I Was Born On Christmas Day*.

★

27 The Orb play an all-nighter at the Brixton Academy, confirming their position as one of the country's favourite live bands.

★

29 Guns N' Roses release *The Spaghetti Incident?*, an album of "punk" covers.

* 21st Jim Brown (1957) * 22nd Tina Weymouth (1950) * 23rd Bruce Hornby (1954) * 26th Tina Turner (1938) * 29th John Mayall (1943) * 30th Billy Idol (1955)

FRANK'S FINALE

December 4, 1993, Frank Zappa, often acclaimed as one of the most important figures in Rock, dies after a two-year battle with prostate cancer, age 52. Obituaries hail him as a genuine enigma, with *Melody Maker* remembering him as a man "on the forefront of the radically unusual."

FULL MOON, DIRTY HEARTS

INXS

December

album of the month

INXS – *Full Moon, Dirty Hearts*

INXS have boots that glitter with gold. They have a singer called Michael who has a girlfriend called Helena, both of whom embody just about everybody's notion and fantasy of sex. But with this Xmas release, Australia's biggest musical export get all experimental. Full Moon, Dirty Hearts *finds INXS trying to "do a U2", with disappointing results...*

"The problem is this: desperate as INXS are to create a mood of U2-like Euro-chic, they are unable write either a decent lyric or a song that resists the temptation to be over-blown." **NME**

"It sounds brilliant. Wouldn't it be great if more rock stars behaved like INXS and simply got on with enjoying the job they're paid such good money to do?" **The Times**

"So, no startling self-reinvention á la U2. (This) is a tenth LP by a band in their 17th year, and sounds like it." **Melody Maker**

"The band succeed in promoting an atmosphere of been there, done that, thanks for all the merchandise revenue." **Select**

"INXS sound impressive without signifying anything beyond bar-band credentials and Michael Hutchence's convincing impersonation of a rock star." **Vox**

"Before going back to their roots, perhaps INXS should've remembered that they really weren't that great in the early days." **Time Out**

Having finally confined the man to life on the *Celebrity Squares* treadmill, the public gets duped into making a hit out of Meatloaf's latest musical effort. The solo albums didn't do much, but call it *Bat Out Of Hell II – Back To Hell*, and it's hit city and back on the road. "This year, we've yawned through shows by U2, Guns N' Roses, Bon Jovi, and two dozen hipper-than-thou hopefuls, and Meat Loaf beats them all for tunes, sincerity and sheer visceral thrills. No contest." Opined *NME*. *Melody Maker*, similarly, gushes love for the man. "Meat's not a difficult chap to appreciate. Something this pure and unsoiled cannot be faulted... it is therefore absolutely wonderful." Enough to make a vegan froth at the mouth with carnivorous instincts.

LIVE

Birthdays: 2nd Michael Macdonald (1952) • 3rd Ozzie Osbourne (1948) • 6th Ben Watt (1962) • 7th Tom Waits (1949) • 8th Sinead O' Connor (1966) Jim Morrison (1943) •

snippets

End of year polls reveal **Bjork**'s *Debut* album as everybody's favourite goody bag of aural delights. She becomes a national hero in her native Iceland and is revered by everyone. "I'm a proud bastard," she says.

Guns N' Roses pay their former drummer Stephen Adler $2.5m in an out-of-court settlement. Adler brought the suit against the band, claiming that he had not received payment for his contribution to the band's success.

*Marie Lamour, a thirtysomething American woman from Massachusetts, has something of an identity crisis and passes herself off as **Madonna** for six months before being exposed. In that time, she fooled charities, film crews and even her own bodyguards.*

Radiohead singer Thom Yorke may make impeccably good music, but when it comes to movies, he proves to possess fairly naff taste. He cites *Arthur* as his favourite ever movie!

"Bono's so absorbed in the idea of himself as almost messianic, and then he realises he looks a complete prat." The Cure's **Robert Smith**, aged 30-plus, dressed in out-sized jumpers, fat trainers, the hairstyle of a toilet brush (used) and lipstick.

2 Pac Shakur, US rap star, is arrested and charged with shooting two off-duty policemen in a gun battle over a traffic dispute. As you do.

The K Foundation, formally the KLF, award sculptor Rachel Whiteread £31,500 (they initially intended £40,000, but £8,500 was stolen!) for being voted the worst artist of the year in a poll they'd conducted via newspaper ads. She also won the Turner Prize for the best work, scooping £20,000.

The scandal over **Michael Jackson**'s alleged child abuse intensifies. All musical activities come to a halt as the investigation continues and escalates.

"The more you fuck with me the more I'm gonna do it! If the women would shut up I'd stop making records about them, but as long as I know I'm gonna bother you I'm gonna bother you! That is how I am!" **Ice T**, a man who lives on the opposite side of town to words like sensitive, caring and understanding.

"You can see it in fucking shopping malls in middle America now, flares and platforms. Six years ago everyone was laughing at me, saying what an asshole I was." **Lenny Kravitz**, dedicated leader of fashion, and no mistake.

Marky Mark releases a workout video featuring the neanderthal rapper himself, barechested and bulging, and surrounded by scantilyclad women, similarly bulging in all the right places.

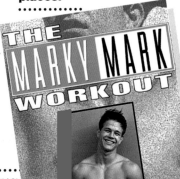

December**Diary**

▲ Oasis

1 John Lydon's bold teaming up with dance gods Leftfield on *Open Up* gives him his first ever Number One independent single and his gloating mug graces the *NME* cover.

★

4 Oasis, new Creation signings, play a one-off show at the Warwick University, and give the kind of performance that has critics not only calling them The New Stone Roses, but also suggesting that 1994 will belong to them.

★

6 Elton John releases an album called *Duets*, an album of, aptly enough, duets with lots of famous stars. Kiki Dee, for one.

8 The The, fronted by that most cerebral of menfolk, Matt Johnson, embark on a national tour, coinciding with the release of a live video, *From Dusk Til Dawn*.

★

10 *CB4*, a spoof rap movie, opens, hoping to do for hip hop what *This Is Spinal Tap* did for rock. Subsequent hindsight reveals it failed.

★

15 Ice T brings his Body Count to the UK for a national jaunt.

★

Howard Jones (who he?) plops back into a suitably dim limelight with a live London date. Only mid-80s keyboard fanatics attend.

18 Latoya Jackson, brother of Michael, appears on TV, discussing her sibling's child abuse allegations and says, "I cannot and will not be a silent collaborator of his crimes against small children. I'm a victim too, I know these kiddies will be scarred for life."

★

Gin Blossom's former guitarist, Douglas Hopkins, is found dead in Arizona. Newspaper reports say he put a hand-gun into his mouth and blew his head off.

★

19 Mr Blobby is confirmed as this year's Christmas No 1 single. Blobby, blobby, blobby... blimey!

★

25 Christmas greetings, like respect, are due.

▼ Ice T

▶ *Kristin Hersh, having temporarily thrown out her muse, releases a solo album of quite staggering depth this month. Hips And Makers is ace, quite ace. A decidedly singular kind of songwriter, Hersh writes from pain, torture and anguish. Far from easy listening maybe, but exquisite stuff nonetheless. And the low-key tour that accompanying its release has the critics reaching for the thesaurus and the audience for their hankies. "Kristin Hersh sits hunched with her guitar cradled in her arms as if she wants to bury herself in its frame. And, as you watch her locked in to some private groove, you know that some people go beyond the parameters of the here and now. I go home and cry like a baby," gushed Melody Maker. "Having gratefully nudged Kristen so far up the deification ladder, you're almost convinced there's a halo hovering above her head," remarked NME. Wow.*

January

album of the month

Tori Amos –
Under The Pink

Tori Amos, the woman who made all things weird into all things wonderful with her 1991 debut LP Little Earthquakes, *is the picture of 90s femininity. Here is a woman into mental penetration, into confronting fears and phobias, and setting them all to music. And here is a woman with a successful second album on her hands ...*

"Twisting and turning, soaring and swooping, ebbing, flowing, coming, going: it's all in a minute or two's work for Tori Amos, a singer whose command of the histrionic gesture is such that, in full flight, she can make Meat Loaf sound about as animated as Chris Rea." **The Times**

"In times past, Women With Weird Ideas were called witches and burned at the stake; these days they are more likely to be given a recording contract. You feel she is just being weird because it is easier and more fun than being normal. But for the most part, *Under The Pink* is a good, odd record." **Daily Telegraph**

"Sometimes reminiscent of the startlingly unhinged quality of Kate Bush, Tori's vocals are supremely powerful, channelling tides of emotion towards the listener with unrelenting force." **Time Out**

"*Under The Pink* is chock full of the emotional twists and turns that are Amos's stock-in-trade. She's exploring a rich vein in taking a long hard look at the relationship between women and at what lies under the coquetry of a certain kind of femininity." **Q**

"To Tori's credit her themes of woman-as-victim-or-not are considered enough to transcend monochrome platitudes, and they acknowledge that there's more to relationships than Punch And Judy." **Melody Maker**

"Where once less was more, *Under The Pink* finds Amos floundering in hopelessly complex arrangements... throughout, misguided ambition clouds vision." **Vox**

"All told, *Under The Pink* is small but likeably formed; ideal for those herbal-tea moments." **The Guardian**

Birthdays: 3rd Steve Stills (1945)• 8th David Bowie (1947) • 9th Jimmy Page (1944) • 10th Rod Stewart (1945), Donald Fagen (1948) • 13th Graham Suggs McPherson (1961)

snippets

The B-52s' singer Kate Pierson faces a year's imprisonment and a $5000 fine after being arrested at an anti-fur demonstration inside the New York offices of *Vogue* magazine.

"... Bodies of energy breaking to get free, kind of like verbal vomiting." **Kristin Hersh** describes her new solo album, *Hips And Makers*.

Black Crowes' singer Chris Robinson becomes a super-waif supermodel for a *Sky* magazine fashion shoot in LA, photographed in cool black and white and draped over his girlfriend, Lala.

"I used to put out information to explain that it was the music that was important, not the clothes of morality the media dressed us up in. We've learnt that lesson. Now we put out disinformation." Born-again **Bono**, *aka The Fly, aka MacPhisto.*

"Famous people are the ultimate star fuckers, which is endearing in a way because it makes them human. Fame is indiscriminate, but once you're in the club it doesn't matter how you got there." **INXS'** Michael Hutchence, very definitely famous, and in the club, so to speak.

Status Quo celebrate the publication of their autobiography, and are 'honoured' with Royal Doulton mugs of their, um, mugs. £90 each!

"I don't think we're fundamentally unmanly. All you have to do is come and watch us live. We're about sexuality, power and emotion." Brett Anderson on the bulging machismo that is Suede.

The **Bee Gees**' label, Polydor, unveil plans to place 45ft high advertising hordings on the Battersea Power Station chimneys, to celebrate the toothsome trio's 30th anniversary. The plans, however, are scuppered by the local council. Phew!

Matt Johnson, **The The** frontman, enters into a war of words with **The Auteurs'** Luke Haines after a major bust-up on tour last month. "I knew we should have booked Mr Blobby," says Matt. Now now, children.

Michael Jackson appears on TV claiming his innocence over the child abuse allegations and talks of his addiction to pain killers. "Don't treat me like a criminal," he begs, "because I am innocent."

Jim Martin, **Faith No More**'s guitarist, has been sacked by the band. Musical differences are cited. Ah, that old chestnut.

9 Chaka Demus & Pliers hit the Number One spot with their rosy rendition of *Twist And Shout*.

★

Bryan Adams, Rod Stewart and Sting rub shoulders and compare bank balances as *All For Love* from the film *The Three Musketeers* tops the singles chart.

★

14 The Cranberries play London's Astoria 2, record it for posterity and future video release, and officially 'arrive' as stars. Their debut album, *Everybody Else Is Doing It, So Why Can't We?*, has now sold over one million copies in America.

★

15 Harry Nilsson, American singer-songwriter and erstwhile partner to John Lennon dies in Los Angeles. Coincidentally, Mariah Carey lifts his best-known rendition, *Without You*, to even shriller heights, and to Number 1 in the US charts. Harry's mellifluous tones will be missed.

★

Elastica play a rammed London show and suddenly everyone realises what the fuss is all about.

★

Snoop Doggy Dogg, the US's biggest new rap star, has the Number One LP in America with *Doggy Style*. Putting the Gangsta back into Gangsta Rap,

he's also out on $1million bail for his part in a drive-by killing in Los Angeles.

★

17 Tori Amos returns with new single, *Cornflake Girl*

★

D:Ream re-release their top tune, *Things Can Only Get Better*

★

Kristin Hersh releases her single, *Your Ghost*, an appropriately haunting duet with REM's Michael Stipe.

★

Michael Stipe (again), Pearl Jam, The Shamen and many others contribute unreleased tracks to an animal benefit album called *In Defense Of Animals*.

★

24 The NME present their Brat Awards (see *Music Awards* in *Off The Record*) the credible alternative to the Brits, at London's Forum. The Boo Radleys, Pulp, One Dove and Credit To The Nation perform live sets.

★

Tindersticks, who scooped Best Album in *Melody Maker*'s End Of Year polls, begin a small UK tour

★

28 Manic Street Preachers sell out Brixton Academy

★

31 Elastica release *Line Up*, and become the most hyped new band since Suede.

▼ D:Ream

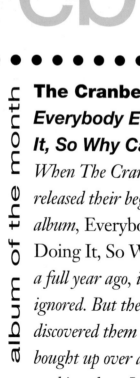

February

LIVE

◄ *And with* Siamese Dream, **Smashing Pumpkins** *coast into genius territory. It's the album, post-Nevermind, the world has been waiting for, swooping and swooning with the most melodically-inclined so-called grunge music you're ever likely to hear. It sells millions, makes the band huge beyond their dreams, and sends their dictator-like leader, Billy Corgan, into a state of confusion and neurosis: The Woody Allen Of Rock! A triumphant tour this month does little to alleviate his problems, it seems.* "Seriously, I don't see what his problem is. He's rich, famous, successful, married even. He has, by any standard, made it. Yet he whines and frets and chides. He's insecure and paranoid, fine. Everyone is. But there comes a point where you've just got to say, 'For fuck's sake! Pull yourself together man!'" *advise MM. NME, meanwhile, felt similar.* "When Corgan sneers 'Thanks for nothing!' after a rapturous response, is he taking the piss or his he genuinely pissed off?" *Hmmm...*

album of the month

The Cranberries
Everybody Else Is Doing It, So Why Can't We?

When The Cranberries quietly released their beguiling debut album, Everybody Else Is Doing It, So Why Can't We?, *a full year ago, it was all but ignored. But then the Americans discovered them and subsequently bought up over a million copies, making them Ireland's biggest export since U2. It was only a matter of time, then, that the rest of the world caught up...*

"Countless times, while listening to this record, I'm on the verge of recognising some favourite, forgotten song, something sad or comforting. But I can't seem to pin any of them down. I think, in fact, it's simply the sound of this record, already all the way through to my bones." **Melody Maker**

"It would be very easy to dismiss Limerick's Cranberries as another Sundays... never mind, this is just the beginning, certainly not where The Cranberries' story will end." **Hot Press**

"Doubts are summarily banished and the album's delicious frisson is affirmed." **Vox**

"There's enough personality here to indicate that they're worth watching." **Creem** (USA)

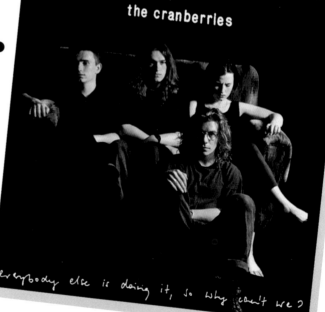

the cranberries

everybody else is doing it, so why can't we?

"A deeper, dreamier unit. They've accomplished a sharp, self-aware debut." **Rolling Stone**

"She eerily duplicates Sinead O'Conner's halting, passionate attack and Suzanne Vega's cold-water Yankee warble. Dolores O' Riordan's homages could fill a gap." **Details**

18

Birthdays: 1st Lisa Marie Presley (Mrs MJ, 1968) • 4th Alice Cooper (1948) • 9th Carole King (1940) • 10th Roberta Flack (1938) • 19th Smokey Robinson (1940)

snippets

Elastica, stars of what the music weeklies are calling The New Wave Of New Wave, get their first front cover. *Select* magazine has singer Justine snarling, chomping on a fat cigar, and looking every inch a star. Their first proper single release has yet to happen.

Alternative NRG, a **Greenpeace** compilation album, comes out, featuring tracks from U2, James, Jesus And Mary Chain, and REM, the latter contributing a live funk version of *Drive*.

"Chocolate is a big part of a lot of women's lives," informs Voodoo Queens singer **Anjali**, on the eve of their debut album release, *Chocolate Revenge*.

"We were there in the early days, making music while Jamiroquai was still taking his exams." **Brand New Heavies** confirm "we was first" to the young pretender.

"I still haven't got the gall to say to someone, 'Take your clothes off because I'm Andy from Therapy?'. With me it's more like, 'Well, I'm no oil painting and I'm shite in bed'. That's my sales pitch." **Therapy?**'s Andy Cairns, a lovely, down-to-earth kinda guy. Crap in the sack, allegedly.▼

"By age 46, I'll be playing Las Vegas." **Milla Jovovich**, ex model, some-time actress (if her starring role in *Return To The Blue Lagoon* can be described as acting), now turned sensitive singer. All this and she's still just 17.

The The's Matt Johnson has his scrotum pierced in Los Angeles. Apparently he's most pleased with his "sexy" new jewellery, despite those tears in his eyes.

K Foundation have been fined by the Bank Of England for defacing the Queen's currency. The devilish duo nailed £1million to a board, entitled it *Nailed To The Wall*, and awarded it to artist Rachael Whiteread.

Michael Jackson **reaches an out-of-court settlement with Jordy Chandler, the 14-year-old boy who accused him of child abuse. He agrees to pay Chandler a whopping – and unconfirmed – $26million over a period of 10 years. Who says money can't buy everything?**

February**Diary**

7 The Cocteau Twins have a new single, *Bluebeard*, out today. ▲

★

Under The Pink, the new album by Tori Amos, is released. Seven days later it's the biggest selling LP in the country.

★

Therapy? release their new album, *Troubelgum*.

★

8 Suede begin a mini-tour, lasting just three dates (Worthing, Blackpool and Edinburgh), in minimalist support of their new eight-minute single, *Stay Together*.

★

10 Snoop Doggy Dog plays his first ever UK show at Equinox in London's Leicester Square. A significant police presence is in full effect, just in case, like. However, a peaceful night is enjoyed by all.

★

14 This year's Brit Awards takes place at London's Alexandra Palace.

★

S*M*A*S*H, the band who seem to be spear-heading the entire New Wave Of New Wave polemic, release their single, *Lady Love Your C****, today, on Valentine's Day. Proof that romance still burns bright.

★

Soundgarden pump back into muscular action with their *Spoonman* single."

19 Carter USM, that eternal duo, become a three-piece! They unveil drummer Wez at a "surprise" guest slot supporting Sultans Of Ping in London.

★

23 Smashing Pumpkins begin a four-night sold-out residency at London's Astoria.

★

26 Bjork plays the Brixton Academy in a special show that lasts until 3 am. The show is entitled Bjork On Legs.

★

28 Hole, featuring Mrs Kurt Cobain, Courtney Love, return with a new single, *Miss World*, a taster for their forthcoming album, *Live Through This*.

★

Saint Etienne release their third album, *Tiger Bay*.

▼ Hole

19th Holly Johnson (1960) • 20th Walter Becker (1950) • 25th George Harrison (1943) • 26th Michael Bolton (1953) • 27th Paul Humphreys (OMD, 1960)

19

LIVE

► *The rise and rise of* **Therapy?** *has been little short of inexorable these past few years. From appealing directly to thrash metal heads to just about everybody in the space of two bloody good, bloody loud albums, has taken all by surprise, not least the band themselves. A relentless work schedule has ensured that their question mark is rarely out of the Top Ten and round about the time of this month's larger than life tour, Therapy? are almighty news. "Therapy? have an innate knowledge of the good aspects of rock,"* decides NME. *"They know that swearing on stage is top, they know that wearing black wins you kudos, and that pointing at individual members of the audience and reaching for their hands is ace. The perfect example of rock without the frills, and thrills without the frocks."* Select, *meanwhile, heartily agree that "Therapy? are going to be massive."* Massive.

March

• • • • • • • • • • • • • • •

album of the month

Elvis Costello
Brutal Youth

How does that old saying go: you can't teach an old dog new tricks? Well, Costello returns, now aged 39, and proves that while he's no Paul Daniels, he's certainly refining those enduring skills of yore. Reunited with The Attractions for the first time since 1986, Brutal Youth is the sound of a songwriter full of life, spite and beautiful bitterness...

"There's no respite from his spite, his bark, his bite. This is vitriolic and perversely, blindingly romantic. This is another bitch of an album from the old dog." **Melody Maker**

"This album has all the knowing pop references, but is infused with a humanity that has been missing on recent works. A man out of time, and back on track." **Vox**

"*Brutal Youth* may be his most immediate collection since *Blood And Chocolate* in 1986, but it lacks the essential, sappy charm of those early albums it tries so hard to emulate. An impressive, but ultimately unnecessary, album." **Sunday Times**

"Costello's 15th album is emotionally fresh and cynically knowing at the same time. The jammy bugger's gone and done it again." **Time Out**

"*Brutal Youth* is the album Costello fans have been begging him to make for years." **Select**

"He has found enough of the old vitality to repair a dented reputation and *Brutal Youth* is as good an album as could reasonably be expected from Costello at this stage of the game." **The Times**

"What has kept Costello going for 17 years is his polished-to-a-lustre anger at interests, global and personal. He can, and usually does, out-vitriol both Van Morrison and Morrissey." **The Guardian**

"Welcome to Costello's best pop album since 1982... confirms that Costello is back in the ring and a shave is nearly always a prerequisite for good pop music." **Q**

"Costello has made an album that sounds like a debut, with all the fire and fury that entails - and he has brought to it a wise man's brain and wit." **NME**

"Driving, feral music and a singer who sounds as if he has swallowed a thesaurus of contempt. No artist ever seemed quite so much in his element when raging about the foibles and failures of human nature." **Daily Telegraph**

Birthdays: 1st Roger Daltrey (1945) • 2nd Jon Bon Jovi (1962), Lou Reed (1942) • 4th Chris Rea (1951) • 6th Dave Gilmour (1947) • 10th Neneh Cherry (1964)

snippets

"Am I ego crazy? No, the opposite – insecure. It's like an insatiable hunger that you have, you need something to make you feel better." **Smashing Pumpkins**' Billy Corgan, becoming increasingly stressed-out as his band become increasingly successful.

"I fucking hate being here." **The Wonder Stuff's Miles** Hunt on tour in America. Judging by the band's Stateside status, Americans feel much the same about them.

"I never thought I'd be at the forefront of anything at all. I wanted to be an electrician or a sound engineer. Or a coach driver!" **Credit To The Nation**'s Matty, a young man at the forefront of the indie-rap crossover.

Pulp release their new single, *Do You Remember The First Time?*, and accompany it with a 26-minute film on the theme of losing one's cherry. Vic Reeves, Jo Brand, John Peel and actress Alison Steadman confess all before the camera.

Nirvana's future is in a state of confusion after Kurt Cobain's recent overdose in Italy. Speculation is rife over the singer's health, his mental state,

his relationship with the rest of the band, and, indeed, with his wife. The world watches and waits...

Smashing Pumpkins are banned from appearing on Tops Of The Pops after refusing to change the lyrics of their current single, *Disarm*. The line, "Cut that little child up inside of me" was thought unsuitable for television in the light of the James Bulger killing.

Morrissey signs copies of his latest album, *Vauxhall And I*, at London's HMV and causes a road-block.

Anna Friel, aka Brookside's Beth Jordache, TV's top sex symbol (and if you disagree, then please step outside), admits a fondness for Sting and Simply Red. Argh! But then she quickly wins back a little credibility by name-checking Nirvana and Manic Street Preachers. Phew.

U2 win a Grammy for Best Alternative Act. In his acceptance speech, Bono said, "We shall continue to abuse our position and fuck up the mainstream." Gasp! Bono swears on American TV!

"Money? Up to now I'm just going to our accountant, 'Take it away. Put it in my bank account.'" **The Cranberries**' Delores on the problems one faces when one has money coming out of one's ears.

◄ "I have a fever when I'm going to write a song. My hair stands on end, it's like rocks in my head. And if I don't write a song, that can turn into a seizure." **Kristin Hersh** on the vagaries of being an artist and suffering for it.

March**Diary**

2 Manic Street Preachers are joined on stage at London's Clapham Grand by Suede's Bernard Butler for a benefit show for the Imperial Cancer Research Fund.

★

4 Kurt Cobain, currently on tour with Nirvana in Italy, is rushed to hospital in a coma after overdosing on alcohol and drugs in a Rome hotel.

★

Paul Weller begins a national tour, as the man enjoys his biggest critical and commercial renaissance since The Jam.

★

7 Elvis Costello returns with his new album, *Brutal Youth*, in which he is re-united with The Attractions.

★

Blur return with their new single, *Boys And Girls*, which goes straight in at Number Five. Stars at last!

★

Inspiral Carpets play a free show at London's Tower Records in Piccadilly Circus.

★

12 Mariah Carey is top of the pile transAtlanticly with her *Music Box* album.

★

13 *Doop*, a song based on the Charleston, by a Dutch band also called Doop

reigns at Number One in the singles chart. And stays there.

★

14 Nine Inch Nails release their new album, *The Downward Spiral*.

★

24 Kristin Hersh begins a small UK acoustic tour before a bewitched and adoring audience.

★

25 Radiohead begin a short UK tour after their triumphant conquering of the 50 states of America.

★

Virgin 1215 air world exclusive radioplay of Floyd single *Keep Talking* from *The Division Bell*.

★

26 Credit To The Nation's MC Fusion receives death-threats on the eve of the release of the band's debut album, *Beat Dis*.

★

S*M*A*S*H, leaders of 1994's most hyperbolic scene, New Wave Of New Wave, are deemed "the least cool band on earth" by *Melody Maker*.

★

28 Nick Cave releases his new single, *Do You Love Me?*, amid cries of "magnificent"

▼ *Credit To The Nation*

Cobain's suicide

Friday, April 8, and Kurt Cobain's body is found in his Seattle home by visiting electrician Gary Smith, where apparently it had been laying for up to four days. Cobain had taken his own life with a shotgun, and a suicide note was found near his body. He was 27.

Cobain was reported to have become increasingly dissatisfied with his position and the pressures it brought. Struggling with heroin addiction and still chasing the highs of early performances, his suicide note made it clear he was unable to cope.

The following day a public memorial is held in Seattle, attended by over 5000 grieving fans. His wife, Courtney Love, thanks the fans for their unity and support and reads out excerpts from the note. "It's not fun for me any more," it says. "I can't live this life."

April

album of the month

Pink Floyd – *The Division Bell*

Hello, is there anybody out there? Well, yes, there is. And hark, it's Pink Floyd, rumbling back into action with something of a comeback album, The Division Bell, *a record that sells aplenty and confirms their obviously enduring appeal. Seriously atmospheric stuff from three blokes whose combined ages total 457. Honest...*

"Just the job for Floydies and a striking listen for anyone else who bumps into it. They remain unique and uniquely enigmatic." **Q**

"To say that this is in the classic Pink Floyd mould would be an understatement. It is a compendium of traditional Floydian hallmarks." **The Times**

"The music on their 16th studio album is just as lavishly pointless. Naturally, no expense has been spared in its sumptuous execution." **The Guardian**

"Musically, the group's slow, patient tread is exactly as remembered. It's as if they're meekly accepting this dullard mainstream as

their natural home, rather than fielding the ball batted back by newer progressive-rock acolytes like The Orb." **Independent**

"Their music is now as unadventurous as their world view, epic only in its emptiness." **The Observer**

"It's not that this album is particularly bad, it's just that it's so damned anonymous. It's very, very boring." **NME**

"While not breaking any significant new ground here musically, the sound is more cohesive and delicately textured than anything the Floyd have recorded since the glory days of the 1970s." **Mojo**

"It comes to something when you go to describe to someone how the best bits of Pink Floyd's new album sound like The Orb, because then you remember that it's actually the other way round, by nearly 30 years." **Time Out**

"Ever since their genius founder Syd Barrett went entirely awry in the brainbox, Pink Floyd have been tilling a turf of 'ambient' music that can only be described as 'soothing' (euphemism for 'greatly boring')." **Mail On Sunday**

Birthdays: 1st Ronnie Lane 1946) • 5th Agnetha Faltsfog (ABBA, 1950) • 11th Lisa Stansfield (1966) • 14th Richie Blackmore (1945) •

snippets

"We've never destroyed a hotel or anything like that. I hate that, cause it's always somebody's mum who's got to go down on her fucking knees and clean up the shit for £1.50 an hour." **Primal Scream**'s Bobby Gillespie, a '90s kinda rock star.

Tori Amos graces the front cover of *Vox* magazine, dressed in vest and Y-fronts, claiming "I'm the Queen of the Nerds!"

"Yes, I am pregnant." **Morrissey** shocks the world again, this time for very different reasons. A new album (*Vauxhall And I*), a baby due (allegedly), and, we presume, a taste for peanut butter and coal sandwiches.

"The Woody Allen Of Pop? That's a new one on me. There are worse things to be called, aren't there?" **Elvis Costello**, tempting fate, clearly.

"This could be our last show for ever as far as I'm concerned. Kurt's death has changed everything. I don't know if I can do it any more." **Pearl Jam**'s Eddie Vedder.

"There's nothing wrong with machismo. I'm into being male. I love having a dick. I love fucking." **Henry Rollins**, a man's man in a man's, man's, man's world.

The Wonder Stuff are having problems. Their latest album, *Construction For The Modern Idiot*, isn't selling as much as hoped. The subsequent World Tour seems to have drained them of all enthusiasm. Rumours abound that they're thinking of calling it a day. But, no matter, for this month they hit the UK and provide possibly the best performances of their lives. "The fierce intensity of tonight never lets up," says *NME*. "After ten minutes you remember why it was that you always loved them so: for the simple cliched reason that they've always made more sense on stage than anyway else." *Melody Maker* agrees: "It's a storming gig - stadium-sized glee crammed into a venue a fifth the size of the steaming audience. This sounds like two hours of nothing but singles, until you realise that everything sounds like a single because they're all that good."

April**Diary**

2 Primal Scream release their new album, *Give Out But Don't Give Up*, to mixed reviews and embark on a mega-successful UK tour.

★

Nirvana's live dates are re-scheduled after Kurt Cobain's recent overdose. It's announced that they are to play four nights at the Brixton Academy on the 17, 18, 19 and 20th April.

★

3 Hold the front page! Nirvana and Hole have now cancelled their forthcoming tours amid continuing speculation about Kurt Cobain's drug problems. It is now believed that the singer and his wife have been booked into a detox clinic to curb their drug problems.

★

5 Kurt Cobain commits suicide by shooting himself in the head at his Seattle home.

★

7 Lee Brilleaux, founder member of Dr Feelgood, dies of lymphoma, a form of cancer. He was 41.

★

Courtney Love is arrested on drugs and theft charges after a reported overdose, unaware that her husband, Kurt Cobain, lies dead in their home.

★

8 Kurt Cobain's body is discovered by electrician Gary Smith and the news breaks around the world.

★

9 Pink Floyd return with their *Division Bell* album and debut at Number One.

★

A public memorial is held in Seattle for Kurt Cobain.

★

10 Reports filter through about the first Kurt Cobain-inspired copycat suicide. Daniel Kasper, who lived just outside Seattle, dies from a self-inflicted shotgun wound. He had attended the Seattle Centre vigil for Cobain the day before.

11 Hole release their new album, *Live Through This*, despite recent events, and it's widely regarded their best effort yet.

★

Pulp, a band in their 13th year of existence, finally release their debut album proper, *His `N' Hers*.

★

Backbeat, a biopic about The Beatles' early days in Hamburg and starring Stephen Dorff, opens to rave reviews.

★

25 Sales of *Nevermind* and *In Utero* continue to rocket worldwide, both climbing back into the Top Ten, following Cobain's suicide.

★

30 Teenage Fanclub drummer Brendan O'Hare has left the band after months of speculation about their future.

★

Virgin 1215 a year old precisely.

★

The Cranberries cancel their forthcoming UK dates (supporting Crowded House) after singer Delores injures her knee in a skiing accident. Rock'n'roll! ▼

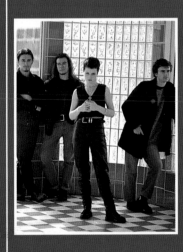

15th Dave Edmunds (1944) • 17th Pete Shelley (1955) • 21st Iggy Pop (1946), Robert Smith (1959) • 25th Andy Bell (1964) • 27th Sheena Easton (1959)

23

May

album of the month

Blur – *Parklife*

From the doldrums of despair come great things. So said some philosopher. Probably. This time last year, Blur's survival looked distinctly iffy, but somehow they bounced back with the defiantly rumbustious Parklife, *a third album of gloriously glorious proportions. Magic, evidently, happens…*

"They've got the attitude of The Faces and bits of psychedelia and English art school zanyness." **Daily Mail**

"*Parklife* is full of guitar pop every bit as impersonal as a shopping mall atrium." **The Independent**

"Young girls have been known to scream at Blur, not necessarily a good sign…but when did they last scream at anyone this brazenly talented?" **Q**

"With all the subtlety of a right-wing cab driver's conversational style, the Essex boys have gone for the jugular and, incredibly, cut it big time. This is an uplifting, triumphant wonderbra of a record." **NME**

"It's obvious that Blur are deliberately making a record which oozes London suburbia, and every now and then it becomes a little too 'cor blimey!', but this is a charming record." **The Telegraph**

"Like rivals Suede, they are committed to reviving The Song. The Kinks and Small Faces may have done it before, but not in this charmingly cynical way." **The Guardian**

"Blur, along with… Primal Scream and … Suede, are one of the three bands currently vying for the title of Greatest British Group since The Smiths." **Sunday Telegraph**

"Most of *Parklife*, you'll not be gobsmacked to hear, sounds like The Kinks in melancholy mode, *Alfie*, Madness' dignified dying days, The Small Faces, *Absolute Beginners*, The Jam and *Quadraphenia*." **Melody Maker**

"And are they really the best British band since The Smiths? On this showing, bloody right they are. Here there's imagination, humour…and a whiff of the devil." **Select**

"At the moment, Blur remain a better idea than a band. But when Blur's execution becomes as deft as their vision, they'll be untouchable." **Time Out**

A sign of the times? Snoop Doggy Dog is Amerikkka's most wanted in more ways than one. Right now, he's the biggest new rap name around, his lazy delivery amid glorious P-Funk grooves exciting and delighting audiences on both sides of the Atlantic. But he's also on a murder charge back in LA, out on a million dollar bail. His first proper UK show, then, could also be his last. Which probably accounts for the feverish reaction he gets wherever he goes. "This is amazing," says *Melody Maker*. "The raps are clear and strong, the music like some phunky fusion of the Fatback Band and surreal 70s TV themes. £16 and worth every penny. The best rap package this side of Public Enemy." **NME**, meanwhile, considers, "This performance ritual of rap as heady hedonism - big fat spliffs, big fat butts, big fat bea

LIVE

snippets

The Levellers plan to fight against the recently published Criminal Justice Bill, which aims to curtail gatherings of 100 people "at which amplified music is played during the night"; in effect destroying travellers' entire lifestyle.

The Lemonheads' Evan Dando graces the *NME* cover, with new cropped hairstyle.

Morrissey causes further controversy by stating in *Select* magazine that the BNP and similar far-right organizations should be given a platform for their views. He declines to comment further, however.

A Kurt Cobain college scholarship fund is set up at Cobain's high school in Seattle to encourage the continuing education of creative minds and to benefit students who show artistic promise regardless of academic ability.

Chrissie Hynde upsets her rather senior-in-years audience when, at The Pretenders' London dates, she invites avant-garde acid noise merchants **Death By Cleavage** to support. The audience are seen pleading, fingers in ears, for the soundman to knock off a few dBs. He doesn't.

Round about now, we learn that **The Stone Roses'** *second album is to be called* The Second Coming. *No-one knows, however, when, or indeed if, it will ever see the light of day.*

"There are only a minority of white people who are cool. The majority are fools. They just want to tell you how much you're suffering and how sympathetic they are." Aki, from Asian/Black rap crew, **Fun-Da-Mental**.

Blur release their third album, *Parklife*, and throw a music biz party at Walthamstow's dog track.

"I'm kind of apologetic when I meet people. It's like, 'I'm the singer of **The Lemonheads**. I'm sorry!'" Evan Dando, the singer of The Lemonheads.

Q magazine tell us "Why Kurt Cobain Had To Die", as do *Select*, *Vox*, *Mojo*, and just about every other music magazine.

Courtney Love has been cleared of all charges relating to her arrest in Beverly Hills on April 7.

MTV, the music video channel with every available finger on every available pulse, report that ex-Clash man, **Mick Jones**, has died of pneumonia.

May**Diary**

▲ **Beautiful South**

9 The Fall release their 18th album, *Middle Class Revolt*.

★

Gene, a new London four-piece, release their debut single, *For The Dead*, all angst and weeping guitars. Critics hail them The New Smiths, a misplaced accolade bestowed before on, ooh, hundreds of bands. But maybe this time...

★

The Beautiful South release their version of the late Nilsson hit, *Everybody's Talkin'*.

★

Seal returns with the moody *Prayer For The Dying* single.

16 Sonic Youth release their *Experimental Jet Set, Trash And No Star* album.

★

The Pretenders release their new album, *Last Of The Independents*.

★

The Auteurs sneer back into town with album number two, *Now I'm A Cowboy*.

★

20 Nine Inch Nails begin a sold-out tour of the UK and succeed in scaring their audience witless.

21 Youssou N'Dour, Africa's biggest superstar, plays the Brixton Academy.

★

The Wonder Stuff announce that they are to split up. Their headlining slot at The Phoenix Festival in July will be their last ever show.

★

23 Jah Wobble releases his new album, Take Me To God, amid a downpour of critical acclaim.

★

The Beastie Boys release their new album, *Ill Communication*, to surprising critical acclaim.

★

Frank Black releases his second solo album, *Teenager Of The Year*.

★

28 That Petrol Emotion play their last ever gig in Dublin. After ten years together, the band finally call it a day.

★

31 The Orb release their new album, *Pomme Fritz*, today.

June

The Spin Doctors –
Turn It Upside Down

New York's Spin Doctors are this generation's Grateful Dead. It's kind of like official, dude. Pocket Full Of Kryptonite *has now registered over six million whopping sales. Sheesh! This follow-up, then, proves two things: 1) Joe Public still loves 'em, and 2) the critics still hate 'em. No change there then...*

"The Doctors won't be cited for trailblazing but their music is precisely their (carpet) bag." **Mojo**

"Enjoyable enough if you are already a sold fan; otherwise, an unessential companion to *Pocket Full Of Kryptonite*." **Sunday Times**

"Music fans will be appalled by the most hideous microwave philosophising since Edie Brickell, but heartened by the absence of anything as insidious as *Two Princes*." **Select**

"Looks like the man with a sock on his head, who looks like Jesus, has run out of ideas for this new slice of Spin Doctors rock'n'roll. Oh dear!" **Smash Hits**

"*Turn It Upside Down* contains a large slab of what we can safely predict will be the chart soundtrack for the rest of the year. It's loud, confident and wrong. If it were up to me, I'd just say, Turn It Down." **Hot Press**

"They still sound like a clever-clever, hippy-dippy 90s update of the Steve Miller Band, but with music so ingenious and enjoyable, who's complaining?" **Sky**

"While they sit smugly on centre-stage, hogging the front covers of so-called 'alternative' magazines and making albums as saccharine and mushy as this, then they'll always be something for us to despise. Odious." **NME**

"Often acclaimed as the 'Grateful Dead of the MTV age', what the Doctors have over the West Coast warhorses is a finely honed pop sensibility... (but) for all their chumminess, the Doctors can tend towards the faceless and anaemic." **Vox**

"The tumbling, bluesy funk, spiralling guitar riffs and open, Hendrix-like jams remain, but the melodies are sweeter, more folk-influenced, and the overall feel is infectiously wistful." **GQ Magazine**

Creation Records celebrates its 10th birthday this year. An almighty "bash" is duly called for. This, after all, is the label that has brought love and meaning into the hearts of indie kids everywhere via the aural delights of Jesus And Mary Chain, My Bloody Valentine, Primal Scream, House Of Love, and more recently, Ride, Sugar, Boo Radleys and Oasis. And so the Royal Albert Hall is hired out and the cream of Creation grace its stage for the unmitigated celebration that is Undrugged. And yet, somehow, the evening disappoints. "Personally," begins *Melody Maker*, "I'd rather have had an all-dayer with more bands, longer sets and a smidgen of atmosphere. Undrugged might have seemed like a good idea at the time, but it's not the yardstick I'll be using to measure Creation's success." *NME* were similarly disappointed. "Our lives have not been changed. Our evening has been starless. We can't tell whether we have just celebrated ten years of Creation or whether we've attended some sort of declaration of the end."

Birthdays: 1st Ronnie Wood (1947) • 2nd Charlie Watts (1941) • 7th ex-Prince (1958) • 8th Mick Hucknall (1960) • 10th Maxi Priest (1961) • 14th Boy George (1961)

snippets

Guns N' Roses are on the verge of splitting, according to US sources. Apparently Axl hates Slash and Slash hates Axl, and the other members all hate each other. Fear and loathing all round, pretty much.

Neil Young has decided never to perform his classic 1979 track *Rust Never Sleeps* after he learned that Kurt Cobain used a line from the song ("It's better to burn out than to fade away") in his suicide note.

"Look, I didn't even pay for intercourse. I would be too scared... it was just masturbation, basically." Richey from Manic Street Preachers, on the fun he had in Bangkok.

"*Ill Communication* is one hell of a long way down the road from laughing at spastics." *NME* on the **Beastie Boys**' new LP.

The Levellers' plans to run a series of high profile ads protesting against the Criminal Justice Bill have been scuppered by London Transport. LT does not accept 'political' anti-government campaigns, apparently.

Courtney Love accompanies REM's **Michael Stipe** to the MTV Film Awards.

Deep breath. Rumours abound that **Evan Dando** and **Meg Ryan** will star in a film about the life of **Kurt Cobain** and **Courtney Love**. Yeah, and pigs will fly and Acrington Stanley will win the Premiership.

A fire destroys the Pyramid Stage at Glastonbury on June 13, just two weeks before the festival is due to begin. Glastonbury owner Michael Eavis insists everything will still go ahead as normal.

"I know we're better than fuckin' anything that's come out of this country. I mean Suede? I played that album and it sucks!" Stone Temple Pilots' **Scott Weiland**.

Ian McCulloch and former Echo And The Bunnymen guitarist Will Sergeant have formed **Electrafixion** together. They play live this month before disappearing into the studio to work on an album.

Public Enemy's Flavor Flav turns himself into New York police after failing to turn up to a court appearance charged with possession of an illegal weapon.

Prince steps into the future as he releases *Interactive*, a CD-ROM, featuring a rare interview, a game, and also a "trip" into his boudoir. A snip at £50.

George Michael *loses his High Court case against Sony in which he was seeking to free himself from a contract which would bind him to the mega corporation for the next 15 years. He now faces court costs of over £3 million, but says he will appeal.*

4 Oasis get their first music weekly front cover. Singer Liam stares nonchalantly in moody black and white on the *NME*.

★

Seal's new album debuts at Number One despite mediocre reviews.

★

Wet Wet Wet reach Number One in the singles chart with *Love Is All Around*, from the hit film of the moment, *Four Weddings And A Funeral*.

★

Legendary music journalist Nick Kent releases a collection of his articles in one book, *The Dark Stuff*.

★

6 Smashing Pumpkins re-release their debut album *Gish*, re-mastered by singer Billy Corgan. It sounds, however, exactly the same as the original.

★

8 Some 16 months after release, The Cranberries' debut album *Everybody Else Is Doing It, So Why Can't We?* reaches Number One in the charts.

★

11 The Fleadh Festival takes place live and large in London's Finsbury Park. Top Irish combo ...er Crowded House headline.

★

13 The Almighty take Best British Live Band from

▲ *Kerrang!*'s Great British Heavy Metal Awards. Metal thirsts suitably quenched courtesy of the major music backer... probably, of this summer's festivals, Carlsberg.

19 The Lemonheads play two triumphant nights at London's Shepherd's Bush Empire.

20 Ride release their third album, *Carnival Of Light*.

★

Dawn Penn rides high in the chart with her 25-year-old single *You Don't Love Me (No No No)*.

24 Glastonbury is upon us. Let the celebrations commence...

★

25 ...Five people shot and injured at Glastonbury by a lone madman.

★

27 Oasis release their second single, *Shakermaker*, which debuts at Number 11 in the charts.

▼ *Glastonbury*

• 18th Paul McCartney (1942) • 20th Brian Wilson (1942) • 21st Ray Davies (1944) • 24th Mick Fleetwood (1942) • 25th George Michael (1963) • 26th Mick Jones (1955)

27

July

Not Suede Away

Well, not quite, but guitarist Bernard Butler leaves the band after reputed disagreements with singer Brett Anderson and producer Ed Buller. The band look for a replacement by placing an ad in *Melody Maker*, asking for a melodic guitarist into The Beatles, Cocteaus and, reasonably enough, Suede. Meanwhile, the band dodge investigative journalists while putting the finishing touches to their autumn-due second album.

ROLLING STONES **VOODOO LOUNGE**

album of the month

The Rolling Stones – *Voodoo Lounge*

They're back! The true inhabitants of that place Noel calls Crinkly Bottom are now all 50 years old, minus a wandering bass player (that Wyman fella's long gone), but still firing on all four cylinders. They're called The Rolling Stones, they've a new album out, and they're the national institution they always were ...

"Rock's old master can still carve out riffs that can make your eyes water, just as Jagger still makes a far more convincing rock god than singers half his age. *Voodoo Lounge* makes it seem that Nirvana never happened." **Daily Telegraph**

"How proud the Stones must be that their new album warrants a sticker reading 'Warning! This CD contains language some may find offensive'. What better confirmation that, though Mick and the 'boys' are now 50, they can still offend like raw young men." **The Guardian**

"*Voodoo Lounge* is an important release, not for what it sounds like but for what it is: a fine rock album made by men old enough to be your grandfathers, for christ's sake. Senile on main street? I think not." **Melody Maker**

"*Voodoo Lounge* is, by a clean pair of lizard-skin cowboy-boot heels, the best Stones album in a couple of decades." **Independent**

"So, *Voodoo Lounge* is some sort of result. It may not enhance the Stones' reputation, but at the very least it doesn't much diminish it." **NME**

"It's no classic, but nor is it the resounding hound it could have been. And with *Out Of Tears* they prove there are still tantalising glimmers of genius." **Q**

Galliano are the country's funkiest, earthiest crew. It was Galliano who paved the way for their jazz-funk-rap label Talkin' Loud back in the twilight of the 1980s, and the subsequent 1990's chart success for its proud roster of acts (Urban Species, Omar); Galliano who single-handedly made the goatee beard fashionable once more; and it was Galliano who put the word 'vibe' back into the English language. In other words, a long, cool pina colada of a band. With ice. Last month came the release of their third album, the impossibly cool *The Plot Thickens*, and a sold-out UK tour (including three rammed London Forum June nights) that marked their transition from cult to sexy mainstream. "... a finely-honed sense of showbiz coursing through their veins," quoth *NME*. "But beneath such tomfoolery, there's the distinct scent of a band who have stumbled upon something noticeably inspiring."

LIVE

Birthdays: 1st Debbie Harry (1945) • 3rd Vince Clarke (1961) • 7th Ringo (1940) • 9th Jim Kerr (1959) • 10th Neil Tennant (1954) • 11th Suzanne Vega (1959)

snippets

Michael Jackson marries Elvis's daughter Lisa Marie in a secret ceremony somewhere in America. From the sublime to the weird to the downright bizarre...

"I'm sexier now, I'm not hung-up about sex. I'm very horny, whereas before I was very hung-up about being horny." Sex-on-a-pogo-stick, **Julian Cope**.

"I was doing as many drugs as I am now when I was working as a computer analyst. Whatever gets you through the night." **The Breeders'** Kelley Deal. Bong!

"When you don't do the right thing it catches up on you and that's what happened to me. So everybody, don't be like me." **Public Enemy's** Flavor Flav after being arrested on more than one occasion for more than one crime.

"You can analyse techno up its own arse if you're not careful." **The Grid's** Richard Norris.

▼ **The Beastie Boys** become a screensaver computer package as a way of promoting their album, *Ill Communication*.

1994 Mercury Prize nominees are announced: **Blur**, **Take That**, **M-People**, **Michael Nyman**, **The Prodigy**, **Ian McNabb**, **Pulp**, **Therapy?**, **Shara Nelson** and **Paul Weller**. The winner will be announced later in the year.

"We love Gary Numan, he's fascinating. The first time I saw him I couldn't beleeeeive it! The blue hair and the white face and those songs! They're just brilliant, brilliant songs." **Shampoo's** Jacqui, too young to know better. Give her time...

Kurt Cobain's suicide note has become available printed on T-shirts in America. And the machine rolls on...

July**Diary**

▲ *The Phoenix rises – with cans on*

4 Julian Cope releases his new album, *Autogeddon*. And shaves most of his head.

★

7 George Michael enjoys a rare interview situation on tele with Sir David Frost. His recent High Court case dominates the chat.

★

9 The NME "interview" dead Rolling Stone Brian Jones via a medium. Hmmm.

★

14 The Phoenix Festival begins...

★

15 The Wonder Stuff play their final gig at the Phoenix before a crowd of 50,000.

★

17 The Phoenix Festival ends.

★

Sod music - it's the World Cup Final. Go Brazil!

★

18 Terry Hall, ex-Specials, Fun Boy Three, and many more, returns for brief UK tour after a two year sabbatical in which he and wifey made babies.

★

24 Shampoo, two teenage grrrls from Plumstead, SE London, coast into Number 14 with their debut EMI single, *Trouble*.

25 Jesus And Mary Chain return with a new single, *Sometimes Always*, a duet with Mazzy Star's Hope Sandoval. It's dead nice.

★

28 Veruca Salt, next-big-things from Chicago in the Breeders mould, play their debut London date to mass acclaim. Their future starts today, here and now.

★

30 The Rolling Stones sit proudly at Number 1 in the album chart with their latest album, *Voodoo Lounge*.

★

Pavarotti, Carreras and Domingo straddle the charts with *Libiamo* from their pre-World Cup "gig". It's classic, innit.

★

Through it all Wet Wet Wet spend their umpteenth week at Number One with *Love Is All Around*.

17th Spencer Davis (1942) • 19th Brian May (1947) • 20th Carlos Santana (1947) • 22nd Don Henley (1947) • 23rd Martin Gore (1961) • 26th Mick Jagger (1943) • 30th Kate Bush

August

◄ *January of this year, and* **Oasis** *are just another new band with big ideas jostling for attention with all the other new bands with big ideas. But come August – already three singles in (Supersonic, Shakermaker, Live Forever: classics all) – and Oasis are synonymous with all things wonderful. A heady combination of The Beatles, Stone Roses and Happy Mondays, and an even headier combination of surly arrogance and prodigious talent, and everybody suddenly worships them. They do drugs. They drink. They crave sex. Singer Liam and songwriting brother Noel constantly beat the crap out of each other. They have a guitarist called Bonehead. Yeeees! Rock'n'roll! They play throughout July to packed venues and the perimeters of rabid excitement are pushed all the way back. "Oasis are a dream come true," babbled NME. "They fight! They flirt! They go fucking mental! And they make music that creeps through your intestines, squeezes your kidneys and proposes to your heart." Right now, Oasis have a significant part of the world in a 'We're not worthy!' position at their feet. By the end of the month, as their debut album is released, they'll have the rest of it. What a year. What a band.*

• •

album of the month

Neil Young –
Sleeps With Angels

Rock stars and their stars wane with age. That's how it goes. Look at anyone still recording over the age of 40 (yes, even the likes of Jagger and Morrison and Dylan ain't what they used to be). But not Neil Young. Different league, Neil Young. As his age and facial hair increases, so does his skill. Sleeps With Angels *is his umpteenth album and is instantly hailed a classic.*

"The bottom line is, Good Old Neil's latest album stands or falls on the 15-minute centrepiece *Change Your Mind*. Yes, we're talking endless guitar solos. And this is where it matters that the backing band are Crazy Horse. And this is where music speaks louder than lyrics. And this is where I doff my cap to the grand master of stringbending and harmonics. Don't you wish everything in life was as reliable as an endless (Forever) Young guitar solo?" **Melody Maker**

"As a body of music, *Sleeps With Angels* is too rich and vivid to digest all at once. The effect is like hearing a whole load of new *Decade*, taken from the most stunning points along Young's 30-year journey. It points to just one thing: Neil Young and Crazy Horse have made a classic." **Q**

"Melodramatic as it may seem, these are the deliberate recordings of a man entering the final third of his lifespan, driving to his last destination, sustained by love in all its ineffable forms. If this sounds quasi-religious, too bad; spirituality is what you're getting on *Sleeps With Angels*. Its 12 songs

neil young and crazy horse

could be construed as a suite of hymns, and probably ought to be, since they are the outpourings of a man with a focused four-track mind." **Vox**

"Another great album from the master, then. Possibly his best in 15 years. And certainly more grist to the argument that Young will still be pumping out the business long after McNabb, Dando and all the other Neil/Crazy Horse thunderstealers have gone back to being unemployed and/or fully-qualified landscape gardeners. Buy it. And then buy it some more." **Select**

Birthdays: 7th Bruce Dickinson (1958) • 8th The Edge (1961) • 9th Whitney Houston (1964) • 12th Mark Knopfler (1949), Tanita Tikaram (1969) • 16th Madonna (1958)

snippets

Woodstock II! What started out as some (lame?) attempt to re-create the legendary-to-end-all-legendary festival (featuring **Pearl Jam**, **Guns N' Roses**, **Metallica**) is embroiled in legal wrangles and arguments between rival factions claiming rights to the festival name. It'll probably still be a legendary event, but for all the wrong reasons.

Billy Idol is admitted into hospital in Los Angeles after a drugs overdose. He is released the day after, surprisingly alive, and apparently full of remorse.

Manic Street Preachers' Richey Edwards is booked into a private clinic to be treated for "nervous exhaustion".

Alice In Chains cancel their forthcoming American tour due to singer Layne Staley's alleged ever-increasing drug problem.

Radio One lose more listeners, according to latest figures. In the past three months, a further 900,000 ears have gone elsewhere for their listening pleasure. Ouch.

"Black kids shouldn't be pointing guns at each other; they should be pointing them at the record company presidents. Then you'll see the shit cease." **Public Enemy**'s Chuck D on the politics of record company politics; his way.

"I can really see us losing it." Ed from New Wave Of New Wavers **S*M*A*S*H**, mid-way through experiencing mild UK success and even milder US success, thus suggesting their days are numbered.

"My mother would force me to lie on the floor and she would stamp on my abdomen with the intention of bursting my womb. That's what she said, I'm going to burst you." **Sinead O'Connor**, coming clean in *Q*.

september...

... and if we squint, we can see September and beyond in all its autumnal glory. Look! If those who make it their business to spread rumours can be trusted, here comes **REM** with a new album of the eagerly awaited variety, with a world tour looming. **Dinosaur Jr** return, majestic of grunge guitar and heavily pregnant with a beautifully bouncing new album. The recently deceased **Wonder Stuff** offer up a Greatest Hits package. As does **Sting**. And as does **Cyndi Lauper**. **Suede** dish up their second album, while departed guitarist Bernard Butler looks for another job. **Kylie** squeaks back into five-foot high life. **Barbra Streisand** is "Live", allegedly, and **Luther Vandross** croons his favourite love songs for us. **Shabba Ranks** returns to remind us why some consider him the Reggae King, while **Gloria Estefan** re-claims her Pop Queen crown. **Sugar** deliver their much-anticipated third album, **Pearl Jam** do similar with *Vitalogy*, while **Nirvana** release a double album of outtakes and live numbers. The days get shorter, the nights longer, and the "imminent" return of the **Stone Roses** seems more and more unlikely. Christmas is just around the corner and so is another new year. Thank you and good night.

August**Diary**

1 Gene, the band some people - in fact, a lot of people - are calling The New Smiths, release their second single, *Be My Light, Be My Guide*, today. Sounds like The Smiths.

★

The National Film Theatre screen a short season of music films in conjunction with the *NME* under the banner, "Punk: Before And Beyond".

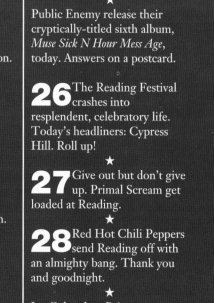

▲ *Echobelly*

★

6 Madness, who played their last ever live gigs two years ago before breaking up forever, play their LAST EVER concert at London's Finsbury Park before breaking up forever. Two words: Status Quo.

★

7 Eleven weeks at Number One for Wet Wet Wet. Two words: Whitney Houston.

★

8 The Farm, baggy heroes from 1990, return with a new album, *Hullabaloo*. A nation... ignores.

★

13 UB40 play The National Bowl in Milton Keynes supported by Chaka Demus and Pliers, Jamiroquai and Bitty Maclean.

Woodstock II begins.

★

14 Woodstock II ends.

★

15 Prince, who recently insisted in an interview that he's not obsessed with sex despite lyrics that suggest otherwise, releases the sexually unambiguous *Come*, his final album as Prince before officially becoming Squiggle.

★

22 Echobelly become a proper band today with the release of their fulsome debut album, *Everyone's Got One*.

★

Public Enemy release their cryptically-titled sixth album, *Muse Sick N Hour Mess Age*, today. Answers on a postcard.

★

26 The Reading Festival crashes into resplendent, celebratory life. Today's headliners: Cypress Hill. Roll up!

★

27 Give out but don't give up. Primal Scream get loaded at Reading.

★

28 Red Hot Chili Peppers send Reading off with an almighty bang. Thank you and goodnight.

★

Ice Cube plays Brixton Academy, his first musical outing since completing filming *Higher Learning* with *Boyz N The Hood* director John Singleton.

★

30 Oasis release their debut album, *Definitely Maybe*, today.

★ 20th Robert Plant (1948) ★ 23rd Shaun Ryder (1962) ★ 25th Elvis Costello (1955) ★ 29th Michael Jackson (1958), Eddi Reader (1959) ★ 31st Van Morrison (1945)

31

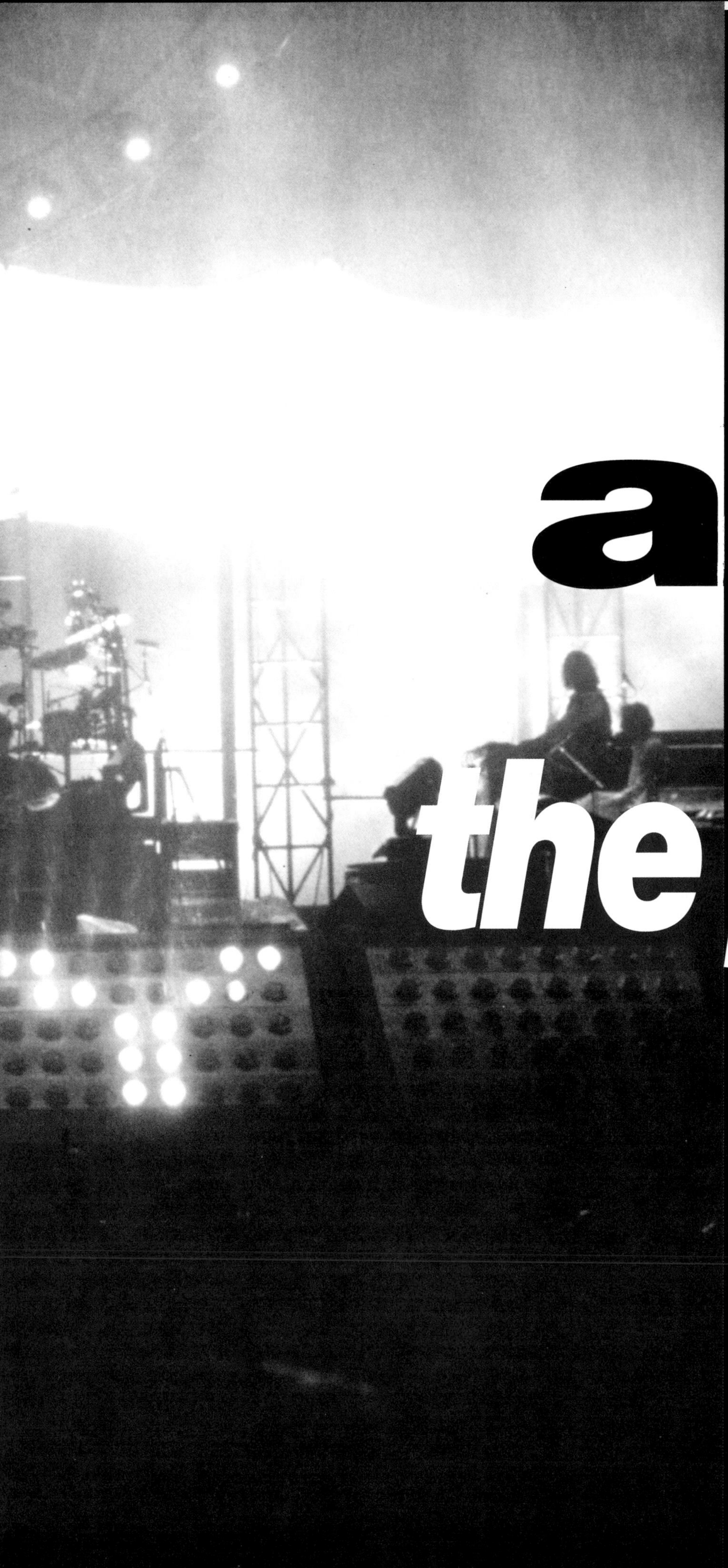

section two

acts of the year

Pink Floyd in concert © 1994 King Street Tours Ltd – photographer: Dennis O'Regan

- the best of '94
- *music styles*
- festivals

blur

"Blur's quantum leap from dippy chancers to agenda-setters had a healthy effect on British pop in 1994. Their critical and commercial success restored the balance after American Rock's near-hegemony of the music industry."

Blur as Britain's most successful alternative pop band? Who'd have thought it? Probably only the four confident-verging-on-arrogant young ex-student lads who make up Blur.

Blur entered last year's college season (September to July) still languishing somewhere around the middle of the indie league, above old-timers like The Charlatans and Ride, but well below flash newcomers such as Suede. By summer '94, however, the Essex boy wonders had been to Number One with *Parklife* (an album compared by one hysterical Sunday broadsheet critic to The Beatles' *Sgt Pepper*), headlined the *NME* stage at Glastonbury and heralded a wave of innovative home-grown pop groups the likes of which we haven't seen since the days of ABC, The Human League, Heaven 17 and Japan in the early '80s.

Who'd have thought it, indeed? Blur started the 1990s promisingly enough, charting with their first two singles, *She's So High* and *There's No Other Way*, and debut LP *Leisure*, riding on the back of unarguably the least sturdy bandwagon in recent pop history – baggy. Baggypop, epitomised by The Stone Roses (the good), The Mock Turtles (the bad) and Northside (the godawful), meant shuffling beats, hooped shirts, floppy fringes and stoned vocals. By the end of '91, Blur had sensibly ditched this dodgy phase, cocky mainman Damon Albarn even going so far as to declare in *Select* magazine that "we killed baggy".

Pretty soon, Blur had upped the ante from mellifluous to malicious, swapping their ravey nonchalance for a decidedly more aggressive stance. *Pop Scene*, from 1992, saw Blur finally bare their teeth, dressing like mods – all DMs, drainpipes and Fred Perrys – and coming on like punks. Not for nothing did this year's crop of New Wave Of New Wave bands (S*M*A*S*H, These Animal Men and Compulsion) cite Blur as an influence. The following year saw the band release another single: *For Tomorrow* wasn't just their first great single, with its glorious, instantly memorable hookline, it also reinvented Blur as the finest quintessentially English – or, more specifically, Londonish – pop group of the modern era. Damon Albarn finally found credit as a wry observer of the British condition, compared regularly to The Kinks' Ray Davies, The Who's Pete Townshend and The Jam's Paul Weller.

1993's *Modern Life Is Rubbish*, Blur's second album, offered an unequivocally critical view of the state of the nation, a landscape blemished by ugly seaside resorts, sanitised shopping malls, desensitising bingo halls and anodyne morning TV programmes. *Modern Life...* portrayed this septic isle as some kind of hell, although the music was heavenly, choc-full of neat melodies and sharp choruses. That autumn's *Sugary Tea* tour, co-sponsored by *Melody Maker*, consolidated Blur's position as student favourites and further evinced the band's commitment to criticising the Great British Way Of Life. Their on-stage set was dotted with huge versions of such suburban standbys as settees, lamps and curtains,

"...the reference points in Parklife didn't so much inform the songs as shine like tiny little sparks from the past."

though somehow Blur's infectious enthusiasm turned *Sugary Tea* into less of a dour caustic condemnation than a wild kitsch celebration.

Early '94 saw Blur further hone their unique vision and change course once more. *Girls & Boys*, which entered the charts at Number 5, took a half-cynical, half-affectionate look at the 18-30 brigade who "follow the herd down to Greece", suggesting that Damon Albarn might have been to a few Shaz & Kev-style discos in his time, even if he couldn't exactly find it in himself to join in the "fun". Musically, *Girls & Boys* was brilliant, Blur's best yet, shimmering with all sorts of sounds from pop's rich tapestry, notably David Bowie's *Boys Keep Swinging* and early '80s techno-pop.

Parklife, the notoriously difficult third album released in April, was an unqualified triumph. Here, the reference points – Pink Floyd, Talking Heads, The Buzzcocks, Madness, Devo, Wire, Magazine, thrashy punk à la The Vibrators and clever-clever post-punk (XTC, say) – didn't so much inform the songs as shine like tiny little sparks from the past through a music that can really only be described now as Blurlike.

Parklife's stylistic variety and breadth of ambition was emphasised by *To The End*, the second single from the album and another hit when it was issued in June. Featuring sumptuous strings, ethereal French backing vocals courtesy of Laetita Sadier of avant-popsters Stereolab, and fabulously over-produced by Stephen "Pet Shop Boys/New Order" Hague, *To The End* sounded like a latterday John Barryesque *James Bond* theme. It was Blur's contribution to the hallowed pantheon of teenage summer snog-athons, their very own *I'm Not In Love* or *If You Leave Me Now*. The reach and range of *Parklife* and *To The End* indicated that, for Blur, and for British pop, anything was possible.

Blur's quantum leap from dippy chancers to agenda-setters had a healthy effect on British pop in 1994. Their critical and commercial success gave the lie to cultural commentators such as Tony Parsons who believe that Pop Is Dead and restored the balance after American Rock's near-hegemony of the music industry over the last few years. Indeed, Blur's unassailable rise seemed to coincide with the demise of grunge following the suicide of Kurt Cobain in April '94, offering a fresh opportunity for the likes of Oasis, Elastica, Pulp, Echobelly and Radiohead to dominate the scene.

All that remained for Blur in autumn '94 was to do what their quintessentially British predecessors failed to do: conquer the States. Reports filtering across the Atlantic during July/August indicated that the peculiar parochialism and idiosyncratic Englishisms of *Parklife* were achieving the impossible – turning the Yanks on.

Who'd have thought it?

paul lester

"No plaid shirts, no US accents, no Made in America posturing. At last, Blur proved to me that once again, Britain can produce a genuinely good rock band without relying on a string of American influences. Instead, flashes of Blighty's finest – Kinks, Bowie, Beatles – shine through their music, and *Parklife* also proves that albums can be genuinely diverse and still hold together. Excellent material from a band that looks like they're here to stay."

Gary Davies

paul weller

"This was the year that Weller proved that he is capable enough to become a mature performer with integrity in the manner of Van Morrison, Elvis Costello, or Neil Young."

★ The first year of the new decade was not a happy one for Paul Weller. First, he was dropped by Polydor after 12 years of loyal carriage-clock-deserving service, his crime being the delivery of a ropy Garage album to the label (which record company legend has it was so poor, it's no wonder it has yet to grace the bootleg stalls). Secondly, his Solid Bond studio, set up with the royalties from his Jam and Style Council days, had gone bust. Worse still, he felt that his creative muse had completely deserted him. With two sturdy Greatest Hits packages to his name at the age of 31, and legendary status as possibly the coolest skinny geezer of all time, it looked like Weller was finished.

"It was a bad time, a low time," he admitted recently. "But I realise now you've got to go through it. It did me good, brought me back down to earth a little bit."

If Weller's critical and popular re-emergence became concrete with the release of *Wild Wood*, his creative regeneration dates back to a series of low-key gigs at second division London venues such as The Paul Weller Movement, and the 1991

release of the single, *Into Tomorrow*, on his own Freedom High label. Long-term Weller fanatics began feverishly broadcasting the fact that the great man had found his voice again. As he now agrees, "The turning point for me was writing *Into Tomorrow*. Until then I thought I'd lost it."

"And if at times it seems insane/All the tears in searching/Turning all your joy to pain/In pursuit of learning..." For the first time Paul Weller had gone beyond trying to be the spokesman for the fashionable end of his generation, the ageing mods, the cappuccino poseurs; he was opening up about his own turbulent emotions.

"When I was in The Jam, I wrote about other people's feelings. Now I write about myself, my feelings. I like the way music can get you through dark periods."

The light at the end of a particularly dark tunnel in sight, Weller's cocky live

performances at packed club venues in 1992, and a deal with Go! Discs, led to a *Top Of The Pops* appearance with *Uh-Huh Oh-Yeh* and dignified sales and reviews for his eponymous debut solo album. But the ace card tucked in his desert boot turned out to be *Sunflower*, the first single off the Mercury-nominated follow-up album, *Wild Wood*. With firmly gritted teeth, wielding his guitar like an offensive weapon, Weller was exhuming the ghosts of The Small Faces, Cream and Traffic just as he had once payed unhealthily obsessive homage to The Who or Stax – but this time he was definitely no one other than Paul Weller.

At 35, and still looking ten years younger and more vital than any of his peers, Weller was performing with a wild-eyed passion and kick-starting his own second coming.

Skinny-rib T-shirts, Levi's hipster cords, Marriot hairdo – he's still the envy of most

"At 35, and still looking ten years younger and more vital than any of his peers, Weller was performing with a wild-eyed passion and kick-starting his own second coming."

blokes and a lust object for many girls, even though the man who at one time promised he would "die a mod" while refusing to listen to records made by anyone with long hair or a beard has almost completely reinvented himself. He's near as dammit turned hippy on us.

His current troupe are certainly the best since The Jam days – long-term drumming sidekick Steve White, bassist Yolanda Charles and axe buddy Steve Craddock of Ocean Colour Scene. Together they incite a fevered audience reaction in sharp contrast to the cool indifference of Style Council crowds. As *Mojo* observed at a Guildford show in April, "the more robust numbers trigger the sort of mosh pit mayhem that used to accompany *Strange Town* and *Billy Hunt* in 1979". As Weller himself pointed out, "When I was a kid and had just started playing guitar, all I wanted to be was in a pop group, be successful and make records. And I don't see anything wrong in that really. I just got side-tracked."

The themes of the *Wild Wood* album acknowledged his regeneration, with song titles like *Has My Fire Really Gone Out?*, the overall imagery indicating a personal struggle with past successes and the fear of failure, a search for the answers to The Big Questions; Weller standing bewildered at *The Foot Of The Mountain* and "chasing dreams across the fields" in *Shadow Of The Sun*, insistent on having it all "while I'm still young". Tracks like *All The Pictures On The Wall* dealt with the numbing death of a relationship, *Country* was a poetic dream of a rural life, *Can You Heal Us (Holy Man)* brought fears that Weller had Got God. But as one particular reviewer at the time commented tellingly, "[The] subjects hardly represent virgin territory for artists of his

age, but he approaches them with conviction and finesse."

Musically, the sound was tight, punchy and bone dry, Weller accepting it could be termed as "retro", buy hey, didn't the old records sound better anyway? He flattened all accusations that he was Doing A Lenny with the sheer intensity and character of his approach, and calmly intoned that Kravitz made "patchwork music". Weller isn't simply pick 'n' mixing his influences. He means it (man). He's grown-up, but he hasn't mellowed; there's still a fiery sparkle in his eye. Better still, his audience has matured with him, even if the odd loser still shouts for *Going Underground* at the gigs.

A growing fascination for Dylan may point the way forward for future releases. Whatever, this was the year that Weller proved that he is capable enough to become a mature performer with integrity in the manner of Van Morrison, Elvis Costello, or Neil Young. The man the music press once dismissed as The Modfather is reaching his creative peak. Joe Strummer's prediction that Weller would become one of this country's greatest-ever soul singers is beginning to sound strangely prophetic. At last, Paul Weller feels at one with himself.

"Now I can look at Neil Young and Van Morrison, who are still valid and prolific," he says. "Do we have a certain time and then it finishes, or can we make it go on forever? I dunno..."

tom doyle

on air

"Where were you in '82? I was in a record queue (not all year!) behind Paul Weller. His purchase was Edwin Starr's *Smooth*, so I asked him if he was a secret soul freak. He replied that his next band would be pretty much a soul outfit. I was so stunned that before I could attack him physically he was gone. For those who feel that the Style Council was a waste of recording equipment, my sincerest apologies. Paul's recent material is a massive return to form and sounds to me like something The Jam might have eventually come up with. So get jamming, get back into Paul Weller."

Gary King

bjork

"It's entirely probable that many neither know nor care who The Sugarcubes were. For better or worse, Bjork has become this decade's Sade – a face, a sound, a cipher, an idea."

 "I've got the right to be an idiot and I've got the right to be clever, both at the same time," Bjork could be found telling a swish American magazine in the summer of 1994. "I insist on being happy, mad, sad, stupid, brilliant, genius, imbecile, horrible, mean, happy. I make an effort not to forget all those different colours: to get hilariously drunk sometimes *and* to pay all my electricity bills *and* to forget what time it is *and* run a band without a fault."

It's probably just as well that the 28-year-old pop diva looks so benignly on the multifarious traits of human behaviour. The past year has seen her evolve from cultish indie yodeller to genuine eccentric crossover star of pop and dance culture. Her face – grinning, gurning or gazing – has appeared on every glossy magazine cover known to the western world. She has become a bemused neo-grunge fashion icon and an amused award-winner. She is very nearly the least pronunciation-friendly household name in Britain, and her solo

album, *Debut*, is clearly just the beginning. It's achieved what are described as "double platinum" sales (ie more than Phil Collins' last effort). Her music will launch the new Levi's jeans ad campaign.

Bjork is not, however, strictly speaking, a newcomer. Through the '80s she was a star – there aren't many – in Iceland. She'd already cut a punk album at the age of 11 (her mother's idea). Titled *Bjork Gudmunsdottir* (but what's in a name?), it sold over 6,000 copies. (Today these collectors' items change hands for three-figure sums.) Around this time Bjork developed the give-a-hoot attitude towards fame which has served her so well of late. Many flailing experiments down the line she joined "hardcore existential jazz punk" outfit Kukl. Kukl nurtured their love of radical art and formed a collective called

Bad Taste. To blow off steam at the weekends they would mutate into a happy-go-lucky "joke band", who'd "write bad pop songs about making love to cats". Along with guitarist Thor Eldon, the father of her child, Bjork found herself in (cue thunderclap) The Sugarcubes.

In late 1987, this group of idiosyncratic mavericks produced an eerily beautiful single, *Birthday*. As chance would have it, a certain *Melody Maker* writer quite correctly declared this the finest record made since the dawn of time, and a succession of cover stories, casting the Keystone Cops in Dante's Inferno, snowballed. Bjork has complained since that the group were patronised as loopy surrealist Eskimos. It is difficult to apologise for this presentation when you have witnessed said band being determinedly loopy and surrealist Eskimos (with a taste for a lethal Icelandic drink known as Brenivin) in four different countries. Bjork's first highly glamorous and exotic words to the British press in London were, "Sorry my hands are wet, I've just been shitting."

Global interest lasted for over four years and three albums, but after the rapturous acclaim that heralded the highly charming *Life's Too Good* album, a minor backlash bubbled up like a lazy geyser. People grumbled at the yobbish/poetic contribution of Einar Orn. It became increasingly evident that what the popular ear coveted was the staggering voice of Bjork without the frenetic filter of the band's wilful perversities. In 1992 they went their separate ways. Bjork fell in with a good crowd, moved to London, embraced club culture (well, she'd *always* liked Boney M), and is now a dinner-party darling, a coffee-table countess. It's entirely probable that many owners of the *Debut* CD neither know nor really care who The Sugarcubes were. For better or worse, Bjork has become this decade's Sade – a face, a sound, a cipher, an idea.

Though much of *Debut* is contrived electronic dance fodder (producer Nellee Hooper of Soul II Soul fame proving as influential to the direction and public perception of the new Bjork as the fashion shoots and sleeve photography of Jean Baptiste Mondino), it still sparks and crackles, thanks to the immense mountain-swallowing vocal range that looms and lurches from the unlikely source of that tiny frame. Singles (married to gently absurd and hyper-real videos) such as *Human Behaviour*, *Venus As A Boy*, *Big Time Sensuality*, and *Violently Happy* force-fed jumping beans to the charts, and Bjork became an unwitting role model, even hailed as "the new Madonna". With *Play Dead*, the theme song from the *Young Americans* British-made movie, she proved she could still tackle a good tune with knowing guts and glory. She became so very very famous that *Spitting Image* devoted a puppet to her. It whirls and rotates with a childlike absence of self-consciousness, imitates fire alarms and mimics microwaves.

Bjork continues to bewilder interviewers as the pop butterfly who won't be pinned down. To our reserved Brit sensibilities she appears to be a euphoric cross between a party-devouring feral urchin and a media-manipulating, bizarre, quintessentially "foreign", drop-out princess.

At the Brit awards, where she elected to perform a duet with PJ Harvey of *I Can't Get No Satisfaction*, she won in the categories of Best International Act and Best Newcomer. How she must've chuckled at the latter. Now, back in Reykjavik, her reputation swoops somewhere between Helen of Troy, Betty Boop, and God.

In August '93, soon after *Debut* began its chart assault, Bjork's first headline live show as a solo artist (at London's Forum) saw another deluge of praise. "Deserves every superlative in the Thesaurus," wittered *The Guardian*. "Melted every heart in the house, as we knew she would," cooed *MM*. These events continued to be highspots of the social calendar, culminating in her bill-topping whirl at the 1994 Glastonbury Festival, where somebody came up with a new accolade: "sexiest short person on the planet. Beautiful children know they can get away with anything." Lads love her; so do loners. And nouveau feminists simply worship her. Never worrying what's right or proper, she can do no wrong.

"Being a woman gets in the way," she's said. "It's like people who explain my music in terms of coming from Iceland, or having Oriental eyes. If I was from Newcastle making exactly the same noises I wouldn't get all this elfin bullshit." Bjork is interested in Georges Bataille, Betty Hutton, Gerard Depardieu, her son Sindri, her peripatetic nature, lack of inhibition, going to clubs and *actually dancing*, and earthquakes.

"Pop music is one of the strongest forces in the world, one of the necessities of life, up there with religion and food."

She finds all the attention "quite flattering". She gets bored easily. She is interested in being violently happy.

on air

"If there's one thing that struck me about Bjork, it was her appeal as quite possibly the first genuine crossover artist. As a singer with the Sugarcubes, she'd already gained credibility with indie rock fans; as a vocalist with an ear for a good tune, pop fans were soon hooked; and as a regular mover in London's clubs, she knew only too well how to get the dance crowd on their feet. *Debut,* her first solo album, proved to me that the combination works, and that boundaries between music styles were made to be broken. And Bjork knows how to break them into pieces."

Richard Skinner

chris roberts

the cranberries

"If it's debatable how much good The Cranberries have done America, there's no doubting that America has done wonders for them."

⭐ In 1994, The Cranberries took almost everything America can give a young band. They sold over two million copies of their album, the lovely and unassuming if cumbersomely titled *Everybody Else Is Doing It, So Why Can't We?*. They played stadiums supporting Duran Duran, and decent-sized college venues supported by Suede and Counting Crows. MTV held "Cranberries Days", where they played nothing but the band's collected works, which hardly amount to a substantial cinematic oeuvre. The band's gentle arrangements and poignant minor chord lilts made them much-requested mainstays of rock radio and restaurant muzak alike. Delores O'Riordan's gorgeous voice inspired devotion, deification and, memorably, a sentence of vintage drivel from the author of *Lipstick Traces* and *Mystery Train*, Greil Marcus.

"It seems to summon," he postulated, "the landscapes and poses of the pre-Raphaelites, where our Christian ideas of innocence and our Enlightenment notions of intelligence break down into paganism."

Well, quite. Keep banging the rocks together, Greil.

If it's debatable, then, how much good The Cranberries have done America, there's no doubting that America has done wonders for them. Aside from making them – one assumes – reasonably wealthy and sufficiently famous to be asked to model suits for *Rolling Stone*, the absolute, uncritical adoration that America bestows on its chosen has helped The Cranberries ripen (wahey!) from the awkward, shy collection that arrived from County Limerick in 1990 to an assured, polished semi-alternative Pop group. It was only three years ago that Delores could hardly bring herself to face an audience, and tapes of her interviews used to summon every dog for miles around but were little use to transcribing journalists. This year, with her head shaved to a defiant crop, she was to be found ending gigs with a bizarre Irish jig and granting breezy interviews from hotel beds, confined so after sustaining a well rock'n'roll skiing injury in the French Alps.

"Since I was small, really small," she explained to *Melody Maker* from behind a leg brace, "I just knew that all this was going to be. I've known since I was a kid that I was going to be really successful. And that's why I was given this voice, so that everybody would hear it."

Indeed, almost everybody now has. But had Delores made her childhood prediction in a bookmaker's office, she'd surely have been invited to write her own ticket. Whatever activity Delores O'Riordan was referring to when she coined the title *Everybody Else Is Doing It, So Why Can't We?*, it certainly wasn't "New bands from this side of the Atlantic stealing the hearts and minds of middle America and laughing all the way to the bank." Since the unlikely ascent of the Billboard charts by EMF and Jesus Jones in 1991, the US has been, in British music terms, something of a graveyard. Every band that's cracked it over here – James, Happy Mondays, The Wonder Stuff, Curve, The Levellers, PJ Harvey, Suede among them – has gone over there and looked like they couldn't get arrested if they burnt down the White House and pissed on the smoking ruin.

When it eventually did happen, it happened to two bands residing very much in Britain's rock'n'roll Endsleigh League: Radiohead, and The Cranberries. Radiohead did it with a song called *Creep*, full of crunching guitars, sneering vocals, a line in self-loathing and nihilism not incompatible with the grunge zeitgeist, and therefore an understandable, if pleasantly surprising, hit. The Cranberries did it with a gentle, plaintive warble called *Linger*, a simple plea for swift release from a faltering relationship.

In Britain, where pop is – and long may it remain so – a continuing triumph of style over substance, of flash over pan, the

"It was only three years ago that Delores could hardly bring herself to face an audience... This year, with her head shaved to a defiant crop, she was to be found ending gigs with a bizarre Irish jig..."

Washington State, cut straight through the static to surmise that "O'Riordan never pushes her vocal gift, she coaxes it straight from the warmth of her heart," before going on to describe said voice as "patrician". And who are we to argue.

Judging by recent interviews, The Cranberries seem to be accepting their fame and fortune with about the right blend of pride and bemusement. They were last heard of working on the follow-up album, again under the supervision of former Smiths producer and Morrissey collaborator Stephen Street. Some of these songs have already been previewed live, most notably *Twenty One, Zombie* – a seething assault on the redundant creed of republican extremism – and the certifiable future classic *So Cold In Ireland*.

All are roughly what you'd expect, the subtle, pastoral guitars that could well drift away like mist if not galvanised by a voice that seems to be hooked to the heavens by God's own jumper cable.

"I think," Delores told *Deadline* magazine, "what I'd like to do in the future is keep writing really strong songs. I suppose some day I'd like to enlighten some people in the human race into thinking in a better way, open their minds."

After The Cranberries' 1994, she could be forgiven for thinking that almost anything is possible.

andrew mueller

on air

"*Everybody Is Doing It, So Why Can't We?* – for me, the album title of the year. The LP's excellent first single, *Linger*, didn't make it here first time around, but then took the States by storm. And after weeks of airplay at Virgin 1215, Island Records finally took the hint and re-issued it in the UK, the band successfully consolidating the resultant success with *Dreams*, their second hit. It wouldn't surprise me if singer Dolores O'Riordan ends up a solo act, but in the meantime, maybe the working title of the second album could have been "*We Can Do It, But What Next?*"

Graham Dene

sentiments of *Linger* had seemed, if touching, perhaps twee, or maybe just embarrassingly honest. In America, where British bands and their manifestos, theories, contrivances, personas, images and, above all, irony have long been greeted with a mixture of derision and bafflement, they heard Delores sing it simple and sweet and they knocked The Cranberries down in the rush. The fact that The Cranberries were a) of Celtic stock, which never goes amiss in the States, even if one hapless MTV jock famously introduced them as from "Limerick, England" and b) very definitely not grunge, didn't hurt, either.

As that feared journal of record, the *Fort Worth Star-Telegraph*, observed, "The Cranberries make the most of the power of simple, strong structures to push their songs across." Similarly, and as usual, the pop columnist on the *Tri-City Herald* of Pasco,

Pink Floyd

acts of the ye

"Pink Floyd have reached a point where they have little reason to take risks and even less to prove. The battles have all been won, unimaginable heights have been scaled..."

★ At the beginning of 1993, four-and-a-half years after Pink Floyd had played the final show of their *Momentary Lapse Of Reason* tour, the leviathan stirred again. Guitarist and singer David Gilmour, drummer Nick Mason and keyboard player Rick Wright reconvened, and spent a fruitful two-week period improvising together, kicking ideas around and laying down the first, hazy foundations of about 50 songs. From these beginnings a new album, entitled *The Division Bell*, would eventually be written, recorded and released in April 1994.

There could have been little doubt about the likely fate of *The Division Bell*. Although temporarily gone, the group had hardly been forgotten. The fallow years had produced a live album, *The Delicate Sound Of Thunder*, a boxed set called *Shine On* and a reissue of *Dark Side Of The Moon* which, in March 1993, celebrated the 20th anniversary of its release snugly installed at Number Four in the UK charts.

Even in their absence, honours were continually being bestowed upon the group ranging from the flattering – an Outstanding Contribution To British Music award at the Ivor Novello ceremony in 1992 – to the preposterous: induction into the National Association of Brick Distributors' Hall Of Fame the year before, in recognition of *The Wall*'s contribution to the American brick industry. The only question mark hanging over *The Division Bell* was exactly how big a hit it was going to be. The answer surprised even the optimists.

An album of bold portentous themes, *The Division Bell* bore all the classic hallmarks that have made the music of Pink Floyd a cornerstone of rock culture. Not overly specific, its lyrics conjured dark oppressive moods of alienation (*Poles Apart*) and emotional numbness (*Wearing The Inside Out*) with occasional moments of uplift and tales of spirits breaking free from earthbound chains (*Coming Back To Life*). Songs of panoramic scope, such as *What Do*

"FM" found enormous empathy with, as they did with the Crash Test Dummies' indecipherable *Mmm* and tremendous cartoon hip-hop gleam of Cypress Hill's *Insane In The Brain*. And then *Doop* went to Number One. Curses.

To Essex we turned, unfeasibly, for shiny Brit-pop in the google-eyed good-lookingness of Blur, with their rousing pop pinger *Boys And Girls* heralding some kind of New British Mod Revival (Part 27). Several billion "indie-pop" groups wore skinny ties and looked like they needed a Pot Noodle or 10, but not as much, of course, as Primal Scream, who attempted to invent old-blokes'-r'n'b-in-a-Louisiana-pub-with-spitoons-in-it with *Rocks* and *Jailbird*, and no one thought they were much cop any more. Blur danced on their barraful of pop plums, gave us the effervescent *To The End*, everyone went "coo" and realised they'd been really quite talented all along. Damn. We always knew that about Sheffield's premier crimpolene superstars Pulp, who finally made televisual glory with *Lipgloss*, *Do You Remember The First Time* and the greatest pop song ever written (this week), *Babies*. A nation of nubiles fancied the corduroy breeks off Gentleman Jarvis,

52, and lots of old people felt much better about themselves. Hurrah!

Then it was the girls' turn. Salt 'n' Pepa 'n' En Vogue had already alighted the hormonal ragings of pop girlies across the globe with the speciality-swing of *Whatta Man*, and then the Salts did it all themselves with *Shoop* and reckoned we should all have a "yum yum scoop", and boy did they know a thing or two. Even weedy Eternal continued their kwahlidee smoochers with *Save Our Love* and *Just A Step From Heaven*, before Prince – or should that be % or @ or whatever he's called these days – took dwarf-pop into a new dimension of wimpfulness with the shimmering *The Most Beautiful Girl In The World*.

You could tell summer was upon us. The sun, as we know, makes everyone all goofy and thus big snogs abounded to Wet Wet Wet's blasted 89 weeks at Number One with *Love Is All Around Us*, Big Mountain's rather more jaunty *Baby I Love Your Way*, Maria Carey's blubmungous *Any Time You Need A Friend*, while ver kids sought solace in East 17's *All Around The World*.

We should have known. Twelve

▲ *2Unlimited: rave music for the under-fives*

months on, Girlie-Bloke Pop was Back! and it was bigger than ever. New tunes floated out from BBI, Worlds Apart, EYC, Let Loose and Take That, who seemed to have taken on drip-pop as a radical new direction with *Love Ain't Here Anymore*. They toured all through the autumn and the tots were jubilant. Old folk contented themselves with The Future via Oasis' paean to the glory of the New Seekers, ie *Shaker Maker*, Shed Seven's paean to the glory of Sham 69, ie *Dolphins*, the Beastie Boys' *Get It Together* and the Manic Street Preachers' New Punk bile-brimmer *Faster/PCP*, and rattled an arthritic knee to the verily kerrlassic Dawn Penn's *You Don't Love Me (No No No)*. New pop was promised by Plumstead's finest shouty-pop troubadours Shampoo.

It was they, with their peroxide curlicues and fabulous shoes with glitter on, who embodied The Voice Of The Kids in 1994. Their favourite bands of the year? East 17 and, er, Gary Numan. Persons over 19 didn't understand anything anymore – which is, of course, precisely as it should be. That's pop, mate.

sylvia patterson

◀ *Take That: girlie-bloke pop is back*

Indie

"*If indie music in 1994 showed anything, it was that the desire to progress, which has gradually been slowing down since punk, has all but stalled.*"

▲ *S*M*A*S*H: New Wave Part Deux*

Ostensibly it's been a healthy time for British indie music. After Kurt Cobain's death we were left with a bunch of shameful Nirvana imitators and MOR shams strutting in their ripped jeans and plaid shirts. Grunge didn't die, but for a while it excavated a few too many tender memories.

And so we looked closer to home for the spiky pop thrill of some new young Pop Stars. What started off as a new glam movement (at least in the eyes of the press) with Suede, Pulp and The Auteurs as its flag bearers, gave way to a clutch of fresh-faced indie terriers with home-made haircuts and sequined sneers. *NME* called it The New Wave Of New Wave, and well… so did the rest of us. S*M*A*S*H and These Animal Men appeared on *Top Of The Pops* within a few weeks of each other, jumping around so much that no end of camera training could contain them.

In sound and fury, both bands seemed at pains to emulate the manifesto of the fledgling Manic Street Preachers when they burst onto the scene four years ago. But the visceral pop kick of S*M*A*S*H's *Real Surreal* and *Lady Love Your C**** wasn't quite

as erudite or assured as the mascara-stained existentialism that the Manics sought to force down our throats. Still, you could jump around to it, a quality that should never be underestimated in a record.

And indeed, so taken was the indie constituency with it, that These Animal Men, spearheaded by the charmingly named Hooligan, thrashed all three chords in the UK Subs' songbook all the way to the bank. However, by the end of the summer, the smart money was on York's Shed Seven, whose second single *Dolphin* – a boiling kaleidoscope of bongos, teen-charged crooning and John Squire guitar shimmers – vaulted into the Top 40 and onto indie dancefloors across the country. The haircuts and clothes may have lumped Shed Seven in with their Adidas-adorned peers, but a hook-stuffed album in the can, plus the shag-me eyes and chiselled features of Rick Witter, flaunted a beauty that marked them out for special attention.

It wasn't just the New Wave Of New Wave bands that contributed to the singularly retrogressive air of indie pop in 1994. Elastica – voted brightest hope of 1994 by readers of *Melody Maker* and *NME* – had a comparatively quiet time leading up

to Christmas. Their *Line Up* single, though, came as a complete microcosm of the Elastica sound – layer upon layer of warped fuzzpop that bore more resemblance to Wire's *Pink Flag* album than anything produced over the past decade. Great if you like that kind of thing.

And if you felt like listening to something a little more modern, then you could always slip on *Insomniac* and *I Can't Imagine The World Without Me* by Echobelly. Sonya's vocals possessed the sneering taunt of one Mr Steven Morrissey without any of the pith and prettiness. As summer came to a close, it became obvious that the latter single – an overstuffed Primitives-meets-Lennon tirade of pomposity, was probably as good as Echobelly were going to get.

At least if you were going to ape Morrissey's singing style, you might care to do it with a little more theatricality and panache than Echobelly can muster. And, in the case of Gene, you might want to take it a step further and reel off several rounds of lethal pop ammo to go with it. In March,

"Some people say that guitars are the problem, that they just sound obsolete compared to the way dance music has eaten up the zeitgeist. Bollocks, I say."

▲ Breeders: staggering

Gene swallowed up the spotlight with *To The Dead*, a wonderfully self-pitying slab of mordant suicide pop. They followed this with *Be My Light, Be My Guide* and a sellout national tour. Silhouetted perfectly against some suitably *noire* lighting, Rossiter, with cigarette in hand, looked already assured of his oncoming stardom.

With Blur, Pulp, Primal Scream and Bjork finally relinquishing their indie following and breaking out into mainstream success, five Mancunians by the name of Oasis appeared from nowhere to follow swiftly in their footsteps. After a carefully orchestrated campaign on the part of Creation records, the Shaun Ryder-esque drawl of Liam Gallagher and his band's post-baggy janglepop could be heard blaring out of every bedsit across the land. Oasis offered a simplicity and a generic familiarity that, even a year ago, seemed far too conservative to catch on (remember Whiteout?). Lyrics like "I know a girl called Elsa/She's into Alka-Seltzer" would have made The La's seem like latter-day TS Eliots by comparison.

Perhaps, in the wake of Cobain's untimely departure, we didn't want the bold, innovative avant-pop offered on the peripheries of indie by the likes of Disco Inferno, Insides and Seefeel. Nor did we want the staggering cross-cultural collages evidenced on Trans-Global Underground's second album, or the masterful, militant hip-hop of Fun-Da-Mental's *Seize The Time* album. No. We wanted derivative urchin pop. By the time Oasis's debut album followed *Shakermaker* and *Live Forever* into the Top 10, and The Stone Roses prepared for the release of their long-awaited second album, Oasis's leaden version of what The Stone Roses used to do seemed more and more like something we were making do with than actually seeking out. So much for the band who sang "You've got to be yourself/ You can't be no one else".

If indie music in 1994 showed anything, it was that the desire to progress, which has gradually been slowing down since punk, has all but stalled. Sure, there are pockets of innovation to be found – be it The Boo Radleys' ability to fashion a planet of sound out of crashing dub riddims, Beatley inflections and Arthur Lee-style insanity; be it Tindersticks' effortless ability to suck all the light out of the stars and leave you gasping for hope; or be it Stereolab's inspired experiments with the mechanics of sound merged with a pin-sharp pop sensibility – but these groups are all too conspicuous by their scarcity.

Some people say that guitars are the problem, that they just sound obsolete compared to the way dance music has eaten up the zeitgeist. Bollocks, I say. For every Ride or Lush, content to let a decent record collection and a hip record label paper over their lack of inspiration, there's the itchy psycho-whimsy of Pavement, Disco Inferno's disturbing avant-pop or the Breeders' percussive narcosis. These are bands that feel totally comfortable with the responsibility of making staggering pop music, yet realise that the more you tease your audience's preconceptions, the more they'll remember you for it a year or two down the line.

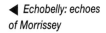

◀ Echobelly: echoes of Morrissey

peter paphides

KATE BUSH
The Red Shoes (EMI)

"A four year gestation period has produced Kate Bush's most complex album... *The Red Shoes* conveys an air of solemn reflection. Kate, in heart-stopping voice throughout, seems somber to the point of melancholia... as moving as anything she's ever committed to tape, this is the sort of record that reveals itself in gradual layers." **The Guardian**

"*The Red Shoes* is Bush at her most vulnerable, exposed, introverted and occasionally shrill: a collection of vivid emotional portraits daubed in thick gashes of acrylic and framed by curtains of purple rouged satin. Not that easy to love, perhaps, but difficult to ignore." **The Times**

"... one is left with a distinct feeling that her involvement is as hedonistic here as it was on *Hounds Of Love* and *The Sensual World*, though applied to matters of the soul rather than the body." **The Independent**

"*The Red Shoes* dances so far ahead of the rest, it's embarrassing. Apparently, the contest for second place is to be allowed to continue, out of magnanimity." **Melody Maker**

DAVID BYRNE
David Byrne (WEA)

"After meandering down some lonely musical pathways, David Byrne has returned to his role as the personification of New York City's neurotic yet compelling energy... just when the finely-honed lyrics begin to seem straightforward, he unwraps another twisted layer." **Mojo**

"... every corner of this album radiates with the realisation that David Byrne, perhaps for the first time, is perfectly happy being David Byrne. It's been a long, strange voyage. Welcome back." **Vox**

C

MARIAH CAREY
Music Box (Columbia)

"With a voice that slices through the mix like a laser beam, lyrics that assail the emotional tastebuds like an oozing dollop of clotted cream and songs that veer from slick swingbeat to soggy soul, Mariah Carey has evolved a formula that is not so much winning as overwhelming. If soul music was required to conform to EC quality guidelines it would sound something like this." **The Times**

"...most of *Music Box* is schmaltzy AOR. The material allows The Voice little scope for showing off, and Ms Carey witters ineffectually from within the anodyne fog." **Melody Maker**

"The thrill of a singer revelling in her own vocal prowess cannot be denied – that's where the pleasure of Mariah Carey resides." **Q**

CARTER THE UNSTOPPABLE SEX MACHINE
Post Historic Monsters (Chrysalis)

"Carter used to be the cheeriest chappies in indie pop. Now they've gone all serious with angry songs about suicide, child abuse and the uselessness of the Royal Family." **Smash Hits**

"... *Post Historic Monsters* comes as a pleasant surprise. Though not that pleasant – after all, it sounds the same as every other Carter album, with fewer of the one with the spaghetti haircut's celebrated punned titles." **Sky**

"Even Carter The Unstoppable PC Machine it seems, is not immune to the silly season's dinosaur cliché-mania; but two months after the film's release, it just seems passé: the T Rex roaring from the cover, and that insipid pun of a title, are as old hat now as most of Carter's targets here." **The Independent**

"The result is a bunch of riffs that sound like rejects from an early Clash album... the overall effect fails either to capture the spirit of the age or raise the spirits in quite the way that was intended." **The Times**

NICK CAVE & THE BAD SEEDS
Let Love In (Mute)

"Arch angst-fiend Nick Cave isn't in the business of making bad records, but *Let Love In* is stunning. Cave's sepulchral baritone is offset by the murky brilliance of the band, and deals in his chosen territory of destruction and damnation like some latter day Heathcliffe." **Mojo**

"... things are a little more explicity personal this time round, but this is still, ostensibly, just another Nick Cave album. Just another Nick Cave record that rides the nine circles of hell like a giant red rollercoaster; that wallows and raves and, ultimately, amazes." **NME**

"*Let Love In* is another freakshow of horribly curdled obsessions, miserable low-life death and impending doom. Records that will keep you awake at night long after you've stopped playing them are few and far between. This, happily, is one of them." **Select**

"*Let Love In* is a loaded gun blasting away all your preconceptions of what lurve should be. Dangerous in the wrong hands, no doubt, but, what the fuck, buy it for the one you love." **Melody Maker**

THE CHARLATANS
Up To Our Hips (Beggars Banquet)

"The Charlatans used to be a treat – fat, vintage Stranglers-like organ riffs, hip-shuffling dance beats, a kissable singer and a sense of youthful urgency. But on their third album, *Up To Our Hips*, they commit the mortal sin of being boring. Only total spliffheads move slowly enough to get this miasmic dirge." **Sky**

"Far from being embittered ex-tabloid sensations, workshy human enigmas or My Jealous God, The Charlatans have made Another Pretty Good Album; just about what we expected, really." **NME**

"Playing the percentages, *Up To Our Hips* is way ahead of its predecessor, *Between 10 And 11*, which was quarter of an album at best. *Up To Our Hips* is half an album, easily." **Melody Maker**

TONI CHILDS
The Woman's Boat (Geffen)

"Intriguing, adventurous album from the deep, dark voice of Californian singer-songwriter Toni. Beneath the rather off-putting new-age feminist surface there's some challenging, exotic music here." **Today**

"... Childs has written an 11-song cycle which begins with womb and ends with death, touching upon birth, love, motherhood, passion and every other interpersonal link that comes in between. It's certainly ambitious, even if not many of the songs really succeed as such on their own." **Mojo**

ALEX CHILTON
Cliches (New Rose)

"With its potential audience at an all-time high, Chilton could easily have cashed in, delivering an album that would define what others are emulating. Instead, he throws a curve. This album reminds us that Chilton is not an artist to be categorised nor exploited." **Mojo**

"On the third Big Star album, Chilton's crazed desperation resulted in songs which provided utterly compelling glimpses of the depths of paranoid delusion. This too is desperate, but only insofar as it suggests that his self-critical faculties have flown the coop." **Q**

"It's just cack. Alex, you've inflicted your worst ever album on your audience. Nice one." **Select**

COCTEAU TWINS
Four-Calendar Café (Fontana)

"From the first bar to the last, *Four-Calendar Café* consists of romanticist rhapsodies and shimmering glissandos played on celestial harps. I know, you're astounded. But here's the real surprise. For the first time ever, discounting last year's *Frosty The Snowman*, you can hear what she's on about." **Melody Maker**

"Some of this newfound focus finds the Cocteaus edging towards power ballad territory, a few of Fraser's mostly thrilling vocal arrangements border on the twee but, overall, *Four-Calendar Café* shows that the Cocteaus can be bewitching without being merely mystifying." **Q**

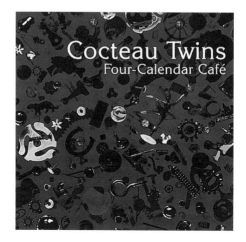

"The Cocteau Twins would never be embarrassed by gentleness but then they don't have a sharp edge or pointy corner between them. Nor, usually, do they have much in the way of meaning, though *Four-Calendar Café* finds Liz Fraser making what are, by her standards, giant strides of comprehensibility." **The Independent**

"...this record knows exactly what it's doing, and how much it's giving away; it has not dirtied its hands with experimentation or daring. If you listen carefully, you can hear the sound of treading water. And it's a lovely sound." **Select**

LLOYD COLE
Bad Vibes (Fontana)

"The problem is Cole's rather ineffectual delivery. He writes nice songs that are often pregnant with emotion and soulful nuance, but then struggles to achieve the vocal performances needed to do them justice." **The Times**

"Forget all your ill-conceived notions of what's credible and what's not and make room for 11 songs that put some aesthetic equilibrium back in your life." **Melody Maker**

"There are real blues lurking in the shadows – if only Cole's bookish, reclusive air would let them out." **Vox**

PHIL COLLINS
Both Sides (Virgin)

"... at his best he's as deft on affairs of the heart as he is cackhanded with politics. Most of *Both Sides'* melancholy yet seductive ruminations eyeball the uncertainties of relationships with an appealingly ruthless sympathy." **Q**

ALICE COOPER
The Last Temptation (Epic)

"Like the carnivals and funfairs that inspire him, Cooper still possesses a certain downmarket, theatrical flair. The thrill may be brief, but this is his best album for 15 years or more." **The Times**

"... amazingly, after centuries of duff and often embarrassing comebacks, Alice Cooper has made a halfway decent album. Blow me, if this was Rigid With Metal magazine we'd probably all be jumping around hailing *The Last Temptation* as a king-sized corker." **NME**

"In which the old rocker gives today's grunge merchants a run for their money and issues a warning to America's youth."
Today

JULIAN COPE
Autogeddon (Echo)

"This is a mixed-up record filled with both musical and conceptual contradictions but that's exactly the man behind it. There are many apprentice rock eccentrics out there – arise Andy Bell, Dave Baker, Kristen Hersh etc – but there's only one Arch Drude. And he's 37 this year so you've got some catching up to do." **NME**

"Frankly, this is a very bad trip. It's like Copey has decided that electricity is an agent of Evil, no longer to be channelled into brilliant, ambitious, self-fulfilling music…" **Select**

"Those tuned into Cope's particular frequency will not be disappointed but it's hardly likely to win him new fans with its determined singularity. Apparently a new phase is just around the corner and something more conventional might be good for the bank balance, if not the soul." **Q**

ELVIS COSTELLO
Brutal Youth (Warners)
(See **The Year In Review** p. 20)

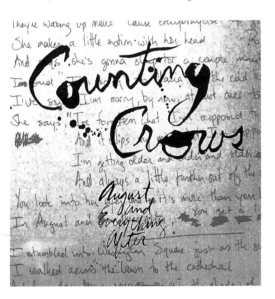

COUNTING CROWS
August And Everything After (Geffen)

"Currently Stateside's hottest property, Counting Crow's debut is lyrical, earnest and engaging Country and folk-inflected rock. Just don't mention REM." **Vox**

"*August And Everything After* is a gorgeous record, and there are never as many of them out there as we sometimes like to think."
Melody Maker

"Counting Crows haven't quite managed to light out from their national disaster zone, but all that flailing and raging makes for a cool drama on its own." **NME**

"If Counting Crows are to capture the attention of a wider public, Duritz needs to dip more deeply into the tub marked 'melodies' and should make more determined efforts to ensure that his band's impressive onstage energy is captured to much better effect next time around." **Q**

CRACKER
Kerosene (Virgin)

"…a rock laboratory of awesome proportions that, had it come out on vinyl in 1974, would have been hailed as a classic." **Vox**

"A band with no inhibitions, Cracker's country rock infusion is a friendly nod at the whiskey-doused world of Lynyrd Skynyrd and, more recently, Counting Crows." **Mojo**

THE CRANBERRIES
Everybody Else Is Doing It… (Island)
(See **The Year In Review** p. 18)

CRASH TEST DUMMIES
God Shuffled His Feet (RCA)

"*Mmm Mmm Mmm* is a truly beautiful masterpiece, but this album is hardly full of barnstormers." **Smash Hits**

"Nick Cave must be seething with envy." **Q**

"What at first glimpse sounds like a great, oddball pop album, soon mutates into forgettable fluff. Crash Test Dummies simply lack the wit or the style to rise above pedestrian MOR." **Vox**

BEVERLEY CRAVEN
Love Scenes (Epic)

"… *Love Scenes* is so light, pink and fluffy, it's probably best served on a stick." **Q**

CREDIT TO THE NATION
Take Dis (One Little Indian)

"No doubt about it, MC Fusion (Matty to his mates) is the king of right-on rap while

most rap crews are tough guys from LA who go on about guns and 'bitches'. For hard-hitting lyrics and top tunes without the dodginess, Take Dis and party." **Smash Hits**

"Even if *Take Dis* is short on any real surprises (apart from a small blast of opera and a recorded interview with John Peel) it works as a succinct documentary of the rise and rise of a diminutive black kid from Birmingham. Take dat and party." **Select**

"In many ways, this is both their *Three Feet High And Rising* and their *De La Soul Is Dead*. Raw, untutored originality and seething idealism meets disillusionment, paranoia and self-defensive instincts." **NME**

SHERYL CROW
Tuesday Night Music Club (A&M)

"Memorable stuff, sung with that unmistakable confidence of an artist who's getting it right all down the line." **Q**

"The content is hardly original, but Crow captures scenes beautifully, sings with a finely sanded rasp and writes melodies custom made for car radios. But inevitably, they will play only too well on MTV." **The Times**

"Her debut album is confident and self-assured, bubbling over with heady music from all sources – folk, jazz and the much-maligned soft rock." **Vox**

CROWDED HOUSE
Together Alone (Capitol)
(See **The Year In Review** p. 10)

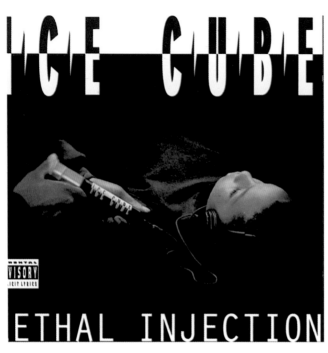

ICE CUBE
Lethal Injection (Island)

"The word 'knowledge' is prominently emblazoned on the CD booklet, evidence of Cube's positive intentions. *Lethal Injection* emphasises the rapper's committment to black empowerment, but its failing is that Cube perceives every issue in, pardon the expression, black and white. There's some nasty violence on this album – it opens with the rapper gratuitously shooting a white man – but for the most part *Lethal Injection* is thought-provoking." **The Guardian**

"No longer shouting the first couplet of invective that comes into his head over loops of automatic gunfire, Cube has matured as both a producer and lyricist. By burying his anger and thinking about what he says before he says it, he's produced the best album of his career so far." **Select**

"12 tracks that mesh ghetto mayhem with chill-out summer grooves worthy of Jazzy Jeff and the Fresh Prince. This is a scorchingly good, heavyweight album..." **Sky**

"It's a potent brew, strongly evocative of 70s blaxploitation movie soundtracks, whose confluence of black anger and superfly criminality is echoed in Cube's work." **The Independent**

CUD
Showbiz (A&M)

"Cud might shudder at the very idea, but they're starting to sound mature. They shouldn't worry, and nor should any long-term admirers. It suits them just fine." **Melody Maker**

"Back again with another set of vaudevillean outfits and high camp posturing, Cud will once again have the pundits struggling to invent new genres to account for their startling strain of absurdist pop. Whatever it is, it's brilliant." **Select**

"This is not a classic. It is probably one of the least ambitious or challenging records you'll hear all year. But wait! Cud's central clutch of ideas remains as gleamingly ace as ever, and Showbiz is as rich and strange as anyone could have wanted." **NME**

CURVE
Cuckoo (Anxious)

"Among other things, 1993 may be remembered as the year Curve came surging into the mainstream with the kind of uncompromising rock music that retains an affinity for the outlandish and atonal within more familiar structures. Aptly titled: it just sits there like a big cuckoo, outgrowing whichever genre it nests in, even as it gobbles up the choicer elements of that style: indie, goth, psychedelia, baggy, ambient, industrial, grunge ..." **The Independent**

"*Cuckoo* is the sound of a disaster happening to someone else. It never unnerves; it consistently overawes." **Melody Maker**

"Curve's problem is still lack of variety but what a sound it is – intense, mesmeric, full of kooky melodrama, and they've managed to up the decorations this time." **Q**

CYPRESS HILL
Black Sunday (Columbia)

"*Black Sunday*, the band's second LP, consolidates Cypress Hill's position by redoubling their assault. The trademark funky swagger and rolling blues licks remain intact, but unlike its predecessor there is no light relief to be had from the diet of dope and guns that is the Cypress Hill staple." **Vox**

"Thankfully absent from their hardcore stance is the brute sexism that normally goes along with such a tough guy routine." **Q**

DEEP FOREST
Deep Forest (Columbia)

"... the formula works fine, but when track after track features native vocal samples subjected to the fundamentalist religion of rigid four-beat repetition, the appeal palls rapidly." **Mojo**

DEEP PURPLE
The Battle Rages On (RCA)

"*The Battle Rages On* is their most persuasive bid yet to recover the colonies. No *Machine Head*, but at least a partial return to form." **Q**

MARCELLA DETROIT
Jewel (London)

"The downside is the occasional sterility and coldness of Detroit's voice. This suited her previous deranged outfit very well, but on *Jewel*, where the songs are far more restrained and tasteful, she sometimes sounds as if she just doesn't care." **Mojo**

"Maybe Marcella has become too used to her role as a consummate professional, verging on muso rather than loosening up as frontwoman." **Vox**

"Few surprises here: always the more sophisticated half of Shakespear's Sister, Marcella Detroit uses her first solo album to lay claim to Annie Lennox's mainstream pop soul crown." **The Independent**

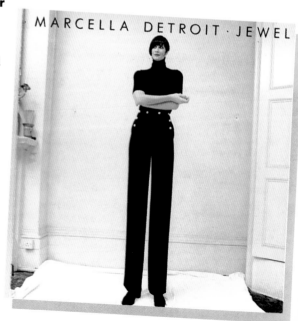

THE DIVINE COMEDY
Promenade (Setanta)

"It's probably too much to hope that The Divine Comedy will be massive, but let's not sully our hands with commerce. *Promenade* is a masterpiece. If you do one brave and imaginative thing this month, be on the side of the angels and buy this record." **Select**

"In its own little way, *Promenade* is a phenomenally audacious record, chiefly because it dares to be straight, to be straight-laced, to be so proper it sounds positively improper in the midst of a million rock stars all trying desperately hard to be debauched." **NME**

"*Promenade* is quite genteel, very witty, almost absurdly literate and very post modern. It also can't help but sound like an imaginary mixture of Michael Nyman and The Walker Brothers. Yep, that good." **Mojo**

"*Promenade* walks the path of indulgence with bravado and a mischevious grin. A stolen masterpiece." **Melody Maker**

BOB DYLAN
World Gone Wrong (Columbia)

"Dylan's 39th album is a bleak sequel to last year's acoustic set, *Good As I Been To You*. Again, he's alone in the studio with his guitar, scratchy sounding harmonica and a fistful of ballads. Most of them are so obscure that Dylan has had to pen liner notes explaining the origin of each, although puzzling through his cryptic notations is a job in itself. No doubt Dylan has his reasons for paying another visit to the music of his youth – is it that, after 35 years, the creative well has run dry?" **The Guardian**

"*World Gone Wrong* finds Dylan strumming again through songs from what he sees as his tradition. It is still, totally, a Bob Dylan record. Hear this man do it, and take courage. How great it could be if everybody struggling to find their own voice were able to just sort of stop struggling and... well, use their own voice. We all got one, unique as a fingerprint." **Mojo**

"... while one sympathises with his search for more enduring values, it's self-evident that the past and the primitive by no means have a monopoly on the truth, though they certainly seem to have a monopoly on Dylan's attentions these days." **The Independent**

"Any similarity to the sound of a pissed-up busker on the London Underground making it up as he goes along is, of course, purely coincidental." **Select**

ERASURE
I Say, I Say, I Say (Mute)

"Erasure are on a higher plane. They make music for adolescent girls who, while their male peers bluster and blaze in a hail of fart jokes, acne and rock, demand and always have demanded a constant stream of gloriously sentimental shiny hard pop. Once again Erasure have proved themselves worthy and the world, as a result, is a slightly nicer place." **NME**

"'I know this one,' claimed my dad when I whacked it on the stereo. And he's got a point – Erasure's latest album does sound like everything else they've ever done. But these boys are onto a winner, and they know it." **Smash Hits**

"Erasure have floated down from their heavenly heights to remind us that great pop music – above and beyond everything else – is a timeless celebration of now." **Vox**

GLORIA ESTEFAN
Mi Tierra (Epic)

"... there is a distinct shortage of pop tunes, and filling all the spaces with Afro-Cuban rhythms and percussion does make it all sound much of a muchness if you don't have the language." **Q**

THE FALL
Middle Class Revolt (Permanent)

"If you're looking for the true sound of the downtrodden, the prejudiced, rotten, grumbling voice of the gutter, only The Fall can commit it to record. *Middle Class Revolt* is more snotty, more inflexibile and more indecipherable than ever." **NME**

"Their 18th LP, *Middle Class Revolt* follows The Fall's first Top 10 album, and finds them back at the peak power of *This Nation's Saving Grace*, with Mark E Smith at the wheel of a muscular vehicle..." **Mojo**

"It's punchy, sour and the perfect antidote to all those pantomime-punk pretenders. And yet it's business as usual from The Fall; no pop gems, no dazzling surprises." **Vox**

FISH
Suits (The Dick Bros Record Company)

"It seems Fish is missing his mates rather more than they're missing him." **Vox**

"On this loosely themed protest against modern-day materialism, bile replaces the passionate sincerity that is Fish's most precious stock in trade..." **Q**

FUN-DA-MENTAL
Seize The Time (Beggars Banquet)

"Dark, relentless and brutal, Fun-Da-Mental's methods leave nothing to chance, or subtlety. Over 90 minutes they wear their listeners out, leave them drained, dizzy, ears ringing, throughly assailed. Which can't be all that far from the effect they hoped to achieve." **NME**

"...Fun-Da-Mental have reworked much of their original material, trading some of the band's innovative musical appoach in favour of a more straight-up rap attack." **Mojo**

"Between the powerhouse grooves, Nazi death threats and real-life radio reports of racist violence intensify the explosive tension." **Vox**

FUTURE SOUND OF LONDON
Lifeforms (Virgin)

"*Lifeforms* is 90 minutes of rolling ambient soup with themes boiling to the surface only to disappear again. FSOL's sound palette is

in a different league to the bedroom ambience pack..." **Select**

"... this is electronic music whose raw iconoclasm is matched by ear-catching melodies and a talent for evoking seductive dreamscapes." **Mojo**

"... compared to the quietly chundering chill-out chud that passes for modern music these days, this is Richard Strauss on a good day. Very, very superior fare." **Sky**

"... it's an electronic extravanganza, a huge, amazingly ambitious set that sounds not a lot like anything on Earth..." **NME**

g

GABRIELLE
Find Your Way (Go! Beat)

"*Find Your Way* won't break any records but it'll make Gaby a few mates. The laid back tempo is a bit repetitive, but this is still an accomplished debut." **Smash Hits**

"She cites everyone from Madonna to Haircut 100 as influences, but mostly you hear the stroll of swingbeat, the relaxedness of Lisa Stansfield and an ear for stylish dance pop." **Q**

"Gabrielle sings cutely and the majority of the 11 easy-on-the-ear cuts here are never less than pleasant. But there's little depth of interpretation to her lyrics; the deeper feelings remain untroubled and she has yet to discover her own voice." **Vox**

GUNS N' ROSES
The Spaghetti Incident (Geffen)

"An album of mainly punk covers, *The Spaghetti Incident* is actually Guns N' Roses' most enjoyable LP, since, though they can play a bit, they have never been able to write a decent song of their own." **The Independent**

"Lots of it is the most rock 'n' rollin, shriekin' 'n' cursin', psycho-chirp, punk-pop you heard. Youths of angst will place this upon their blasters, turn the volume up to 11, set fire to Dad and fling him out of the attic window." **Smash Hits**

"In which Axl and his boys hamfist their way through a bunch of other people's songs. This will undoubtedly sell millions, why?" **The Guardian**

"As it says, perhaps unwisely, on the sleeve, 'a great song can be found anywhere. Do yourself a favour and go find the originals.' No petard ever hoisted its owner higher." **Select**

h

TED HAWKINS
The Next Hundred Years (Geffen)

"Still possessed of a voice comparable only to Sam Cooke's, Hawkins again sings heartfelt songs that draw deeply from soul and country music traditions." **Q**

"This album, Ted's major label debut, brings out the best of Ted's unique blend of acoustic guitar and husky, impassioned soul voice, at times reminiscent of Sam Cooke, Otis Redding and Percy Sledge." **Mojo**

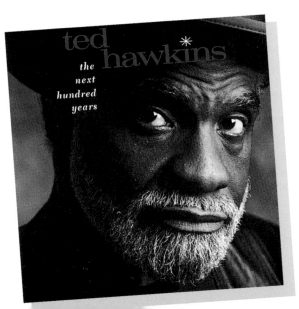

"He's certainly no angel, but Ted Hawkins sings like one and it's his musical record, as opposed to his State penitentiary one, that deserves our attention at the moment." **Vox**

KRISTIN HERSH
Hips And Makers (4AD)

"While never getting specific on any topic, Hersh's voice is so naked you wonder how painful all this is supposed to be. *Hips And Makers* has so much you forget what it's missing. And Kristin Hersh is once again way, way up there." **Select**

"...Kristin Hersh is daring to tell it like it is and take some chances with how it can be told. *Hips And Makers* is a wounded masterpiece." **Melody Maker**

"Fifteen tracks of such scant variety make this a demanding listen... Like the Muses, interesting but not necessarily good." **Q**

"Nothing could fully prepare you for the compelling case of Kristin Hersh's first solo album, *Hips And Makers*. It is the naked truth." **Vox**

HOLE
Live Through This (City Slang)

"Courtney Love's singing style went out of fashion 15 years ago. You know, that bronchially-challenged-squirrel-puking scream that is meant to signify some kind of anger. But *Live Through This* has some superb moments..." **Sky**

"It is Love's heroically scrawny voice that makes Hole distinctive, carrying them through the odd Sonic Youth-like middle eight, and raising the ghost of Pat Benatar only to banish it for all eternity. If anything, Hole's new command of light and shade heightens the impact of Courtney's visceral word-play." **Mojo**

"*Live Through This* is the kind of record that makes you want to lie on the floor in the foetal position with your thumb in your mouth, going 'Mama, mama'. It wakes rock from its cliché coma, leads it, laughing, to a lake of stinking mud and honey, and there drowns it: quietly, efficiently and with surprising gentleness." **NME**

"As an LP designed to transform Courtney from a professional rent-a-gob and habitual Rock Missus into a proper star, *Live Through This* should do the job with a few misery-infused giblets to spare." **Select**

HONKY
The Ego Has Landed (ZTT)

"Far more tuneful and energetic than the spaced-out Stereo MC's, Honky's multi-ethnic daisy-age attitude is unlikely to trouble the lucrative gangsta rap fraternity; this is the best British rap album yet." **Sky**

"This is hip-hop as bouncy liberation music, refreshingly free of misogyny, motherfuckers and menace. Hard? Maybe not. But Honky? Definitely." **Q**

"At their best, Honky are an engaging combination of Stereo MC's and De La Soul. Not bad. Though it's probably a good idea to stick with their singles and forget they ever made an album." **Select**

HORSE
God's Home Movie (Oxygen)

"Horse McDonald is one of the finest singers in Britain..." **Q**

"... *God's Home Movie* dawdles, its grand ballads treading water in a soup of over-wrought, emotional histrionics and over-dramatic, orchestral flourishes." **Vox**

IDHA
Melody Inn (Creation)
"*Melody Inn* is a singer/songwriter album, with the twist that Idha is audibly head over

heels in love with her husband Andy Bell of Ride. The couple share songwriting credits on three songs, and awesomely romantic they are too. A sweet album." **Select**

"Idha's chief concerns appear to be departing lovers, spiritual homesickness, a vague but constant craving – and yet her open-ended delivery frequently undermines these sentiments. The coldness here may result less from language barriers than sheer inexperience and untested ideals." **NME**

"... her uniformed talent doesn't connect with the authentic backing. The result is non-stop emotional detatchment, too polite to demand attention." **Vox**

INSPIRAL CARPETS
Devil Hopping (Mute)

"Maybe it's just as well Inspiral Carpets have saved their best album yet for this moment. After all, coming from Manchester carries diddley squat kudos in 1994... this album is a rare treat throughout, and it's good to see a feted act actually getting better with age." **Sky**

"They've ploughed on with the 'good workrate' that's always given them an uncool charm. But, this workaday spirit ultimately drags this fourth album down after a pretty inspired start." **Select**

"It looks like we're stuck with the gurning buggers for another year." **Melody Maker**

"Tougher, cleverer and more driven than you might think, Inspiral Carpets pluck one more victory from the jaws of derision." **NME**

INXS
Full Moon, Dirty Hearts (Mercury)
(See **The Year In Review** p. 14)

JAMES
Laid (Fontana)

"*Laid* is about paranoid love songs, ecstatic laments and perverse lullabies. In conventional terms some of it makes no sense at all, yet by abandoning Seven's hectoring in favour of a ping-pong mental free-jazz, Tim Booth has come up with thoughts and scenarios that are far more involving." **Select**

"Imagine the Hothouse Flowers without the soul, Deacon Blue without the personality and U2 without the songs, and you're getting close to the mysteriously content-free charm of *Laid*, the latest offering from the veteran Mancunians." **The Times**

"Producer Brian Eno's touch is clearly apparent on most of the songs. Tim Booth's voice is just another fine-spun texture among the many that comprise *Laid*. This is seriously lovely." **The Guardian**

"The proliferating wisps of slide guitar are given room to float free and lightly elevate the songs. Any sense of emotional uplift was (in the past) inseparably linked to a more epic approach, with guitars blazing and Tim Booth lost in banshee wailing. Indeed, in its gentler approach, it could be said that Eno's involvement has resulted in something of a return to their folk-rock roots."
The Independent

ELTON JOHN
Duets (Rocket)

"Chris Rea, Don Henley, PM Dawn, Marcella Detroit, Bonnie Raitt, Nik Kershaw; they are all here. Wot, no Rod?" **Vox**

"...with nothing really left to prove, *Duets* is ultimately a missed opportunity to be a little less self-reverential and to let down his hair; that is if we didn't know any better." **Q**

RICKIE LEE JONES
Traffic From Paradise (Geffen)

"The sound is folkier than before with a more organic flavour to performances which incorporate a range of textures derived from instruments such as mandolin and bowed dulcimer, bodran and marimba. She's singing as well as ever..." **The Independent**

"Rock's most achingly hip singer has produced this album for herself, and it may come as close as she has come in a while to the grandeur of *Pirates*." **Q**

JULIANA HATFIELD THREE
Become What You Are (East West)

"Those left cold by PJ Harvey's bodily functions and shouting may find much to love in these darkly cute songs, nearer to Raymond Carver than so-called Riot Grrl." **Q**

"... *Become What You Are* is too unambiguous and too bare-faced to move as much as it should." **Vox**

KILLING JOKE
Pandemonium (Butterly)

"With a foundation-rocking bottom end and all-powerful grooves, *Pandemonium* is a raucous celebration that instigates the renaissance of one of Britain's most influential acts." **Vox**

"... like a pneumatic drill through the head. Such analogies are unfortunately all too appropriate for Coleman's occasionally disgusting, militaristic passion plays, so bring a strong stomach and a bullet-proof vest." **Mojo**

"Never ones to give a clip around the ear when a punch in the face will do, Killing Joke's latest assault is noisy, intense, brutal and as uncompromising as ever, yet at times also irresistably danceable." **Q**

KD LANG
Even Cowgirls Get The Blues (WEA)

"kd lang is a thrilling performer, but *Even Cowgirls Get The Blues*, the soundtrack to Gus Van Sant's film, will hardly quench her fans' thirst, with only six new songs punctuating the instrumental mood-pieces." **Sky**

"Continuing the collaboration with Ben Mink which produced the nearly perfect *Ingénue*, kd lang's half dozen vocal performances here are as charming and winsome as any she's ever done. Interspersed with incidental instrumental interludes by Mink, the result is a delightful blend of ancient and modern, making for one of the most satisfying soundtrack albums of recent years." **The Independent**

"... this is an album that wipes out at a stroke the carefully nurtured image of her as a contemporary torch singer... she immerses herself in the kind of gilt-edged, traditional country style that may not appeal to the mainstream audience she has worked so hard to acquire." **The Times**

THE LEMONHEADS
Come On Feel The Lemonheads (Atlantic)

"This is what the world needs more of: pop stars like Evan Dando and albums that dazzle you while they affix jumpleads to your legs." **Mojo**

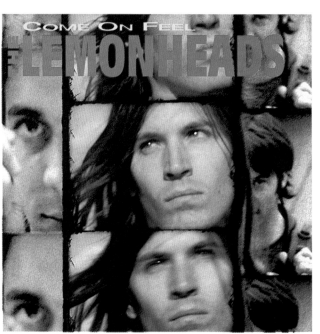

"This is a glimmering tune-fest of goofy punk frenzy, harmonic rock and poetic country-rock wibblers to float off to on a gigantic, magic stetson. Favourite T-shirts, guitars and girls... it's Evans' world and the sun has got its shades on. Man. Triumphant!" **Smash Hits**

"*Come On Feel The Lemonheads* proves that lead singer/main songwriter Evan Dando and his writing partner Tom Morgan can dash off the kind of tuneful, effortless songs most of the oh-so serious grunge boys could write only if they locked themselves in their Led Zeppelin-postered bedrooms for a year." **Sky**

"Pursuing a parallel course to the grunge pop that brought success with *It's A Shame About Ray*, the new Lemonheads album finds songwriter Evan Dando working to a clearer template than before. Dando is clearly more abundantly gifted than most of his grunge co-workers, able to skip nimbly between genres where they seem mired in riffs." **The Independent**

LEVELLERS
Levellers (China)

"... it's clear that describing anything by the Levs as 'actually quite good' is akin to declaring yourself a child molester and proud of it. Still, *Levellers* is actually quite good. The best thing being that for large stretches of time you can forget that it's them altogether." **Select**

LUSH
Split (4AD)

"Anybody remember melody? Lush's latest features plenty of it, along with harmony and guitars, too. This is cool, smooth, pretty – and Lush's best album yet." **Today**

"... Lush must have made this when they were hungover as it's hardly pub jukebox material, but it's not an unpleasant listen either." **Loaded**

"With *Split* they've recovered their own vision with their most complete and varied album to date. The dreamy female vocals are still to the fore, but lashed on to the ethereal harmonies are punk, dance and pop styles..." **Vox**

KIRSTY MacCOLL
Titanic Days (ZTT)

"... in which self-doubt seems finally to resolve into something joyous and MacColl herself emerges from behind the wit and the wordplay with a new emotional directness." **Q**

"... this is certainly her most even album. It's also her most translucent one, being another traceried strum-fest... Songs for springing lovers." **Mojo**

MADDER ROSE
Panic On (East West)

"Madder Rose have painted a beautiful landscape here, a sort of pink fluffy portrait complete with cotton wool clouds and unfathomably blue skies. Pretentious, but true." **Mojo**

"It's a common enough slip-up with second albums, trampling oneself to death in an effort to cover all bases, but it's especially unhappy in this case, in a band who were sounding so great when they were being themselves." **NME**

"If it's supposed to be night-time in their world, it's an hour stuffed with possibilities. Madder Rose are good to listen to, in the same way that not sleeping and being addicted to coffee are good to talk about." **Select**

"Madder Rose do simple things well and the tortuous things with sang-froid. Fuzzy underbellies and hazy veils clothe each precise parable. They follow a grand tradition of apathy and unrest with superbly indolent aplomb." **Melody Maker**

AIMEE MANN
Whatever (Imago)

"With a voice that can shift from sensuous warmth to frosty cool in a way that's sometimes redolent of Chrissie Hynde, Mann embraces dark and brittle emotions... the best songs are mostly bunched up in the first half, and the album sends to sag towards the end. But the sweet and sour flavour lingers on." **The Times**

"Ex-Byrd Roger McGuinn helps out on guitar, sounding more like himself that he's done since 1969, clearly relishing the priviledge of conjuring up perfect licks for Mann's intelligent, emotional and, above all, singable songs." **Q**

"... she has produced a collection of songs which are 'mature' meaning adult, rather than mature hijacked to mean wilfully neurotic." **Vox**

MAZZY STAR
So Tonight That I Might See (Parlophone)

"To enjoy this album properly, first turn the lights off, recline back on your bed and then float along as the acoustic guitar and the ethereal female vocals lift you to a higher level." **Sky**

"... little has changed. They've still got two tricks – either the piss-easy three-chords-and-a-tambourine hazy pop tune, or the freaky Doors-dropping-acid number. Fans already have an LP identical to this and should feel cheated, but expect the Chris Issak market to gobble it up this time around." **Select**

"... fans of Dylan, the Velvet Underground and that uniquely American ennui are encouraged to investigate." **Q**

"Frozen psychosis is mixed with a drifting calm, as though paranoia has eaten so deeply into these songs that they have fallen into a state of near-catatonia. Achingly beautiful." **Melody Maker**

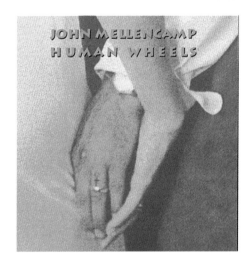

JOHN MELLENCAMP
Human Wheels (Mercury)

"... Mellencamp now presents himself in more lyric, mythic mode on *Human Wheels*, with a sound half American radio rock moderne and half Flannery O'Connor." **Q**

"If over the years Mellencamp had ever stirred himself to work the British market in the way that his contemporaries like Tom Petty have done, *Human Wheels* would surely be a huge hit. It remains a classic." **The Times**

MOOSE
Honey Bee (Play It Again Sam)

"... *Honey Bee* reaches for more rarefied highs, soul-mining the maverick talents of Lee Hazlewood and Fred Neil." **Q**

"... *Honey Bee* is an accomplished set of tunes that dips into folk streams without sounding wet." **Vox**

MORRISSEY
Vauxhall And I (Parlophone)

"The record fascinates so much because Moz himself is still fascinating – only now he's not hiding behind a remnant of the 70s or a smart line. *Vauxhall* is better than *Your Arsenal*, so it's his best record since *The Queen Is Dead* – and if he keeps making records like this, you won't want The Smiths back." **Select**

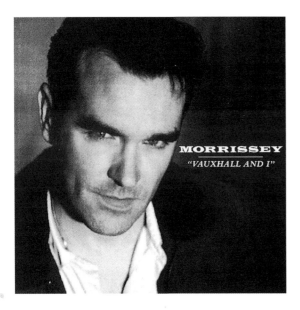

MORRISSEY
"VAUXHALL AND I"

"The most instantly notable thing about *Vauxhall And I* is how serene it sounds, after the frisky glam-a-billy riffing of *Your Arsenal*. The late Mick Ronson's tartly powerful settings for that album have been replaced here by a more sedate production from Steve Lillywhite, which matches perfectly the material's mood of reproachful resignation." **The Independent**

"*Vauxhall And I* is pure nostalgia, a collection of wry, vulnerable and petulant classics, a reminder of why we need Morrissey so much; there are so many pretenders, so few contenders to the pop star throne." **Mojo**

"... it ends with this bizarre address to the critics and what Moz views as an unrelenting witch-hunt. But what exact breed of critic might these people be? The fawning monthly writers? The carefully-vetted interviewees from elsewhere? The enraptured Americans? Shall we forgive him? Will he forgive us? Isn't he the oddest, richest, most royally messed-up fish in the pond? The debate continues." **NME**

SHARA NELSON
What Silence Knows (Cooltempo)

"Best known for her work fronting Massive Attack, Shara Nelson's solo debut stands out proudly from the usual run of soul diva offerings: there's far more imagination and more chances taken on *What Silence Knows*, though it sticks to the bare soul essentials of beats, strings and voice for the most part." **The Independent**

"It's a tremendous record, with Nelson's searing voice matched to a full spectrum of musical textures and resonant lyrics that will frighten the pants off Derek and Shirley canoodling on the sofa in Swindon." **Select**

"The result is highly atmospheric, providing room for both the plaintive songs (mostly about a woman's vulnerability and the uncertainties of relationships) to breathe and Nelson's powerful, yearning voice to engage the listener." **Q**

"*What Silence Knows* is a gloriously troubling record. This is the most exquisite piece of down-trodden, love-lorn claustrophobia released so far this year. Possibly ever." **Melody Maker**

NINE INCH NAILS
The Downward Spiral (Island)

"Glamorising the house in Death Valley where Roman Polanski's wife Sharon Tate was hideously stabbed to death by the Manson Family – that's not too clever... It certainly doesn't make *The Downward Spiral* as good as *The White Album*. Unlike life, the whole thing's pointless." **Select**

"Trent is clearly frozen in a state of hormone-crazed adolescent angst. But rage has its rewards: in this case the music, a raging stew of what can only be termed 'industrial max'. Search and enjoy." **Sky**

"This record is Reznor's most painful and brilliant statement to date. If they play music in hell, it's what you'll hear in the seventh circle. It makes sense." **Mojo**

"The frustrating aftertaste of *The Downward Spiral* suggests that if only Reznor had the lyrical and vocal skills to match his obvious emotional turmoil into something more than one-dimensional rants, NIN might live up to their formidable reputation." **NME**

NIRVANA
In Utero (Geffen)
(See **The Year In Review** p. 8)

ONE DOVE
Morning Dove White (Boy's Own)

"Produced by veteran DJ and studio alchemist Andrew Weatherall, this is an album of breathy, bubbling, ambient vibes littered with echoing back beats, tinkering keyboards and a whole range of ethnic samples." **Q**

"We were promised an album that sounded like the future, but this is how the future sounded in 1990. *Morning Dove White* is beautifully made cake that has been left out in the rain too long – its edges have blurred." **Melody Maker**

"... their album has the kind of easy grace and effortless depth Saint Etienne would swap a wardrobe full of 'cheeky' samples for. *Morning Dove White* (a title derived from the American-Indian name of Elvis Presley's grandmother) is truly a thing of beauty." **Select**

THE ORB
Pomme Fritz (Island)

"All desultory doodles and unneccessary noodles, *Pomme Fritz* is a guide round the mixing desk for sloppy stoners only too happy to try on the emperor's new clothes." **Vox**

POMME FRITZ

"The Orb have stuck a 'Gone Fish N' Chipping' sign on their door and headed for the North Sea. Without a compass. Or a paddle. Climb aboard. Grab a worm. You've got nothing to lose but your marbles." **Melody Maker**

"As ever the band tread a fine line between genius and taking the piss. So for every moment of greatness, there is something that sounds like Jon Pertwee arseing around with his sonic screwdriver, but, hey, that's The Orb!" **Loaded**

PAVEMENT
Crooked Rain Crooked Rain (Big Cat)

"This is Pavement growing up a little less absurd. Maturity made attractive. You won't necessarily expect it, but you may well love it. Nevertheless, the way *Crooked Rain Crooked Rain* arrives splattered with so many wry, but blatant, nods to antiquated American rock, is still something of a shock." **NME**

"Of *Crooked Rain Crooked Rain*'s 12 songs, selected from a pool of 30, six can justly be called great, two are merely excellent, two are fine, one is dull and one should be erased forever from the human memory with celestial Tipp-Ex." **Mojo**

"Cast your preconceptions aside. Pavement are new and improved, back with something bigger, funnier and more touching than before. A delightful surprise." **Select**

PEARL JAM
Vs (Epic)
(See **The Year In Review** p. 12)

MICHAEL PENN
Free For All (RCA)

"*Free For All* finds this idiosyncratic songwriter deep in REM-zone, offering a series of enigmatic, slightly bitter reflections on the gulf between people, set to various shades of folk rock in which folk and rock take turns to determine the cast of the songs." **The Independent**

"An idiosyncratic melodic style, a nice line in bitter and cryptic lyrics and a wheezy, Dylanesque delivery make this second album from Sean's kid brother a success." **Q**

PET SHOP BOYS
Very (Parlophone)

"As lovers of the pop charts, Pet Shop Boys were miffed when their wonderful 'serious' LP *Behaviour* yielded only minor hit singles. Now they've tried to amend that by going all poppy again... Three years ago this would have been a nice collection of pop songs but in 1993 we expect a little more." **Smash Hits**

"Naturally, there is no air of fun or revelation about *Very*... not a bad effort as Pet Shop Boys albums go, but still stricken with that knowing sense of ennui that besets all their work." **The Times**

"*Very* confirms the Boys as one of the rarest treats in pop – a wonderful group who are actually getting more wonderful as they get older. Choruses to die for and lyrics to cry over. Or, then again, commercial rubbish that's all on tape. But very Pet Shop Boys." **Select**

"Before you say it, they say it for you: *Very* is indeed "very Pet Shop Boys", much the same as before, only more so. The cool intelligence, but ironic detatchment, the huge pop hooks, the spruce production – are all firmly in place, to the point where the album is at times in danger of sounding merely generic." **The Independent**

PINK FLOYD
The Division Bell (Geffen)
(See **The Year In Review** p. 22)

PJ HARVEY
4 Track Demos (Island)

"Should you hear these recordings and remain unmoved by them, then it's probably time for you to forget about pop music. It simply doesn't get any more powerful than this." **Melody Maker**

"This is Polly's vision in its purest form, songs played at the moment they were written (voice and guitar with the odd bit of percussion and cello), unproduced and undiluted by the interpretations of band members and engineers." **Sky**

"There's truly a beauty in PJ Harvey's claustrophobic punk rock. And there are queer currents swimming through all of it: Chicago blues and British folk music are there below the surface, emerging here and there... She walks like Bo Diddley, and she don't need no crutch." **Mojo**

"It's immensely powerful. Aside from being one of the greatest garage/blues records in years, it's a monument to how people must suffer after they've loved. You'll play it to death..." **Select**

THE PRETENDERS
Last Of The Independents (WEA)

"There are no instant classic like *Kid* or *Brass In Pocket*, but you wouldn't expect them: they were three or four rock generations ago. But the fact that Chrissie still sounds committed to her art, unlike so many ageing rockers, is testament to her strength." **NME**

"Four years in the mix, and *Last Of The Independents* sounds much fresher than the dull rock 'n' roll of 1990's *Packed!*" **Vox**

"... Hynde may indeed be, as the album title seems to brag, the last of the independents. And for now, she's resisting all take-over bids." **Q**

"...it's not a bad record. The participants are far too skilled to let that happen and I confess that at the eleventh hour, some of the melodies are beginning to haunt me – it just takes a little time." **Mojo**

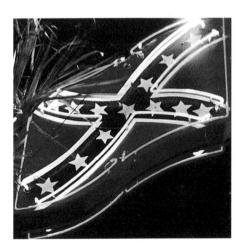

PRIMAL SCREAM
Give Out But Don't Give Up (Creation)

"Primal Scream are the masters of their profession. Three years ago they blew us away with the delicious *Screamadelica*. Now they're back and they've changed to bottom kickin' rock 'n' roll with a dirty 60s feel. If you know early Stones, you'll know this." **Smash Hits**

"Next to the degenerate swing of *Exile On Main Street*, this album doesn't sound quite

PULP. HIS 'N' HERS.

so hot, but anyone who obsesses about the accusations of plagiarism will end up missing out on one of 1994's most enjoyable albums." **Sky**

"While not quite as grittily authentic as Gillespie would hope, it's a superb, artful simulation of the past that's even better than the real thing, an animatronics version of everything you could want from the years 1970 to, well, 1972, in one conveniently accessibile package." **Select**

"Echoing The Stones' most productive period, the majority of these tracks are little more than riffs, the lyrics apparently compiled from a random selection of meaningless early 70s catchphrases... one is left with the feeling that the album would have been little different if Dowd, Hood and Hawkins had been left in the studio on their own, so indiscernible is the band's personal musical signature." **The Independent**

THE PROCLAIMERS
Hit The Highway (Chrysalis)

"Where *Sunshine On Leith* had something of a country rock feel, *Hit The Highway* draws more on R&B, blues and gospel flavours... it becomes clear that soul singing is alien to them, their enunciation and harmonies are too formal. It's a brave attempt but it's not really happening." **The Independent**

"Ignore the lyrics and you might, I suppose, enjoy all that acoustic upfulness and those fabulously authentic accents which, like prunes and wholemeal, must surely be good for us." **Melody Maker**

"Uncool they may well be, but in terms of soul, passion and actually meaning it, their only British rivals of the past decade are the far more lauded Dexy's. Who cares about fashion anyway?" **NME**

PULP
His 'N' Hers (Island)

"... *His 'N' Hers* mixes the venom of the voyeur with the flamboyance of the flirt so naturally that one can only writhe around the shag-pile wondering when on earth the record's main protagonist is going to be awarded his own Viz cartoon strip. 'Jarvis Cocker, The Sleazy Rocker'." **NME**

"Pulp are Eric Morecambe and Errol Brown as The Brothers Karamazov. Pulp

are palpably dancing round the handbags of your brain. Pulp are... palpitations." **Melody Maker**

"Pulp songs tend to fall into two distinct camps; big singalong epics culled from Lionel Ritchie's erotic dreamscape, or long, itchy, semi-spoken carnal melodramas. If anyone out there thought that PulpIntro – last year's compilation of early Pulp material – might be more an end than a beginning, this album proves them wrong." **Mojo**

"Vocal-wise, Jarvis isn't exactly the Mariah Carey of Eccleshall, but his battery of breathy inflections make the whole record sound like it's on heat. Whatever else, you can tell why the French like Pulp." **Select**

BONNIE RAITT
Longing In Their Hearts (Parlophone)

"... Bonnie Raitt is now – with her tequila and cocaine years behind her – playing with an intuitive looseness that no amount of drugs will ever bestow on Primal Scream." **Sky**

THE RAMONES
Acid Eaters (Chrysalis)

"A covers album was inevitable, and while the odd choice might raise an eyebrow or two, The Ramones' interpretations don't throw too many curves. An album to make you smile, smirk and cringe in turn." **Mojo**

"Most bands only resort to doing covers after they've run out of songs. But The Ramones never had more than one tune in the first place. The ancient Sumerians had a word for it, and that word was 'cack'." **Select**

"The visage framed by that nest of split ends may be that of a tax-paying fortysomething these days, but Joey Ramone still hasn't grown up. The latest edition of his Ramones, featuring one C Jay Ramone in place of bassist Dee Dee, is as loud and speed-driven as if it were 1975 and they were bottom of the bill at New York's infamous punk hangout CBGB." **The Guardian**

CHRIS REA
Espresso Logic (East West)

"Rea's latest treads the tasteful path of its 14 forebears, which is to say that it's dominated by its slide guitar playing and wrought gut-and-fags prowl. These, and his relentless pessimism, are what separate him from his Armani-suited peers. Given its dourness, this album shouldn't work, but it's more than the sum of its parts. Another winner from pop's mister sunshine." **The Guardian**

"... generally Rea's voice rumbles up from its smokey depths over a wide range of idiosyncratic yet listener-friendly songs." **Mojo**

"... despite the album's predominately depressed tone, there are enough shafts of light to make his negative prognoses bearable. Rea's good on futility – of continued relationships, of political efficacy, of personal fulfillment – but he still manages to sound as if a few shreds of hope drive him along." **The Independent**

"... an album of such exacting beauty and quiet politesse that its charms are in constant danger of being swamped by the background glare of modern life. If the man gets any more relaxed he will keel over." **The Times**

the record the critics' a-z

EDDI READER
Eddi Reader (Blanco Y Negro)

"... you will love *Eddi Reader*. But it does not mean that you're getting old, or turning a mouldy mellow yellow; it just means that you're a generous spirited soul, with an ear for a good tune, who doesn't want to have to listen to Guns N' Roses for every day of your life. Well, good for you." **Mojo**

"It remains to be seen whether Ms Reader can woo the audience her talent deserves without bending that unique voice to more overtly commercial fare." **Vox**

RED HOUSE PAINTERS
Red House Painters (4AD)

"There's no talking anyone round to Red House Painters. These dolorous, rainy-day drifts either resonate to your very soul or not. And if you find them too mournful, too bone-scrapingly plain, then they were never singing for you." **Melody Maker**

"Eight helpings of spare instrumentation and self-pity isn't a traditional recipe for fun, but unrepentant Galaxie 500 fans everywhere will love it." **Select**

"Redolent of empty spaces and recalling both American Music Club and Marty Balin's work with early Jefferson Airplane, they nevertheless have both tension and slow-burning energy, plus a nice line in melodies." **Q**

RIDE
Carnival Of Light (Creation)

"*Carnival Of Light* is aristocratic in its refusal to recognise such petty concerns as fashion or commerciality. It is bold and flamboyant, self-assured of its cool. It virtually reeks of patchouli oil and calls you maaan. It is, therefore, the first official hippy album of the 90s and if you aren't on its wavelength, it's absolute bollocks." **NME**

"Make no mistake, if Ride had released *Carnival Of Light* in 1969, they'd have probably cleaned up." **Q**

"In *Carnival Of Light*, Ride play in a house of mirrors papered with pop posters – here a Traffic, there a Stones... Ride put on disguises only to lose themselves in the process." **Mojo**

"*Carnival Of Light* is a great, great album. One of the albums of the year, in fact. This time around, Ride don't confound expectations, they just exceed them. Splendid." **Melody Maker**

ROLLING STONES
Voodoo Lounge (Virgin)
(See **The Year In Review** p. 28)

ROLLINS BAND
Weight (Imago)

"Utterly unrelenting, *Weight* gets you in its grip and shakes, hard. Henry Rollins isn't for the faint-hearted, but this record is damn fine." **Mojo**

"... it seems unbelievable that he remains unmellowed by the intervening years... this is a primal raunchfest that will make up for all those crap grunge albums you wasted your money on." **Sky**

"Perhaps due to commercial considerations, this album marks something of a retreat. As a funk-metal album, it's well above par, but from Mr Rollins, it's slightly disappointing." **Select**

MICK RONSON
Heaven & Hull (Epic)

"Poor old Ronno. Still, here's something new to remember him by. It was nearly finished when he died last year... a timely reminder that Ronson had touch and grace as well as power and flash." **Q**

"Ronson elevates the songs with big-scale, heart-warming, glitter-blues guitar solos. As a fitting finale, after all the big name guests have gone, Ronno and his guitar close the album..." **Vox**

DAVID LEE ROTH
Your Filthy Little Mouth (WEA)

"You have to admire Dave... sorry David Lee Roth. He climbs mountains. He makes great videos. Yep. A Man You Have To Admire. Not, of course, a man whose records you have to buy." **Select**

"Dave the MTV tart can be highly entertaining, and doubtless Dave the drinking buddy is a real laugh, but Dave the product is beyond a joke. The chrome may be polished and the paintwork immaculate, but there's nobody behind the wheel." **NME**

"What a sad epitaph it is that his finest moment remains a throwaway cover of *Californian Girls*. Too many early nights for our hero, it seems." **Q**

ROXETTE
Crash! Boom! Bang! (EMI)

"Guitars keep a'squealin', drums keep a'crashin', vocals keep a'screamin'... blimey, what's happened to the 'Ette? Everyone's favourite Danes, er Norwegians, um Scandinavians, have transformed themselves into tough rockin' 'muthas'. And despite the dodgiest lyrics in pop, they're rather good at it..." **Smash Hits**

"Now, as befits their middle age, they're less inlined to rush in with a 'Hello, you fool, I love you' and have entered a wishy-washy pastoral reflective phase. Bad news for rocky pop fans, good news for people who think Bon Jovi are a bit too punky." **NME**

"... lazy lyrical obsessions with Harleys and highways still dominate over the crushingly inevitable sound of overly polished, processed metal thunder..." **Vox**

OTIS RUSH
Ain't Enough Comin' In (This Way Up)

"... he's back, refreshed and refocussed, with his best album in two decades. Producer John Porter, instantly recognising Rush's strengths, recaptures his fog-over-the-West Side guitar sound and furnishes an unfussy setting for intensely delivered modern blues standards..." **Mojo**

"His Stax-like voice and jazz-edged guitar influenced Robert Cray, yet Rush has been away for so long that listeners will think he's impersonating his own protege. Still, there's some fine swinging blues here, if no spirit of anything new." **Vox**

"If there's a better blues album this year, it'll be a good year." **Q**

St ETIENNE
Tiger Bay (Heavenly)

"St Etienne trip from the sublime to the subconscious with this lucky dip of an album. But although it contains some of their best-ever tracks, *Tiger Bay* also has some really bobbins B-sides with token instrumentals. More effort next time." **Smash Hits**

"...the shortcomings of Sarah Cracknell's fey, sugary vocals are cruelly shown up. The result is an album entirely composed of what sounds like soundtrack fragments from a paralysingly dull film." **The Independent**

"Just when you hoped St Etienne would finally return to form they've managed to come up with a third album consisting purely of half-singles and utterly anonymous ambient-chicanery. Isn't *Tiger Bay* just a little too far off the map for us to bother going there?" **NME**

"Too clever. You're upsetting the slower ones at the back, St Etienne. Could do better. But not much better." **Select**

SEAL
Seal (ZTT)

"Jesus Christ, Marvin Gaye or Fairport Convention – either Seal has to make up his mind, or fully integrate the three influences. It doesn't hurt to be direct." **Vox**

SEAL

"The album's ultra-contemporary mix of the most modern synthesizer and drum machine technology with delicate layers of acoustic guitar, piano and the sweep of real strings moves Seal a little further from the dancefloor in its coolly calculated, measured musical approach." **Q**

"The corporate machine and the general way of things will make Seal a coffee table/wine bar/dinner party success, but this is hardly the point. Once, Seal could have been a contender. Now, he just sounds like product." **Melody Maker**

SENSER
Stacked Up (Ultimate)

"A massive overload of gripes and sideswipes, *Stacked Up* lasts for a soul-draining, oft compelling, 63 minutes and features the longest lyric sheet in the history of record packaging. In there somewhere lurks a genuinely great, gripping album waiting to get out." **NME**

"I'm still waiting for Senser to show me a good time, to come up with the horseshit I can believe in, to convince me, for the duration of their records, that they were right all along. Until they do, I'll have to suspect that Senser aren't what those festival audiences so desperately wanted, but what they were prepared to settle for." **Melody Maker**

"Too eclectic to be the hard-core masterpiece some were expecting, *Stacked Up* is sprawling but effective, and Senser score extra points for being the first funky anti-fascist thrash-pop outfit to feature a flautist." **Mojo**

"... depending on whose musical personality is the strongest, Senser could one day find

themselves either blowing the minds of thousands, alongside Metallica and FNM, or playing in front of a small gathering at the Stoneybridge Annual Free Festival." **Select**

SHAGGY
Pure Pleasure (Greensleeves)

"Anyone expecting *Pure Pleasure* to be a string of 'Oh Carolina's' will be disappointed. Nevertheless, there are several tunes here with that oh-so-crucial, hit-making irritability factor." **Vox**

SHARKBOY
Matinee (Nude)

"Turn the lights down low. Start smoking Gauloises. Split up with your lover. Do whatever you have to do to appreciate this dusty pearl of an album. Because, against all odds, it's the soundtrack to the post-rage comedown." **NME**

"... an LP that belies its title with music more suited to late nights than late afternoons." **Select**

"Using cello and trumpet onstage as well as guitars, she has proved an intense, if somewhat formal, prospect. Vocally (Avy) is not dissimilar to Polly Harvey, but although not nearly as blood-caked... A fine debut." **Mojo**

"Perhaps Sharkboy's greatest achievement is that they make romantic music that you can adore without embarrassment; music full of mystery and longing that sounds thoroughly real." **Melody Maker**

SNOOP DOGGY DOGG
Doggystyle (Death Row/Interscope)

"... *Doggystyle* has certainly earned its title of most eagerly awaited rap album of all time. Sad to report, then, that it doesn't live up to the hype, and the content fails to reflect the remarkable facts of their creation." **Q**

"If Snoop doesn't get banged up long-term, a phenomenally successful future awaits. If he does, then he'll need these lyrics about oral sex for the next 20 years as a reminder of what he's missing." **Vox**

SONIC YOUTH
Experimental Jet Set, Trash And No Star (Geffen)

"*Experimental Jet Set, Trash And No Star* will probably confuse the hell out of Sonic Youth's post-Geffen audience, but as part of their 13-year soundscape, it makes perfect sense." **Vox**

"... they've pulled back into their private shell. Maybe it's the pressure of impending actual mom and dad-hood – as opposed to the surrogate 'Godparents of Grunge' variety – which has turned Kim and Thurston back in on themselves. Whatever the reason, this is a very personal, often a rather saucy record." **Mojo**

"... for all their glaring faults, they're still out there in search of the raw nerve, forever young." **Q**

"Yup, you've got the Sonic Youth album that most certainly bloody well WILL NOT go to the 24-hour rave, drop a tab and take its trousers down in the middle of the dancefloor. Yet again." **NME**

SOUNDGARDEN
Superunknown (A&M)

"Like *In Utero*, *Superunknown* has a depth and maturity which isn't easily assimilated on the first few listenings." **Melody Maker**

"... never as deranged or articulate as Pearl Jam, as bitter and twisted as Nirvana, as definitively useless as Alice In Chains. What that leaves you with is another at-least-they're-trying result – and from a band clearly destined, despite everything, for imminent megastardom, it's not enough." **NME**

"... *Superunknown* veers from psychedelic near-poignancy to unreconstructed, slabbering rifferama, and shows why other Seattle bands cite them as godfathers – they have to look way up to see them." **Sky**

"At over 70 minutes, *Superunknown* may be over-long, but it still oozes the quality to put it at least one amp setting above its hard rock peers." **Select**

SPIN DOCTORS
Turn It Upside Down (Columbia)
(See **The Year In Review** p. 26)

AL STEWART
Famous Last Words (Permanent)

"Al's most airwave-friendly album since *Year Of The Cat*, *Famous Last Words* finds him on familiar territory, songs that are never limited by over-achievement or high ambition." **Vox**

"Devotees will be glad to see that the attractive qualities of Stewart's music are still in evidence: the fresh and uncomplicated melodic gift, the plaintive and distinctive voice and the absence of the over-weening self-obsession often compulsory in the singer-songwriter brief." **Q**

SQUEEZE
Some Fantastic Place (A&M)

"Should lyricist Chris Difford and tunesmith Glenn Tilbrook wonder why the freedom of Deptford has so far not been extended into the wider world, they might consider whether, given their volatile line-up, being a beat group isn't selling some of their songs short." **Q**

TEENAGE FANCLUB
Thirteen (Creation)

"All that remained was for them to move on. Curiously, they have not really done so. With another nod to Big Star in its title, *Thirteen* attempts to distance itself from

Bandwagonesque primarily in its instrumentation. But the feel is the same: plaintive, misfit rock 'n' roll music, sung mostly apologetically over a lazy groove. Coming back with half a corker in 1993 is a risky business." **Mojo**

"... it's the same blancmange of 'influences'. It's like trying to work out which Beatles song is being sent up by which Neil Innes song in *The Rutles*. All great rock steals from the past, but you get the picture. Teenage Fanclub are spreading themselves rather thinly on a slice of bread that's getting a tad mouldy." **Select**

"...a certain gravitas goes missing along with the angst, but now that groups like the Lemonheads have made it cool to be carefree, perhaps the Fannies will receive their just desserts." **The Times**

"... *Thirteen* is the first Teenage Fanclub album to sound like Teenage Fanclub. Me, I preferred them when they were Big Star." **Melody Maker**

TERRORVISION
How To Make Friends & Influence People (Total Vegas/EMI)

"Whether such cleverly-edited, chunky pop tales can reap commercial success is another matter, but those willing to dip into their quirky display of anthemic wit won't be disappointed." **Q**

"Produced by Gil Norton, Terrorvision come on like Bradford's answer to *Kick*-era INXS: big, bold and extremely confident." **Vox**

TEXAS
Ricks Road (Vertigo)

"The dozen songs here are good enough but never great, and too monochromatic to ever surprise or really stir. Shame." **Vox**

"... although *Ricks Road* is as good an album as any they've made, it lacks the qualities that have marked out the recent collections by newcomers like Aimee Mann and Sheryl Crow." **The Times**

"... the crisp urban boogies that support most of the songs are so strong that the swampy guitars are allowed to exert themselves to a greater degree without becoming overbearing. It gives their trademark rural blues greater confidence..." **Q**

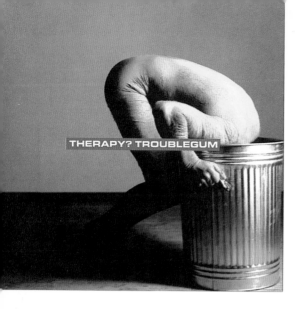

THERAPY? TROUBLEGUM

THERAPY?
Troublegum (A&M)

"Their first great album, *Troublegum* is the sweet you can eat between meals that will actually increase your appetite." **NME**

"*Troublegum* is a fun, fresh epitome of new generation, heavy-edged pop. Without Therapy?, the state of British/Irish music in the 90s would be much the poorer." **Mojo**

"*Troublegum* is a refreshing blast of cross-generic guitar noise, more focused and rhythmic than grunge, more tuneful and rocked-out than industrial. Anyone who finds the notion of Irish indie rock singularly unappealing should hear Therapy?'s new sub-genre..." **Sky**

"The 14 songs on *Troublegum*, Therapy?'s fourth album, detail a hellish spiral towards death, yet it's a hammerhead, in-your-mouth rock album, more exhilarating than depressing, with more than one moment of pure freefall." **Select**

RICHARD THOMPSON
Mirror Blue (Capitol)

"Some magazines will probably make this their album of the year: they get their records for free. If I'd paid for *Mirror Blue*, I'd have to confess to being rather disappointed." **Mojo**

"Well, sorry to be predictable but *Mirror Blue* is a tiny masterpiece." **Melody Maker**

"In Mitchell Froom, Richard Thompson has found his perfect producer, one who favours a wider, more varied sound palette than most, and who's also handy for adding a little emotional guts, courtesy of a Hammond organ. Not that Thompson's

ever in need of added emotional guts: this, their third collaboration, is as honest as its predecessor, *Rumour And Sigh*, in its depictions of contemporary realities of the heart and the head." **The Independent**

TINDERSTICKS
Tindersticks (This Way Up)

"Some might consider releasing a double album as your debut a mite ambitious, but Tindersticks have that much to offer. This album moves like a camera through a night in the heart of town. Behind the lens, a stranger, a lover and a fighter." **Melody Maker**

"... free-flowing, more than a little mysterious, each member a little star in his own right and with big, deep coat pockets full of daytime and night-time songs." **Select**

"The fact that some of this band have, if not skeletons in their cupboards, at least a rubber dog bone, should not be an embarrassment to them. It just makes their current efforts all the more impressive." **Mojo**

TRAFFIC
Far From Home (Virgin)
"Winwood's muse seems to have largely deserted him here, and the moments where the light shines through are rare..." **Vox**

"... those fans who lost the plot with the pair's respective solo albums might not neccesarily appreciate all the old spirits being exhumed. Nevertheless, this is a sturdy collection which avoids being pointlessly nostalgic." **Q**

UNDERWORLD
Dubnobasswithmyheadman (Junior Boys Own)

"*Dubnobasswithmyheadman* is the most important album since The Stone Roses and the best since *Screamadelica*." **Melody Maker**

"It's a form of sound sculpture whose roots lie as much in 70s German groups such as Faust and Can as in the dance scene, though it's the latter's slick gear changes that make the longer pieces so seamlessly engaging. Here, each new element in the groove is ushered in by a treated percussion fill like a

cartoon sound effect, while Hynde's vocals are both sinister and sensual in the manner of Jim Morrison." **The Independent**

"... it's a masterstroke. Quite how Underworld have pulled it off will remain one of those enduring mysteries, like what makes gravity work? For sheer exhuberance and invention there isn't much around to touch it." **Select**

"... there are song structures here for techno-phobes and techno-structures for songophobes. Underworld occasionally edge onto Beloved territory – music that sounds more real in clothes shops than it does in the home – but mostly this is gripping stuff." **Mojo**

VAI
Sex & Religion (Epic)

"From a teenage apprenticeship with Zappa to high-profile stints with Dave Lee Roth and Whitesnake, Vai is beyond City & Guilds standard in his chosen line of work; fast, skilful, histrionic guitar playing in a variety of FM rock settings. If not for the cloth-eared, then certainly for the thick-skinned." **Q**

![W]

TOM WAITS
The Black Rider (Island)

"Waits has now drifted off into the realms of self parody. What began, on albums like *Swordfishtrombones* and *Rain Dogs*, as a skilfully judged strain of junkyard R&B, has descended here into a self-conscious attempt to mimic the weirdness of European writers like Jaques Brel and Kurt Weill, with shambolic results." **The Times**

"Roll up for ringside seats and prepare to be amazed, astounded and bedeviled. For this ringmaster has no living equal." **Melody Maker**

"At times, the ancient twang of dead strings and the dry-gulch clunk of percussion brings to mind Ennio Morricone, another musical narratist gifted with the ability to tell stories in sound; but Waits remains essentially sui generis, a law unto himself. There is odd myth in his madness." **The Independent**

PAUL WELLER
Wild Wood (Go! Discs)

"There's a distinct retro feel here, which isn't surprising, but it manages to stop short of being derivative... every track seems to reveal a new and revitalised Weller." **Sky**

"*Wild Wood* is an album of good pop songs to some; to others, a reassuring sign that the man is back on track and not yet ready for care in the community." **Select**

"Song after song here suggest that Paul Weller is in some kind of transitional limbo – beset by worries about future directions, past achievements, time wasted, an early mid-life crisis in all but name – and certainly, in musical terms, he still seems stuck at the moment when mod turned psychedelic." **The Independent**

"The performances are economical yet heartfelt and, after a long period of uncertainty, Weller has clearly found his voice again. How odd that it should echo so clearly and with such empathy an era of rock he once came to bury." **The Times**

JAH WOBBLE'S INVADERS OF THE HEART
Take Me To God (Island)

"Punk's original creed dictated that exciting music was the sole province of raw, angry young men: punk veteran Wobble explodes this notion effortlessly. This is Godlike indeed." **Melody Maker**

"*Take Me To God* is not without its frailties, chief among them being its dependency on playback volume to ensure that its sonic weight matches the weight of its ideas. And it's possible that, instead of being intrigued, you might find yourself being irritated by its self-conscious mix of jokes and spiritual waffle." **Mojo**

"... the array of glittering guests can't make this LP really shine. For that to happen, Jah Wobble would have to take a complete backseat – and he wouldn't do that, would he? Stop taking the piss, Mr Wobble." **NME**

THE WONDER STUFF
Construction For The Modern Idiot (Polydor)

"*Construction For The Modern Idiot* is less folky than its predecessor, with Martin Bell's fiddle, accordian and mandolin buried deeper in the mix, but there's been little added to give the music some compensatory character: it's generic smug Anglo-indie, the kind of music that's way too pleased with its own supposed cleverness, its show-off aspects shading into misguided arrogance." **The Independent**

"For misanthropes, The Wonder Stuff sound remarkably cheerful. In the course of this album they rail against everyone from paedophiles to a friend's mother, without deviating from a single immaculately tuneful chorus. Heaven knows what's ailing them, but the result is excellent." **The Guardian**

"Call them a pub band now and be forever ashamed. The Stuffies always were going to come back in style. Thir appeal was never constructed on the balsa foundations of fashion, hype, novelty, good sleeves or even timely innovation. Just great songs. Those old things." **Select**

YES
Talk (Victor)

"At its worst, Talk recalls the lengthy guitar-and-synth blitz of Todd Rungren's Utopia; at its best, it stands shoulder-to-

THE WONDER STUFF

patchouli-scented-shoulder with the band's best work. They're not going to give up, are they?" **Vox**

"... the vapid feel good spiritualism of Jon Anderson's lyrics is ill accompanied by the thumping pedestrian beats – has Alan White bothered listening to any other music over the last decade? – and the ego-riddled soloing of Trevor Rabin and Tony Kaye." **The Independent**

Z

FRANK ZAPPA & THE ENSEMBLE MODERN
Yellow Shark (Zappa)

"Having, it seems, played his last guitar solo, Frank Zappa has returned to his initial goal: making his mark as a classical composer. After lacklustre LSO sessions and stiff-necked renditions by Pierre Boulez, he has now found musicians who sound like they were born to tackle his complex, modernistic miniatures with fluency and finesse." **Mojo**

"Frank Zappa's understanding of the classical avant-garde is in no doubt. His own compositions in this vein reflect a prodigious and quixotic mind that can handle polyrhythms, weird time signatures, radical sonorities and still chuck in scarbrous satire." **Q**

ZZ TOP
Antenna (RCA)

"ZZ Top, in case anyone was asleep, still rock. *Recycler* in 1990 was a smart record and so is this. The groove is still liable to be mechanically generated at drum level, but the prowling bass can only be the work of Dusty Hill, a man now well into his 50s." **Select**

"Working on the tenet that if it ain't broke, don't fix it, Billy Gibbons, Dusty Hill and Frank Beard deliver their usual blend of high-octane Houston sass, seemingly to order." **Vox**

"Basically: ZZ Top are shite. Surprise your friends with that one." **Melody Maker**

books

ROUTE 666: ON THE ROAD TO NIRVANA
Gina Arnold
(Picador £9.99)

For Gina Arnold (of *Rolling Stone*, *Elle*, and *The LA Times*) it all started with a Sex Pistols gig in San Francisco. Until then, she thought "everything had already happened", but seeing Johnny and Sid up there on the boards opened "a great chasm of possibility ... and I leapt into its breach my friends. I dove on in."

From that moment on, Arnold has devoted her life to punk, and its after-birth, grunge. This excellent book takes us on a super-fan's journey of discovery as Arnold, aided and abetted by the likes of Jello Biafra, Courtney Love, Eddie Vedder and the late Kurt Cobain, traces the progress of herself, her generation and the bands – Black Flag/The Dead Kennedys/The Pixies/Hole/REM/Husker Du/Jane's Addiction/Tad/Fugazi and most significantly Nirvana – she loves so much.

From that fateful night in 'Frisco to the last time she saw Nirvana playing live in 1993, it's an exuberant, beer-fuelled, plaid shirted mosh across a thousand myths and memories. All of them worth investigating.

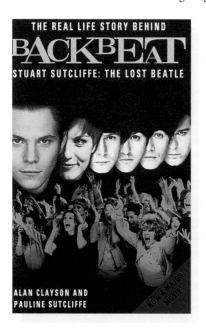

STUART SUTCLIFFE: THE LOST BEATLE
Alan Clayson and **Pauline Sutcliffe**
(Pan £4.99)

Anyone wishing to put some flesh on the bones of the characters they encountered in the film *Backbeat* could do worse than read this informative and insightful paperback. The portrait that emerges is of a thoughtful, articulate character who, had he not died of a brain haemorrhage at the tragically young age of 22, could've made his mark, if not as a musician, then certainly as an artist or writer. His paintings, as the full colour plates reveal, vibrate with vital energy and the extracts from his letters display a lyrical eloquence that rivals anything that Lennon and McCartney went on to write.

Inevitably, there's the low-down on how Sutcliffe met Lennon at art college and why two such obviously different characters – Sutcliffe was studious, philosophical and committed to his art, Lennon was lazy, loudmouthed and "living off the top of his head" – should become friends. There's all the dirt about the early days touring with the Silver Beatles and the hostility that arose between Paul McCartney and Sutcliffe as a result of the latter's musical limitations. Plus, there's local colour aplenty in the earthy descriptions of the Beatles' pill-popping and prostitute-plying adventures in Hamburg.

But the heart of the book lies with the recounting of the love affair that developed between Sutcliffe and German photographer Astrid Kirchherr. Wealthy and sophisticated Kirchherr was originally wary of the wild young rocker in the shades, but once the pair had connected they became inseparable soul-mates. As doomed romances go, you won't find anything better anywhere, and if the description of the pair's final meeting, in the back of the ambulance rushing Sutcliffe to hospital, doesn't bring a lump to your throat, you should hire a stone mason to carve "cynic" on your heart.

HOLLYWOOD ROCK: A GUIDE TO ROCK 'N' ROLL IN THE MOVIES
Marshall Crenshaw
(Plexus £12.99)

Yes, that's right. It's *that* Marshall Crenshaw – the one that Elvis Costello once described as his favourite songwriter. Only this time he's not writing songs, he's writing *about* them. Showing a dedication to his task that can only be envied, Crenshaw has produced a catalogue of virtually every movie with a music connection released since the late 1940s.

Painstakingly rated and cross-referenced, Crenshaw's collection gives details about the song, where it appeared in the film, any noteworthy dialogue connected with it and a critique of the film to boot.

All of which makes for an impressive piece of work that will keep dedicated trainspotters happy for many years to come.

THE ICE OPINION: WHO GIVES A FUCK
Ice-T
(Pan £9.99)

In the foreword to this thought-provoking book, Ice-T claims that "this is not a biography" but rather an opportunity for people to "clarify where I'm coming from and where I've been."

Subsequently, he goes on to offer his thoughts about ghetto and gang life, prison, sexuality, rap, religion, racism, the LA riots and the controversy that has surrounded his own career.

And while you'd have to be a complete dunderhead to disagree with his opening premise that poverty and deprivation in a society that values money, consumerism and privilege above justice, compassion and equality are inevitably going to lead to crime, you might baulk at some of his opinions on male and female sexuality.

However, he paints a picture of an articulate, perceptive and compassionate man who has obviously thought long and hard about what he says. So, when he claims "the biggest role model I have is just the fact I'm achieving. Fuck what I'm rapping about. Fuck *Cop Killer*... I want people to say 'this brother was down here with us and now he's making something and he's attempting to tell us how to do it'", you can't help but believe him.

A BONE IN MY FLUTE
Holly Johnson
(Century £15.99)

The former Frankie Goes To Hollywood frontman's open, engaging and delightfully warm and witty autobiography takes us from his lonely and relatively loveless childhood, to the summer of 1991 when he was diagnosed as suffering from AIDS.

The title is taken from the term used in the Johnson household to describe an erection. Which is quite appropriate, since between the tales of Frankie's exploitation at the hands of record company ZTT, or the rivalry that was always present between Holly and his sidekick Paul Rutherford, or the teenage years Holly spent playing the Liverpool club scene with bands such as Big In Japan, the book positively bristles with them.

Celebrating his sexuality, Johnson has no qualms about describing his first homosexual encounter in a toilet in Newsholme or the difference in taste between a white penis and a black one. Neither has he any reservations about damning the people who have crossed him, thus Rutherford, Horn, Sinclair, Paul Morley, Boy George and especially "The Lads" of Frankie, all come in for criticism.

As for his illness, Johnson is philosophical. Quoting a line from the *Liverpool* album, he asks, "If I could change the things I've done/Would I be the only one?" and replies "no I would have done all those things much more often."

THE DARK STUFF
Nick Kent
(Penguin £9.99)
Along with Charles Shaar Murray and Mick Farren, Nick Kent was one of those celebrated music writers who clambered from the wreckage of the alternative British press of the late '60s/early '70s, and set about making a name for himself via the pages of the *NME, The Face* and *The Sunday Times*.

As a journalist (and a musician – he was briefly a member of the Sex Pistols and also fronted his own band, The Subterraneans) Kent walked it like he talked it, figuring that if he was going to write convincingly about the rock stars of the day he had to have a thorough understanding of their lifestyle. Thus, if his pals Keith Richards and Johnny Thunders had a smack habit, he would get one too. This method-like approach to his craft eventually lead to a decade-long fight against addiction and a canon of work that is essential reading for anyone with more than a passing interest in rock music.

Kent's strength as a writer was his willingness to put in his articles what fainter-hearted souls would leave out. *The Dark Stuff* is an 18-strong collection of what Kent considers to be his best pieces. In some cases, for reasons of his own, he has re-written or updated them, but the power still remains.

ROTTEN: NO IRISH, NO BLACKS, NO DOGS
Joe Lydon with **Keith** and **Kent Zimmerman**
(Hodder & Stoughton £14.99)
Lydon, nee Rotten, lets rip on the punk era he spearheaded on this autobiographical yet ghostwritten yarn. Tracing his roots from his honestly-portayed adolescent insecurities, through his wilder claims that he single-handedly invented punk, Lydon thrashes out at all around him in a predictable manner. Former Pistols manager Malcolm McLaren, designer Vivienne Westwood and fellow "punk rockers" The Clash all get a whip of his petulant tongue, though the story does get the necessary padding by pulling in a few opinions from the likes of Billy Idol, Chrissie Hynde, plus dad and wifey. Excellent picture backup including a pre-punk Lydon looking exactly like the type of '70s hippy he claimed to abhor.

BEATBOOM: POP GOES THE SIXTIES
Dave McAleer
(Hamlyn £10.99)
A sort of book version of the Beeb's *The Rock And Roll Years* without the political content, McAleer's fun-packed little tome reminds us just how exciting, silly, trivial, mundane and excruciatingly embarrassing the pop world of the '60s could be.

Hilariously embroidered with dumb quotes from the popular music press of the time – "the audience really go for the big beat US negro style", claimed the NME – and quaintly illustrated with black and white pics of the fashions, the movies, and the TV programmes, it's a hoot from cover to cover.

PHILIP LYNOTT: THE ROCKER
Mark Putterford
(Castle/Penguin £9.99)
For most people, the abiding image of Phil Lynott, bass player and singer with Thin Lizzy, will be the one that appears on the front of this impressive piece of work by Mark Putterford; ie the heavy lidded, leather and denim clad rocker, standing legs astride and caressing his giant Fender as tenderly as if it were a much cherished, swan-necked paramour.

It's a picture that paints a thousand words about the man's character; a lover, a fighter, a rock 'n' roll animal, a gentle family man, a moody prima donna, an easy-going Irishman, a drug user and abuser who, as Midge Ure testifies, took great care to shield younger, more impressionable musicians from the illicit allure of the narcotics he himself was experimenting with.

Compiled from interviews with 40 of Lynott's relatives, friends, roadies, managers and fellow musicians – including Gary Moore, Brian Downey, Bob Geldof, Scott Gorham and Brian Robertson – Putterford turns in a well written document of Lynott's rise from the popular half-cast lad from the Dublin suburbs, to the charismatic leader of one of the most important and influential rock bands of the 70s.

As you would expect, there is much anecdotal evidence of Lynott's capacity for wild, and often self-destructive behaviour, but it's the less sensational details about Lynott's loving and close relationship with his mother Phyllis, and his generosity towards other struggling musicians, that give this book a warmth and authority that make it essential reading for all Lynott fans.

THE I HATE MADONNA HANDBOOK
Ilene Rosenzweig
(Virgin £4.99)
If you hate Madonna as much as Ilene Rosenzweig does, then you'll want to get your hands on this entertainingly bitchy little tome, because it's packed to the gills with all manner of nasty facts about the Material Girl. Under headings such as Desperately Seeking Stardom, Feminist Or Slut, America's Most Unwanted and PriMadonna, and using a combination of quizzes, quotes and cut-out-and-keep cards detailing Madonna's treatment of her various lovers and boyfriends, Rosenzweig dishes out the dirt big time. "The backlash starts here", blurbs the cover. Put it next to *Sex* and see which one gets the most laughs.

THE ELECTRIC GUITAR
Edited by **Paul Trynka**
(Virgin £16.99)
From the moment Segovia announced the electric guitar was an "abomination", this whippersnapper of an instrument was destined to change history. In *The Electric Guitar*, Paul Trynka traces this history through words and pictures, peppering the solidly researched text with profiles of pioneering guitar models. Unlike other guitar books, *The Electric Guitar* doesn't forget the player; guitar pioneers from Charlie Christian and T-Bone Walker, through to Steve Vai and Johnny Marr get their say. As essential as a pack of plectrums.

IDLE WORSHIP
Edited by **Chris Roberts**
(HarperCollins £5.99)
Virgin Rock Yearbook contributor pulls together superbly diverse tales of idol

worship from a selection of contemporary popular icons: Bono's stream of consciousness diatribe recalls his first nervious meeting with Frank Sinatra; author Joseph O' Connor remembers a young Bob Geldof playing the backdrop to his childhood. Equally enthralling pieces from Rob Newman, Thurston Moore, Mark E Smith, Caitlin Moran and Roberts himself, who wraps his own life around the career of Debbie harry seamlessly. He wishes.

THE BEST OF ROLLING STONE
Various
(Virgin £7.99)
"When I started *Rolling Stone* in 1967," says proprietor Jann S Wenner in his introduction to this compilation of articles, "I wrote that 'the magazine is not just about music but also about things and attitudes that the music embraces.' As time went on I began to interpret that charter rather broadly. We understood that music was the glue holding a generation together. And through music, ideas were being communicated about personal relationships, social lives, political ethics and the way we wanted to conduct our lives."

It was this possibly more than anything that was the key to *Rolling Stone*'s success. Whereas other magazines wanted to keep music apart from other aspects of contemporary culture, Wenner had the courage and foresight to throw them all in together. The benefits of his all-embracing editorial policy can now be enjoyed in this enjoyable bedside reader.

Covering a 21-year period from 1969-1990, the 32 features presented here cover everything from the legendary lost weekend described by Hunter S Thompson in *Fear And Loathing In Las Vegas*, to Tom Wolfe's revealing profile of the all-American astronaut, "Post Orbital Remorse", which later expanded into the book *The Right Stuff*, to Bill Zehme's witty profile of "Dick Tracy – period Warren Beatty".

CRAZY DIAMOND: SYD BARRET & THE DAWN OF PINK FLOYD
Mike Watkinson and **Pete Anderson**
(Omnibus £9.95)
Everybody knows the legend of Syd Barrett: Handsome Cambridge-born genius forms envelope-pushing band, gets carried away with his interest in LSD, burns out and retires to his home town to concentrate on his art and avoid sensation-seeking reporters. Or *anyone* else.

Using the legend as the peg on which to hang a series of interviews with Dave Gilmour, Roger Waters plus members of Barrett's family and other Floyd era friends

and associates, Watkinson and Anderson trace the rise and fall of Syd. The story follows his life from a personable and popular art school student obsessed with The Beatles, to the Acid crazed casualty who once tried to flag down a jet on a runway like it was a bus on Oxford Street.

Of course, this makes for some pretty hilarious reading, but underneath the amusing anecdotes runs the tragic tale of a man who became unhinged by his own talent and his desire to live constantly on the edge. A man whose ideas were so far ahead of his time and the other members of his band, that eventually he became impossible to work with and they had to sack him.

And so on and so forth. Through the solo albums, the failed engagements and the increasingly violent and schizophrenic behaviour, right through to the present, where we learn, via his brother in law, that Syd is happy and contented and living in Cambridge, writing The History Of Art and still turning down offers to come up with new musical material. Maybe he's not so crazy after all.

SCOTT WALKER: A DEEP SHADE OF BLUE
Mike Watkinson and **Pete Anderson**
(Virgin £15.99)
"I am beginning to get a bit fed up with Scott Walker saying he wants to avoid everybody and playing a big moody scene. As a loyal fan, is it too much to ask for the occasional appearance or single record."

This quote, taken from this unauthorised but immensely readable biography, shows that even in 1967, less than a year after *The Sun Ain't Gonna Shine Anymore* topped the British charts, Noel Scott Engel (aka Walker) was indulging in the kind of reclusive behaviour that, in 1992, prompted a national newspaper to launch The Great Scott Walker Hunt.

We learn that Scott was something of a child prodigy, and that he and his LA friends used to get their teenage kicks from vandalising the Hollywood homes of the rich and famous. We hear about the stage fright that eventually ended Scott's career as a live performer: about the attempted suicide; about his marriage to a Danish nurse and about the serious artist whose distaste for commercialism and quest for integrity caused constant problems for record companies and producers and put an unceremonious end to more than one attempt to revive his career.

As for the present, Scott Walker remains unavailable for comment, although rumour has it that a new album could appear at any moment. Don't hold your breath. ■

BLUR
Starshaped (PMI £10.99)
Ho, ho, it's all aboard the jolly Blur tour bus as the smudgy pop tops flit around the rock festivals of Europe, starting at Reading in 1991 and ending at Glastonbury less than a year later. So what do we learn about the Boys Who Like Girls? Well, Damon gets very sick at the prospect of air-travel, guitarist Graham is a bit of a wag (as indeed are all the lads) given to wandering off without telling anyone where he's going, and the band can perform live stacks of tracks like *She's So High, There's No Other Way, Chemical World, Sunday Sunday*, etc. All this, and a chance to see again all the band's promo vids to date.

DAVID BOWIE
The Video Collection (PMI £14.99)
The original cross-dressing super hero, Dame David, is featured here on a fine compilation of his singles from pre-Ziggy Major Tom, to (thankfully) pre-Tin Machine *Fame '90*. Highlights include Spider From Mars' bass player Trevor Boulder's certifiable silver sideburns, the late Mick Ronson's silk stockings and Jacobean golfing trews, David doing comedy in *Blue Jean*, David looking grotesque and Berlin-ish in *Be My Wife*, David camping it up desperately in *Boys Keep Swinging* and David looking dangerously tanned and healthy in the outback on *Let's Dance*. Good enough, but nothing a few words from the Zig-man himself couldn't have improved.

CROSBY STILLS AND NASH
Long Time Coming
(Wienerworld £12.99)
Kicking off with their first hit, *Marakesh Express*, from only their second live performance at Woodstock ("We're scared shitless man,"

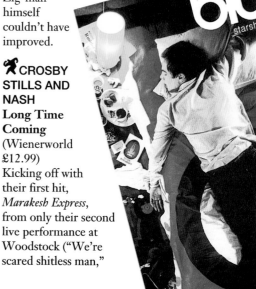

admits Steven Stills in a very smart poncho), this bio-vid traces the life and legend of CSN in an acceptable enough fashion. Heaps of out-takes from heaps of old TV shows are appropriately inter-cut with footage of Graham Nash getting evangelical about pop music, Stephen Stills telling how C&S pinched N off The Hollies, and the boys having a squabble about the size of a recording studio. There's some nice shots of whales too.

☆ THE EURYTHMICS
Greatest Hits (BMG £6.99)
As we all know by now, nobody in the world has a bigger dressing-up box than Annie Lennox. Here we find the delightfully daffy old bird running through a whole gamut of characters as we take a backwards look at the excellent video life of The Eurythmics. Starting with the crop-wielding dominatrix of *Sweet Dreams Are Made Of This*, we quickly progress – without the interference of mini-interviews or related frippery – to the leather-clad butch-birdery of *Missionary Man*, through the frumpy housewife on the edge of a breakdown (*I Love To Listen To Beethoven*), who in turn becomes the strutting strumpet of *I Need A Man* (her finest hour?) to the bruised and battered waif of *You*

Have Placed A Chill In My Heart. Finally, we get *The King And Queen Of America*, where Annie goes completely and utterly bats and plays at being a cowgirl, a bunny girl, a heavy metal priestess, a president's wife, an ordinary Joe-ess, an astronaut, a television evangelist, a cheerleader, a film starlet and a wheel of fortune-type hostess!! Quick nurse, the screens.

☆ PETER GABRIEL
All About Us (PMI £12.99)
If it's state-of-the-art video making you're after, then look no further – it's all here in spades. Describing *Us* as "an album about relationships", the disturbingly Prince Charles-like Gabriel, plus assorted producers, directors and artists, guide us through the inspiration behind, and the making of, the seven videos (including the previously unseen *Come Talk To Me* and *Kiss The Frog* (which, fact fans, was the first video ever to be turned into a theme park ride) contained within. Utilising every technique in the book, from computer

generated morphing to clay animation, this is a jolly good show actually.

☆ IRON MAIDEN
Donington Live 1992 (PMI £12.99)
This live extravaganza captures Britain's premier Metal Heads at their most ferocious, headlining the annual Monsters Of Rock shindig. And as anyone who has ever waded knee deep through the mud, the bin liners and the plastic beer bottles will tell you, watching Donington on video is far superior to actually being there. So what do you get for your £12.99? Views of the band from every possible angle using every possible kind of camera, much thighs-akimbo plank spanking, plenty of screeching and hollering and heaps of sword and fantasy blathering about playing with madness, bringing daughters to the slaughter and running to the hills. A final, florid testament to the reign of Bruce Dickinson.

☆ JETHRO TULL
25th Anniversary Video (PMI £10.99)
Oh, how we all gasped in amazement all those years ago when Ian Anderson, backed by his band of fashion disasters, appeared on Top Of The Pops standing gamely on one leg while tootling his flute and crooning about some old Witch's Promise or other. Strange to think that that mad-eyed, lascivious, lip-licking troubadour would still be going strong 25 years later, successfully combining his fish breeding business with much more minstrelly malarkey. But he is, and this Tullophile-pleasing package includes interviews from most of the former and current members of the band as they gather for a bald-pate comparing 25th reunion in, yes, you've guessed it, a rustic Brit-pub. This all adds up to a diverting 85 mins worth of nostalgia, videos and interesting facts for those people who want that sort of thing. Did you know, for instance, that Clive Bunker now owns an engineering factory and breeds dogs? See, fascinating innit?

PAUL McCARTNEY
Paul Is Live In Concert On The New World Tour (PMI £12.99)
Billed as the biggest rock and roll production ever staged anywhere in the known universe, the Macca world tour came complete with firework displays, giant slide shows and the ageing moptop's retina-threatening collection of waistcoats. Paul shows that he can still rock out with the best of 'em, working his way through a royalty-spinning collection of classics, including *Hey Jude*, *Helta Skelta*, *Drive My Car*, *Penny Lane*, *Lady Madonna*, *All My Loving* and *Let Me Roll It*. But be prepared as you near the end of the concert footage, as Paul tries to prove there's more to him than the cheery thumbs-up stance and family singalongs by tagging on a blood soaked anti-cruelty to animals film.

M-PEOPLE
Elegant TV (BMG £10.99)
The brainchild of ex-Hacienda DJ Mike Pickering, M-People had a pretty good year of it in 1994. This visual accompaniment to their Top 20 album *Elegant Slumming* captures the band in live and promo video form, working their way through eight excellent tracks, including *One Night In Heaven*, *Natural Thing*, *How Can I Love You More* and *Don't Look Any Further*. Well mannered, polite and thoroughly professional, it offers little information about the band, how they got together or where they hope to be going. Otherwise as fine a piece of visual candy floss for the eye as you could want.

NEW ORDER
The New Order Story
(Polygram Video £12.99)
The whole, definitive, nuts and bolts story of Manchester's finest. TV clips from the early Joy Division days in which Ian Curtis danced like a spastic and Barney and Peter looked very nice and tidy in their short sleeved shirts; boozy round-the-kitchen-table nostalgia sessions with Gillian; that brilliant wibbly wobbly video for *The Perfect Kiss*; the New Order quiz show; the marketing strategy; the artwork; what went wrong with Factory; Tony Wilson being hard assed and telling us it was "One long wonderful nightmare"... All this and excellent music to boot.

PET SHOP BOYS/DEREK JARMAN
Projections (Artificial Eye £12.99)
A compilation of the seven short films that Jarman made for background projection on the PSBs' 1989 world tour. Although intended to accompany tracks such as *Opportunities*, *It's A Sin*, *Heart*, *Paninaro*, *Domino Dancing* and *Kings Cross*, there's little if any sign of Neil or Chris here. Instead, Jarman was allowed to indulge his creative muse to the fullest extent. Result – a riot of colour and texture in which violent and shocking images are juxtaposed with the friendly and familiar.

Also included to bump up the value-for-money angle are Jarman's general thoughts on his other work with musicians, *A Garden In Luxor*, which was used at a 1992 benefit gig at The Hacienda and Studio Bankside, his Super-8 cinematic debut.

THE ROLLING STONES
25 x 5 The Continuing Adventures Of...
(SMV £12.99)
Re-issued by popular demand, this satisfyingly in-depth profile of the Glimmer Twins et al includes everything the Stones completest will already know, and everything the neophyte fan might still be wondering about.

Yes, folks, roll up and hear about the moment when Keef and Mick met on a train station; witness the early days when the immaculately-coiffured Brian Jones spoke in an accent that was subsequently borrowed by Mr Chumley Warner; and view how the Stones' appearance on American TV show *Hollywood Palace* was greeted with green eyed sarcasm by dipso Dean Martin. Also present and incorrect is the notorious pissing against the wall incident, the drug busts, clips from the infamous "on the road" film *Cocksucker Blues* and the never-released collaboration with The Beatles, *Rock And Roll Circus*. As if that wasn't enough, there's great tracks aplenty, individual interviews, plus footage from Brian's funeral and Mick, Keef and Bill's weddings. If you want any more than this, you'll have to join the band.

SISTERS OF MERCY
Shot Rev 2.0. (East/West £11.99)
The Mr and Mrs of the Goth world, Patricia Morrison and Andrew Eldritch ham it up gloriously on this impressive Greatest Hits package.

On *This Corrosion*, Pat strides about Amazon-like, looking ravishingly unapproachable, while in the foreground a rain (machine) soaked Andrew, all pigeon chest and aviator shades, wields his microphone stand. And there's more, as Andrew forms a new Sisters line-up with ex-Sigue Sigue Sputnik japester Tony James and proceeds to crash through the killer-riffed *More*, *Dr Jeep* and *Detonation Avenue*.

U2
Zoo TV Live From Sydney (Polygram £12.99)
After two years of pinging around the globe with its giant banks of video screens, its lithesome belly dancers and its cryptic slogans, the Zoo TV telethon finally unplugs on a steamy night in Sydney. For those who couldn't be there, U2 recorded the whole shebang on video. So now from the comfort of your very own home you can watch the leather clad MacPhisto prowling round the stage like some deadweighted demi-devil, playing with his glorified remote control and spurring on Mr Edge and the lads as they plough their way, for the umpteenth million time, through a set list that includes, *One*, *Angel Of Harlem*, *Mysterious Ways*, and *Where The Streets Have No Name*. An outrageously impressive show, but not just because of the assorted FX and gizmos. For all their pomp and pretentiousness, U2 remain at heart a truly great rock band.

VARIOUS ARTISTS
Future Shock (Prism £13.99)
Ambient vibes ahoy as the likes of Banca De Gaia, Attic Attack, Higher Intelligence Agency, The Orb, Future Sound Of London, Brian Eno and the Aphex Twin lay down the soundtrack for what is claimed to be "The World's First Techno Pagan Video". Strangely enough, it's only really Future Sound Of London's *Papua New Guinea*, in which ancient ruins are taken apart by state-of-the-art editing technology, that fits the Techno-Pagan theme, but that's a small quibble. For the most part, this is a cut above the rest of the pack, and taken with the right quantities of the right substance could give many hours of psychedelic pleasure. ∎

films

THE PIANO (15) ▲

Mute Scottish widow and piano-freak Ada (Holly Hunter) is dispatched to the other side of the world (New Zealand, to be exact) to marry a dull, curmudgeonly farmer (Sam Neill) she's never met.

On her arrival, Ada is most put-out to find that the miserable git who has ordered her hand in marriage won't even arrange for her beloved joanna to be moved from its far from ideal position on the beach to somewhere more appropriate. Consequently, their relationship gets off to a start so slow that it never recovers.

Luckily for Ada, the piano falls into the hands of Mr Baines (Harvey Keitel), a passionate Irish man turned Maori, and he agrees to return it to her if she gives him piano lessons. Thus begins an unlikely courtship that, against all the odds, evolves slowly but surely from unrequited lust into a genuine love affair.

In short, a beautiful story, brilliantly told and acted.

BACKBEAT (15)

Stuart Sutcliffe was the so-called fifth Beatle. He played bass badly, he painted brilliantly, he never took off his shades, he was a big mate of John Lennon and he died tragically young.

Set against the seedy backdrop of Hamburg's Reperbahn, this swelteringly atmospheric film tells the story not only of the Fab Four's early flirtations with drugs, drink and the demon rock and roll, but more importantly, of the fraught three-way relationship between Sutcliffe (brilliantly played, despite a slightly dodgy accent by Stephen Dorff), his photographer girlfriend Astrid Kirshner (Sheryl Lee) and John Lennon (the excellent Ian Hart).

Sad, sardonic and stunningly soundtracked, it was the best film to come out of Britain in a donkey's age.

CB4 (18)

Albert Brown (Rock), Euripides Smalls (Payne) and Otis O Otis (D) play the three boyz 'n the hood aiming to make it big as rap stars. When the local mobster Gusto gets hauled off to the Pen, the trio seize their opportunity. Taking over his identity, they become CB4, more than willing to turn the air blue while clutching their codpieces and glorifying violence. Things go swimmingly until Gusto escapes from his jailers and takes issue with the boyz for taking advantage of his incarceration. To make matters worse, the band are also targeted by a right-wing bigot who takes exception to them wearing their headgear back to front.

Spot on with its send-up of rap's rampantly macho posturing, CB4 offers a reasonably successful mix of comedy and social commentary – plus a cracking soundtrack.

PHILADELPHIA (15)

Landmark soundtrack album for landmark film, perhaps, as AIDS-infected (and Oscar-winning) Tom Hanks struggles to keep his job with top law firm while lawyer Denzel Washington represents him despite a chronic case of homophobia. With such a hot "issue" movie, director Jonathan Demme (no slouch with rock music films á la Talking Heads/*Stop Making Sense* feast) was able to engage the talents of, among others, two superstars who had never written songs specifically for a film before: the Boss and Neil Young. Springsteen's sombre but uplifting *Streets of Philadelphia* opens the movie and plays in its entirety. An Oscar for best song was only an acceptance speech away. Young's dignified and plaintiff piano piece *Philadelphia* plays in full under the final scene. Aside from a classical piece by Howard Shore (who scored the incidental music to the film), a nod to opera by Maria Callas, and an Haitian ensemble piece, Demme otherwise selected some classy rock 'n' soul, viz. Spin Doctors, Sade, Peter Gabriel and Indigo Girls.

SCHINDLER'S LIST (15)

Steven Speilberg's film about the enigmatic German industrialist Oskar Schindler swept all before it at the 1994 Oscars.

Studiously avoiding anything that could have been interpreted as sentimentality, Spielberg adopted a stark neo-documentary tone to tell the tale of the man who single-handedly saved 1,100 Jews from the gas chambers of Auschwitz. The result was a numbing three-hour ordeal which relied for its impact on the depiction of individual moments of terror – a small boy jumping into a cess pit to avoid being captured by the Germans; the look on a jeweller's face when he is presented with a bag of teeth complete with their gold fillings – rather than grand displays of obscenity.

Although it's never completely clear as to exactly why Schindler changed so suddenly from indifferent onlooker to heroic philanthropist, the morally uplifting message that the actions of one good man amongst many bad ones can make a difference comes over loud and clear.

FOUR WEDDINGS AND A FUNERAL (15)

The surprise American hit of the year, this British (hurrah!) made film, written by Black Adder's Richard Curtis, provides plenty of screwball comedy-esque laughs as it follows the progress – through the five titular functions – of the central character Charles (Hugh Grant in serious career-advancing form) as he tries to win the heart of mysterious Yank Andi MacDowell, who he meets at splicing number one.

The bizarre plot-twists, razor sharp characterisations and a superb script which makes full use of Grant's prodigious charm and comic talent, made this one of the must-see films of '94.

SIRENS (15)

Based on a fictionalised episode in the life of infamous Australian artist Norman Lindsay, writer/director John Duigan's erotically charged film tells what happens when a naive young clergyman, Anthony Campion (Hugh Grant), and his wife Estella (Tara Fitzgerald) are dispatched to the home of the legendary sketcher in order to try and persuade him to withdraw a controversial painting (a naked woman being crucified) from an exhibition.

So what exactly does happen? Well, to cut a long story down to its bare essentials, Estella arrives chez Lindsay all prim and proper and leaves as a right little raver, having been successively seduced and sexually liberated by the bohemian

▼ Sirens: making a big splash

▲ 4 Weddings... a warm reception

characters she encounters there.

In the hands of a less sophisticated director, this could've been a second-rate flesh fest, but thanks to Duigan's subtle script and skilful direction, Sirens comes across as a truly sensitive appreciation of sensuality, filled with warmth, humanity and humour.

TRUE ROMANCE (18)

A much better film than its poor box office showing suggested, this marriage between the mega-bucks of Warner Bros, the slick direction of Ridley Scott's bro' Tony and the mighty pen of Quentin Tarantino took the familiar movie device of an on-the-run-from-the-mob movie and added a few extra twists.

Basically the plot goes as follows: disillusioned film freak Clarence Worley (Christian Slater) falls for oddly named prostitute Alabama Whitman (Patricia Arquette), guns down her pimp, steals his coke and whisks Alabama off to California, whence the hapless pair are pursued by some extremely unbalanced Mafia types.

Yes it's violent, yes at times it's downright racist, but there's more than enough excitement, humour and telling characterisation to compensate.

WHAT'S EATING GILBERT GRAPE (12)

Johnny Depp stars as Gilbert Grape, a likeable adolescent trapped in the small mid-western American town of Endowa. Armed

with nothing more than his wages from his dead-end job in the town's ailing grocery store, Gilbert must care for his two younger sisters, his hugely overweight, housebound mother and his mentally retarded 18-year-old brother, Arnie. Life, as you can imagine, is pretty tough for Gilbert, but he bears his burden with admirable fortitude. When, however, he meets up with Becky, a temporary visitor to the town, Gilbert is able to momentarily forget his woes, and envisage what life must be like outside the Endowa city limits.

It's on these pegs of character and plot that My Life As A Dog director Lasse Hellstrom hangs some sharply focused observations about personal responsibility. The result is an utterly enchanting, off-beat film that makes its point with wit, subtlety and charm.

THE WRONG TROUSERS (U)

Aardman Animations supremo Nick Park picked up his second Oscar for The Wrong Trousers. In the follow-up to his highly acclaimed short, A Grand Day Out, Park's dazzling double act Wallace and Grommit take in a penguin as a lodger, little realising that the black and white bedsitter is, in fact, the master criminal Feathers McGraw. Subsequently, Grommit is ousted from his place at his master's feet and Wallace becomes the unwilling accomplice in Feathers' dastardly plan to heist a large and heavily guarded diamond.

Cleverly observed, breathtakingly detailed and packed with the kind of comic invention and timing that Little and Large would kill for, The Wrong Trousers is an ageless comedy classic that cuts across all age groups and masonic lodges. Long may it run. ∎

BRITISH REGGAE INDUSTRY 13 ANNUAL AWARD WINNERS 1993/94

Best British Male Singer: Don Campbell
Best British Female Singer: Deborahe Glasgow
Best British DJ/MC: Top Cat
Best British Newcomer: Don Campbell
Best British Reggae Album: *Undiluted* Roger Robin
Best British Reggae Group: Rough Cut
Best British Songwriter: Don Campbell
Best British Radio DJ: Trevor Sax
Best British Radio Station In Support Of Reggae Music: WNK 103.3 FM
Best British Producer: Mafia and Fluxy
Best British Sound System: Saxon
Best International Reggae Single: *Murderer* Buju Banton.
Best British Album: *Voice Of Jamaica* Buju Banton
Best British Artist: Beres Hammond
Best British Newcomer: Luciano
Best British Producer: Donovan Germaine
Contributary Award presented to Deborahe Glasgow

BRITS

Best British Male Solo: Sting
Best British Female Solo: Dina Carrol
Best British Group: Stereo MC's
Best British Dance Act: M-People
Best British Newcomer: Gabrielle
Best Single By British Artist: *Pray*/Take That
Best British Video: *Pray*/Take That
Best British LP: *Connected* /Stereo MC's
Best British Producer: Brian Eno
Best International Solo Artist: Lenny Kravitz
Best International Female Artist: Bjork
Best International Group: Crowded House
Best Soundtrack: The Bodyguard
Outstanding Contribution To Music Industry: Van Morrison

GRAMMYS

Album of The Year: *The Bodyguard*/Whitney Houston.
Record/Song Of The Year: *A Whole New World (Aladdin's Theme)*/Alan Meken and Tim Rice

Best Short Video: *Steam*/Peter Gabriel
Best Long Video: *Ten Summoner's Tales*/Sting
Best New Age Artist: Paul Winter Consort
Best Rock Performance By A Group: *Living On The Edge*/Aerosmith
Best Producer: David Foster
Best New Artist: Toni Braxton
Best Female Pop Song: *I Will Always Love You*/Whitney Houston
Best R n B Song: *That's The Way Love Goes*/Janet Jackson, James Harris III, Terry Lewis
Best Hard Rock Performance: *Plush*/Stone Temple Pilots
Best Metal Performance: *I Don't Want To Change The World*/Ozzy Ozbourne
Best Alternative Album: *Zooropa*/U2
Best Reggae Album: *Bad Boys*/Inner Circle

KERRANG! HEAVY METAL AWARDS

Best New British Band: Terrorvision
Best Alternative Metal LP: *Troublegum*/Therapy?
Best International Live Act: Bon Jovi
Best Video: *Embers Fire*/Paradise Lost
Best British Live Act: The Almighty
Album Of The Year: *Chaos AD*/Sepultura
Best New International Act: Pantera
Best British Band: Def Leppard
Kerrang! Kudos Award: Ozzy Osbourne
Monster Of Rock Award: Peter Grant
Kerrang! Kreativity Award: Aerosmith

MTV MUSIC VIDEO AWARDS

(Sept 93)
Best Video: Pearl Jam/Jeremy.
Best Alternative Video: Nirvana/*In Bloom*
Best R'n'B Video: En Vogue/*Free Your Mind*
Best Male Video: Lenny Kravitz/*Are You Gonna Go My Way*
Best Female Video: kd lang/*Constant Craving*
Best Group Video: Pearl Jam/*Jeremy*
Best New Artist: Stone Temple Pilots/*Plush*

Best Rap Video: Arrested Development/*People Everyday*
Best Heavy Rock Video: Pearl Jam/*Jeremy*
Best Video From A Film: Alice In Chains/*Would*/*Singles*

NME BRATS

Best Album: *Giant Steps*/Boo Radleys
Best Solo Act: Bjork
Best Newcomer: Elastica
Vibes Award (Best Dance Act): Orbital
Best Band: Suede
Best TV Programme: The Smell Of Reeves & Mortimer
Best Single: *Creep*/Radiohead
God Like Genius Award: John Peel
Philip Hall Memorial Award: Credit To the Nation
Best Rap Act: Cypress Hill
Bastard Of The Year: John Major
NME/XD Premium Lager Live Event: Mega Dog

SMASH HITS POLL WINNERS

Best British Group: Take That
Best British Single: *Boom Shake The Room*/Jazzy Jeff & Fresh Prince
Best LP: *Everything Changes*/Take That
Best Video: *Pray*/Take That
Best Dance Act: 2 Unlimited
Best Male Solo Artist: Michael Jackson
Best Indie Act: Nirvana
Best Rock Act: Meatloaf
Worst Film: *Body Of Evidence*
Worst Group: Bad Boys Inc
Worst Male Singer: Jason Donovan
Worst Female Singer: Madonna

▶ *Best British Dance Act: M-People*

music on tv

THE ALBUM SHOW (ITV)

No fuss or bother here at all, thank you very much, as the disembodied voice of one Lynne Parsons took us through a weekly look at the album charts and presented a profile of a leading pop person along the way.

THE BEAT (ITV)

Gary Crowley's late-night effort wisely dropped the fashion section, re-invented the band slot by dropping lip syncing in favour of live performance, and generally did very well for itself, winning various plaudits from the music press. Hidden among the predominantly indie-slanted roster that included Jah Wobble, Madder Rose, Senser, Tool, The Sandals, Sheep On Drugs and St Etienne was a rare telly interview with The Cocteau Twins, an even rarer film (the first ever apparently) of Christy Moore performing at The Finsbury Park Fleah and a series of interviews in which stars of the silver screen rubbed shoulders with the often unsung heroes of the music biz, such as producers and journalists. To date, there have been 76 editions of *The Beat* and there's still no end in sight.

BEAVIS AND BUTT-HEAD (C4) ▲

The disturbing spread of loser culture continued apace with the arrival on our terrestrial screens of the animated chunderheads from MTV land. The usual cries of "must we fling this filth at the kids" arose from all the usual places, leaving defenders of the twatish twosome to claim that, "hey!

it's just a joke, nobody's suggesting that they're role models." Good job too. Needless to say, whether you loved 'em, hated 'em or found 'em too moronic to even contemplate, Beavis And Butt-head came, saw and messed about in their pants. Huh-huh, huh-huh, huh-huh.

BPM (ITV)

Dave Dorrell and Brenda Touhy's clubber-friendly guide was still slotted away in early morning no-man's land, which was fine for recently returned ravers with a head full of E, but not much use to the casual viewer (postmen and milkmen excepted). Pity really, because there was some good stuff going down. Refreshingly cosmopolitan, it reached the parts of this and other countries that other programmes couldn't or wouldn't. Regular reports from clubs like Brilliant in Stevenage, the Ace in Manchester and Rezzerrection in Edinburgh, where the denizens displayed an alarming preference for dancing with day-glo tubes in their hands, plus a stimulatingly diverse playlist. All this and a tasty selection of video clips, interviews, BPM charts and Video Diaries from around the world provided those that needed to know with what they needed to know. Wicked.

BUTT NAKED (C4)

Extended showcase for bands who'd previously appeared on *Naked City*. Tucked away in the wee small hours, it took a lot of dedication to tune in regularly. Among those strutting their stuff were Pulp, Manics, Blur, Urban Species, The Charlatans, Brand New Heavies, Carleen Anderson, Arrested Development and D:Ream. More proof, if it were needed, that simply allowing bands to perform live doesn't always work.

THE CHART SHOW (ITV)

The show that proved that when it comes to pop music the last thing you need is a presenter, continued on good form: it won a confidence-boosting award as Best TV Music Programme from the readers of *Vox*; changed sponsor, and replaced the creaky old animated roller coaster with rocket

ships. Other than that, not much changed; the indie charts were still indie, the Exclusives were still Exclusive and the Video Vault was still opened on a weekly basis and the whole thing ran as smoothly as the trains under Mussolini. Rapidly becoming a Friday night/Saturday morning institution, why, sometimes you watch it without even realising.

LATER (BBC 2)

If it ain't broke don't fix it, runs the old adage, and consequently Jools Holland's highly respected, live musical soirée entered its third season with nothing more drastic than a change of jacket for the ivory-tickling host. As ever, the musical agenda was alarmingly eclectic. Where else would you get The Pretenders rubbing shoulders with Erasure, David McComb with Angelique Kidjo, Nick Cave with the reformed Traffic, or Elvis Costello, whose muscular performance with the reassembled Attractions of *Thirteen Steps Lead Down* provided one of the musical highlights of the televisual year? Nowhere, that's where.

LOUDON AND CO (BBC 2)

A sort of sequel to last year's *No Stilettos*, *Loudon And Co*, introduced by much-loved American balladeer Loudon Wainwright III, followed the same live format herding together a whole host of bands aimed at, shall we say, the more mature viewer. So what you got for your viewing minutes was John Martyn, Roachford, Marcella Detroit, Des 'Ree, Daryl Hall, Paul Young, James Taylor, Iris DeMent, Texas, Chris Rea and Carlene Carter, turning up, tuning in and wiggin' out.

MTV (MTV)

This cable/satellite phenomenon continued to offer as cosmopolitan a mix of programmes as anyone could wish for. Top of everybody's list in the popularity stakes came *Ray Cokes' Most Wanted*. The mixture of music videos, quizzes, fax and phone-ins, and Cokes' spontaneity – on

what other show would you get the host wandering off-set and around the building in search of a fish to interview? – kept things constantly bubbling.

Elsewhere, *120 Minutes* offered videos and up-to-the-minute news from the indie scene; *Headbangers' Ball* continued its comprehensive coverage of all things hard and heavy; while the early morning *Chill Out* provided an ambient-coloured wind-down zone for the rapidly flagging raver.

NAKED CITY (C4)

Out went: the rather pretentious this-is-Caitlin's-squat-where-all-her-kooky-friends-hang-out-munching-crisps angle, Cred Or Dead and Busk Or Bust.In came; luvvable slaphead Smiley, They Might Be Giants (talent slot), Who's In The House (a sort of Unplugged for the disconnected), music hacks Stewart Maconie and Andrew Collins with their droll dissertations on drugs, pop festivals and other crucial matters, and much, much more of the increasingly manic Johnny Vaughan, whose promotion to frontperson thankfully spared us a lot of self-conscious blathering from Ms Moran.

Staying the same was an adventurous musical policy which covered everything from New Wave Of New Wavers S*M*A*S*H through The Brand New Heavies, Bhangra through D:Ream, and Fundamental through lesbian rockers Fem 2

▼ *'Spontaneous' Ray Cokes – ...Most Wanted (MTV)*

Fem. Result: a stronger, fitter and leaner slice of nightlife.

NOISY MOTHERS (ITV)

Was actually just *Raw Power* with a new patch on its denim jacket. Consequently the format – regular visits to HM shrines, (Donington, etc), promo vids, interviews and low profile presenters Ann Kirk and Krusher – stayed the same, and everyone who was happy with it before was happy with it still.

THE ROCK 'N' ROLL YEARS (BBC1)

The best ideas are often the simplest, and as proof of that particular pudding Auntie Beeb served up *The Rock 'n' Roll Years*. Splicing together grainy old black and white film footage (which worked quite brilliantly for the '60s and '70s) and colour video (which didn't quite cut the mustard for the '80s) we were treated to a soundtrack that included The Rolling Stones, The Cure, Simply Red, U2, The Pet Shop Boys, New Order and The Proclaimers. Subsequently, we were invited to witness the assassinations of Bobby Kennedy and Martin Luther King, the kidnapping of Terry Waite, the Tiannemann Square massacre, the break-up of The Beatles and the deaths of Jimi Hendrix and Janis Joplin, while simultaneously tapping our feet and poppin' our fingers. This is how they should teach history in schools.

TOP OF THE POPS (BBC1)

"Will it still be here next year?", we asked last year. And the answer would appear to be a resounding "yes". Flying in the face of all the rumours that suggested its demise was imminent, the doddering old granddaddy of music shows took a deep breath, pulled itself together and dropped the bland and boring frontmen Tony Dortie and Mark Franklin in favour of bland and boring Radio One DJs. Their return was slightly tempered by the use of occasional guest presenters like Jack Dee, Meatloaf, Smashy And Nicey, Angus Deayton, etc, and the show soldiered on towards the millennium. Will the bugger ever die? It seems not.

▲ *Later's Jools Holland: a little bit of chat and tickle*

UNPLUGGED (BBC 2)

Not much to say about this bought-in-from-MTV show, which generally featured noisy types exchanging their electrical goods for acoustic instruments. Among the highlights were Nirvana's prophetically wasted attempts to do something different with grunge, k.d. lang's dykey-diva-ness and Rod Stewart and Ron Wood's boozy bonhomie, fuelled with a nice line in self-effacing humour and some belting songs.

THE WORD (C4)

And still it went on; plumbing depths of bad taste with the They'll Do Anything To Get On TV spot, wherein sad and lonely people in desperate need of lives allowed themselves to be covered in piss, shit and God knows what else for a transient moment of fame. Oh dear. But there was some good stuff too; Snoop Doggy Dog being attacked by Rod Hull's Emu, bald-headed Hufty lapping up the gay vibes at Sidney's Mardi Gras festival and a canny selection of hip and happening bands including K7, Cypress Hill, Soul Asylum, Oasis, Salad and, while we're on the subject of food, Smashing Pumpkins. A fifth series is yet to be confirmed, so don't hold your breath... unless, of course, you're sitting in a bath full of horse manure. ■

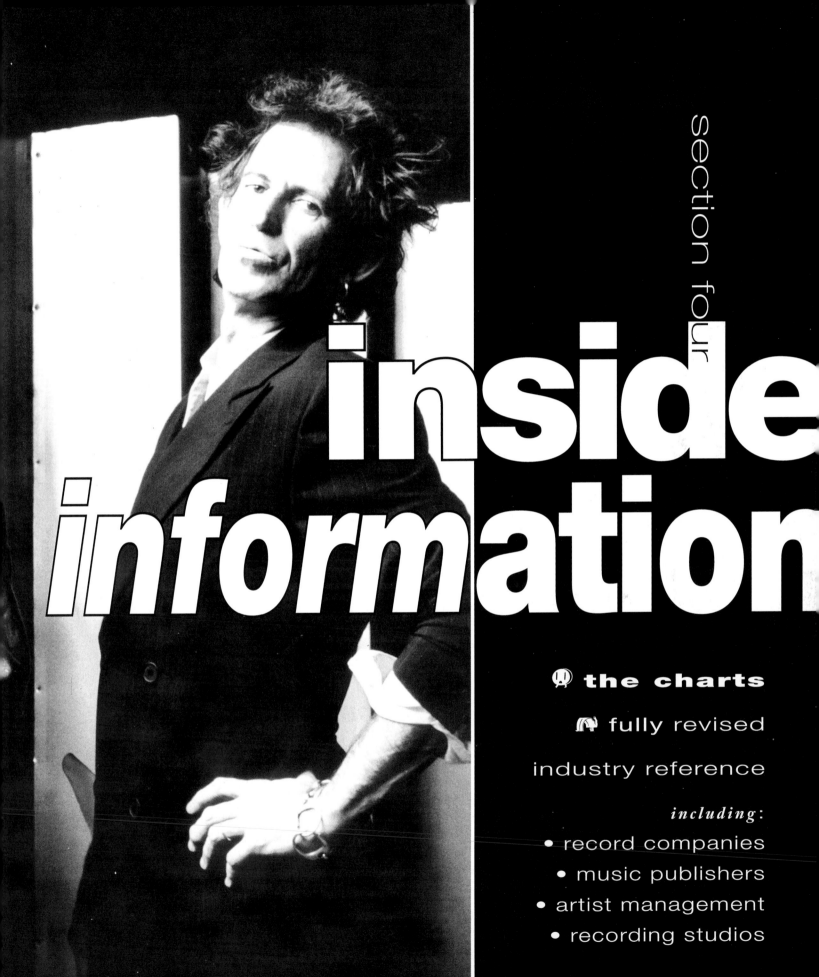

section four

inside information

🎵 **the charts**

🎵 fully revised

industry reference

including:

• record companies

• music publishers

• artist management

• recording studios

uk virgin Crunchie albums

1	**Promises And Lies** UB40	Virgin
2	**Levellers** Levellers	China
3	**Pocket Full Of Kryptonite** Spin Doctors	Epic
4	**River of Dreams** Billy Joel	Columbia
5	**Automatic For The People** R.E.M.	Warner Bros
6	**Zooropa** U2	Island
7	**Antmusic – The Very Best of Adam Ant** Adam Ant	Arcade
8	**Keep The Faith** Bon Jovi	Jambco/Mercury
9	**Ten Summoner's Tales** Sting	A&M
10	**What's Love Got To Do With It** Tina Turner	Parlophone
11	**Debut** Bjork	One Little Indian
12	**Bigger, Better, Faster, More!** 4 Non Blondes	Interscope/East West
13	**The Freddie Mercury Album** Freddie Mercury	Parlophone
14	**Waiting for Herb** Pogues	PM/WEA
15	**Are You Gonna Go My Way** Lenny Kravitz	Virgin
16	**Unplugged...And Seated** Rod Stewart	Warner Bros
17	**Republic** New Order	London
18	**Rage Against The Machine** Rage Against The Machine	Epic
19	**Connected** Stereo Mc's	4th + B'way
20	**Siamese Dream** Smashing Pumpkins	Hut

us albums

1	**River Of Dreams** Billy Joel	Columbia
2	**Sleepless in Seattle** Soundtrack	Epic Soundtrax
3	**Blind Melon** Blind Melon	Capitol
4	**janet.** Janet Jackson	Virgin
5	**Black Sunday** Cypress Hill	Ruffhouse
6	**Core** Stone Temple Pilots	Atlantic
7	**The Bodyguard** Soundtrack	Arista
8	**Promises and Lies** UB40	Virgin
9	**Get A Grip** Aerosmith	Geffen
10	**Unplugged...And Seated** Rod Stewart	Warner Bros
11	**Zooropa** U2	Island
12	**Grave Dancers Union** Soul Asylum	Columbia
13	**The World Is Yours** Scarface	Rap-A-Lot
14	**It's About Time** SWV	RCA
15	**Back To Broadway** Barbra Streisand	Columbia
16	**For The Cool In You** Babyface	Epic
17	**Breathless** Kenny G	Arista
18	**Ten Summoner's Tales** Sting	A&M
19	**Are You Gonna Go My Way** Lenny Kravitz	Virgin
20	**Bigger, Better, Faster, More!** 4 Non Blondes	Interscope

uk singles

1	**Mr. Vain** Culture Beat	Epic
2	**It Keeps Rainin' (Tears...)** Bitty McLean	Brilliant
3	**Right Here** SWV	RCA
4	**The River Of Dreams** Billy Joel	Columbia
5	**Heart-Shaped Box** Nirvana	Geffen
6	**Living On My Own** Freddie Mercury	Parlophone
7	**The Key The Secret** Urban Cookie Collective	Pulse
8	**Faces** 2 Unlimited	PWL Continental
9	**Nuff Vibes (EP)** Apache Indian	Island
10	**Dreamlover** Mariah Carey	Columbia

us singles

1	**Dreamlover** Mariah Carey	Columbia
2	**Can't Help Falling In Love** UB40	Virgin
3	**Whoomp! (There It Is)** Tag Team	Life
4	**If** Janet Jackson	Virgin
5	**Runaway Train** Soul Asylum	Columbia
6	**Right Here (Human Nature)/Dow** SWV	RCA
7	**Will You Be There** Michael Jackson	MJJ
8	**Lately** Jodeci	Uptown
9	**The River Of Dreams** Billy Joel	Columbia
10	**If I Had No Loot** Tony! Toni! Tone!	Wing

indy albums

1	**The Levellers** The Levellers	China
2	**Debut** Bjork	One Little Indian
3	**Siamese Dream** Smashing Pumpkins	Hut
4	**Giant Step** The Boo Radleys	Creation
5	**Levelling The Land** The Levellers	China

dance singles

1	**Sound of Eden/Sweet Sensation** Shades of Rhythm	ZTT
2	**Move** Moby	Mute
3	**Hey Mr. DJ** Zhane	Epic
4	**World (The Price of Love)** New Order	London
5	**Right Here** SWV	RCA

garth brooks

uk virgin Crunchie albums

1	**Bat Out of Hell II – Back Into Hell** Meat Loaf	Virgin
2	**Wild Wood** Paul Weller	Go!
3	**Promises and Lies** UB40	Virgin
4	**River Of Dreams** Billy Joel	Columbia
5	**Pocket Full of Kryptonite** Spin Doctors	Epic
6	**Levellers** Levellers	China
7	**Ten Summoner's Tales** Sting	A&M
8	**Automatic For The People** R.E.M.	Warner Bros
9	**Antmusic – The Very Best of Adam Ant** Adam Ant	Arcade
10	**Zooropa** U2	Island
11	**Debut** Bjork	One Little Indian
12	**Are You Gonna Go My Way** Lenny Kravitz	Virgin
13	**Keep The Faith** Bon Jovi	Jambco/Mercury
14	**The Definitive Collection** Kinks	Polygram TV
15	**What's Love Got To Do With It** Tina Turner	Parlophone
16	**Bigger, Better, Faster, More!** 4 Non Blondes	Interscope/East West
17	**Republic** New Order	London
18	**The Freddie Mercury Album** Freddie Mercury	Parlophone
19	**Unplugged...And Seated** Rod Stewart	Warner Bros
20	**Core** Stone Temple Pilots	Atlantic/East West

us albums

1	**In Pieces** Garth Brooks	Liberty
2	**Music Box** Mariah Carey	Columbia
3	**River Of Dreams** Billy Joel	Columbia
4	**Blind Melon** Blind Melon	Capitol
5	**Sleepless In Seattle** Soundtrack	Epic Soundtrax
6	**janet.** Janet Jackson	Virgin
7	**Core** Stone Temple Pilots	Atlantic
8	**Black Sunday** Cypress Hill	Ruffhouse
9	**Promises and Lies** UB40	Virgin
10	**The Bodyguard** Soundtrack	Arista
11	**Get A Grip** Aerosmith	Geffen
12	**Unplugged...And Seated** Rod Stewart	Warner Bros
13	**Zooropa** U2	Island
14	**Grave Dancers Union** Soul Asylum	Columbia
15	**It's About Time** SWV	RCA
16	**The World Is Yours** Scarface	Rap-A-Lot
17	**Toni Braxton** Toni Braxton	LaFace
18	**Are You Gonna Go My Way** Lenny Kravitz	Virgin
19	**Ten** Pearl Jam	Epic
20	**For The Cool In You** Babyface	Epic

uk singles

1	**Mr. Vain** Culture Beat	Epic
2	**Go West** Pet Shop Boys	Parlophone
3	**Boom! Shake The Room** Jazzy Jeff & Fresh Prince	Jive
4	**It Keeps Rainin' (Tears...)** Bitty McLean	Brilliant
5	**Right Here** SWV	RCA
6	**The River Of Dreams** Billy Joel	Columbia
7	**Creep** Radiohead	Parlophone
8	**Faces** 2 Unlimited	PWL Continental
9	**Heart-Shaped Box** Nirvana	Geffen
10	**Dreamlover** Mariah Carey	Columbia

us singles

1	**Dreamlover** Mariah Carey	Columbia
2	**Whoomp! (There It Is)** Tag Team	Life
3	**Can't Help Falling In Love** UB40	Virgin
4	**If** Janet Jackson	Virgin
5	**Right Here (Human Nature)/Dow** SWV	RCA
6	**The River Of Dreams** Billy Joel	Columbia
7	**Runaway Train** Soul Asylum	Columbia
8	**Will You Be There** Michael Jackson	MJJ
9	**Lately** Jodeci	Uptown
10	**Baby I'm Yours** Shai	Gasoline Alley

indy albums

1	**Last Splash** The Breeders	4AD
2	**The Levellers** The Levellers	China
3	**Debut** Bjork	One Little Indian
4	**Siamese Dream** Smashing Pumpkins	Hut
5	**Levelling The Land** The Levellers	China

dance singles

1	**Boom! Shake The Room** Jazzy Jeff & Fresh Prince	Jive
2	**Hey Mr. DJ** Zhane	Epic
3	**Sound of Eden/Sweet Sensation** Shades of Rhythm	ZTT
4	**Move** MOby	Mute
5	**Heaven Knews** Luther Vandross	Epic

indy albums

1	**The Levellers** The Levellers	China
2	**Debut** Bjork	One Little Indian
3	**Last Splash** The Breeders	4AD
4	**Mind And Soul Collaborators** Back The Planet	Parallel
5	**Siamese Dream** Smashing Pumpkins	Hut

dance singles

1	**Moving On Up** M-People	Deconstruction
2	**Life** Haddaway	Logic/Arista
3	**Boom! Shake The Room** Jazzy Jeff & Fresh Prince	Jive
4	**Fascinated** Lisa B	London
5	**What Happened To The Music** Joey Negro	Virgin

nirvana

uk singles

1	**Boom! Shake The Room** Jazzy Jeff & Fresh Prince	Jive
2	**Go West** Pet Shop Boys	Parlophone
3	**Mr. Vain** Culture Beat	Epic
4	**Moving On Up** M People	Deconstruction
5	**Right Here** SWV	RCA
6	**She Don't Let Nobody** Chaka Demus & Pliers	Mango
7	**It Keeps Rainin' (Tears...)** Bitty McLean	Brilliant
8	**Life** Haddaway	Logic/Arista
9	**Condemnation (EP)** Depeche Mode	Mute
10	**On The Ropes (EP)** Wonder Stuff	Polydor

us singles

1	**Dreamlover** Mariah Carey	Columbia
2	**Whoomp! (There It Is)** Tag Team	Life
3	**Right Here (Human Nature)/Dow** SWV	RCA
4	**Can't Help Falling In Love** UB40	Virgin
5	**If** Janet Jackson	Virgin
6	**The River Of Dreams** Billy Joel	Columbia
7	**Will You Be There** Michael Jackson	MJJ
8	**Runaway Train** Soul Asylum	Columbia
9	**Lately** Jodeci	Uptown
10	**Baby I'm Yours** Shai	Gasoline Alley

us albums

1	**In Pieces** Garth Brooks	Liberty
2	**Music Box** Mariah Carey	Columbia
3	**River Of Dreams** Billy Joel	Columbia
4	**Blind Melon** Blind Melon	Capitol
5	**Sleepless In Seattle** Soundtrack	Epic Soundtrax
6	**janet.** Janet Jackson	Virgin
7	**Human Wheels** John Mellencamp	Mercury
8	**Core** Stone Temple Pilots	Atlantic
9	**Barney's Favorites Vol. 1** Barney	SBK
10	**Black Sunday** Cypress Hill	Ruffhouse
11	**Get A Grip** Aerosmith	Geffen
12	**The Bodyguard** Soundtrack	Arista
13	**Unplugged...And Seated** Rod Stewart	Warner Bros
14	**Promises And Lies** UB40	Virgin
15	**Grave Dancers Union** Soul Asylum	Columbia
16	**Zooropa** U2	Island
17	**It's About Time** SWV	RCA
18	**Toni Braxton** Toni Braxton	LaFace
19	**Ten** Pearl Jam	Epic
20	**Are You Gonna Go My Way** Lenny Kravitz	Virgin

uk virgin Crunchie albums

1	**In Utero** Nirvana	Geffen
2	**Bat Out of Hell II – Back Into Hell** Meat Loaf	Virgin
3	**Wild Wood** Paul Weller	Go!
4	**The Hits/The B-Sides** Symbol/Prince	Paisley Park/Warner
5	**The Hits 1** Symbol/Prince	Paisley Park/Warner
6	**The Hits 2** Symbol/Prince	Paisley Park/Warner
7	**Promises and Lies** UB40	Virgin
8	**Elements – The Best of Mike Oldfield** Mike Oldfield	Virgin
9	**The Singles Collection 1981-1983** Kim Wilde	MCA
10	**River Of Dreams** Billy Joel	Columbia
11	**Automatic For The People** R.E.M.	Warner Bros
12	**Pocket Full Of Kryptonite** Spin Doctors	Epic
13	**Ten Summoner's Tales** Sting	A&M
14	**Debut** Bjork	One Little Indian
15	**Are you Gonna Go My Way** Lenny Kravitz	Virgin
16	**Levellers** Levellers	China
17	**Zooropa** U2	Island
18	**The Definitive Collection** Kinks	Polygram TV
19	**Antmusic – The Very Best of Adam Ant** Adam Ant	Arcade
20	**Some Fantastic Place** Squeeze	A&M

uk singles

1	**Boom! Shake The Room** Jazzy Jeff & Fresh Prince	Jive
2	**Moving On Up** M People	Deconstruction
3	**Go West** Pet Shop Boys	Parlophone
4	**She Don't Let Nobody** Chaka Demus & Pliers	Mango
5	**Mr. Vain** Culture Beat	Epic
6	**Relax** Frankie Goes To Hollywood	ZTT
7	**Life** Haddaway	Logic/Arista
8	**Right Here** SWV	RCA
9	**Going Nowhere** Gabrielle	Go.Beat
10	**It Must Have Been Love** Roxette	EMI

us singles

1	**Dreamlover** Mariah Carey	Columbia
2	**Right Here (Human Nature)/Dow** SWV	RCA
3	**Whoomp! (There It Is)** Tag Team	Life
4	**The River Of Dreams** Billy Joel	Columbia
5	**If** Janet Jackson	Virgin
6	**Can't Help Falling In Love** UB40	Virgin
7	**Will You Be There** Michael Jackson	MJJ
8	**Another Sad Love Song** Toni Braxton	LaFace
9	**Runaway Train** Soul Asylum	Columbia
10	**Baby I'm Yours** Shai	Gasoline Alley

indy albums

1	**Debut** Bjork	One Little Indian
2	**Cuckoo** Curve	Anxious
3	**The Levellers** The Levellers	China
4	**Last Splash** The Breeders	4AD
5	**Into The Labyrinth** Dead Can Dance	4AD

dance singles

1	**Relax** Frankie Goes To Hollywood	ZTT
2	**Joy** Staxx	Champion
3	**Boom! Shake The Room** Jazzy Jeff & Fresh Prince	Jive
4	**Going Nowhere** Gabrielle	Go!
5	**Moving On Up** M People	Deconstruction

us albums

1	**In Pieces** Garth Brooks	Liberty
2	**Music Box** Mariah Carey	Columbia
3	**Bat Out Of Hell II: Back Into Hell** Meat Loaf	MCA
4	**River Of Dreams** Billy Joel	Columbia
5	**Blind Melon** Blind Melon	Capitol
6	**Sleepless In Seattle** Soundtrack	Epic Soundtrax
7	**janet.** Janet Jackson	Virgin
8	**Core** Stone Temple Pilots	Atlantic
9	**Human Wheels** John Mellencamp	Mercury
10	**Black Sunday** Cypress Hill	Ruffhouse
11	**Unplugged...And Seated** Rod Stewart	Warner Bros
12	**Get A Grip** Aerosmith	Geffen
13	**The Bodyguard** Soundtrack	Arista
14	**Toni Braxton** Toni Braxton	LaFace
15	**Promises And Lies** UB40	Virgin
16	**Barney's Favorites Vol. 1** Barney	SBK
17	**It's About Time** SWV	RCA
18	**Grave Dancers Union** Soul Asylum	Columbia
19	**The Hits/The B-Sides** Symbol/Prince	Paisley Park
20	**Zooropa** U2	Island

uk virgin Crunchie albums

1	**Bat Out of Hell II – Back Into Hell** Meat Loaf	Virgin
2	**In Utero** Nirvana	Geffen
3	**The Beatles 1962-1966** Beatles	Parlophone
4	**The Beatles 1967-1970** Beatles	Parlophone
5	**Elements – The Best of Mike Oldfield** Mike Oldfield	Virgin
6	**The Hits 2** Symbol/Prince	Paisley Park/Warner
7	**The Hits 1** Symbol/Prince	Paisley Park/Warner
8	**Wild Wood** Paul Weller	Go!
9	**Promises and Lies** UB40	Virgin
10	**The Singles Collection 1981-1993** Kim Wilde	MCA
11	**The Hits/The B-Sides** Symbol/Prince	Paisley Park/Warner
12	**Automatic For The People** R.E.M.	Warner Bros
13	**Pocket Full of Kryptonite** Spin Doctors	Epic
14	**River Of Dreams** Billy Joel	Columbia
15	**Ten Summoner's Tales** Sting	A&M
16	**Are You Gonna Go My Way** Lenny Kravitz	Virgin
17	**Debut** Bjork	One Little Indian
18	**Keep The Faith** Bon Jovi	Jambco/Mercury
19	**Zooropa** U2	Island
20	**Levellers** Levellers	China

uk virgin Crunchie albums

1	**Bat Out Of Hell II – Back Into Hell** Meat Loaf	Virgin
2	**Laid** James	Fontana
3	**Love Scenes** Beverley Craven	Epic
4	**The Hits 2** Symbol/Prince	Paisley Park/Warner
5	**Elements – The Best Of Mike Oldfield** Mike Oldfield	Virgin
6	**In Utero** Nirvana	Geffen
7	**The Beatles 1962-1966** Beatles	Parlophone
8	**The Hits 1** Symbol/Prince	Paisley Park/Warner
9	**The Beatles 1967-1970** Beatles	Parlophone
10	**Promises And Lies** UB40	Virgin
11	**Wild Wood** Paul Weller	Go!
12	**The Singles Collection 1981-1993** Kim Wilde	MCA
13	**Pocket Full Of Kryptonite** Spin Doctors	Epic
14	**Are You Gonna Go My Way** Lenny Kravitz	Virgin
15	**(Big Red Letter Day)** Buffalo Tom	Beggars Banquet
16	**Automatic For The People** R.E.M.	Warner Bros
17	**The Hits/The B-Sides** Symbol/Prince	Paisley Park/Warner
18	**Debut** Bjork	One Little Indian
19	**Ten Summoner's Tales** Sting	A&M
20	**River Of Dreams** Billy Joel	Columbia

us albums

1	**In Utero** Nirvana	DGC
2	**In Pieces** Garth Brooks	Liberty
3	**Music Box** Mariah Carey	Columbia
4	**Bat Out Of Hell II: Back Into Hell** Meat Loaf	MCA
5	**River Of Dreams** Billy Joel	Columbia
6	**Blind Melon** Blind Melon	Capitol
7	**janet.** Janet Jackson	Virgin
8	**Sleepless In Seattle** Soundtrack	Epic Soundtrax
9	**Core** Stone Temple Pilots	Atlantic
10	**Black Sunday** Cypress Hill	Ruffhouse
11	**Toni Braxton** Toni Braxton	LaFace
12	**Unplugged...And Seated** Rod Stewart	Warner Bros
13	**Get A Grip** Aerosmith	Geffen
14	**Human Wheels** John Mellencamp	Mercury
15	**The Bodyguard** Soundtrack	Arista
16	**Yes I Am** Melissa Etheridge	Island
17	**Barney's Favorites Vol. 1** Barney	SBK
18	**Grave Dancers Union** Soul Asylum	Columbia
19	**Promises And Lies** UB40	Virgin
20	**Siamese Dream** Smashing Pumpkins	Virgin

uk singles

1	**Relight My Fire** Take That/Lulu	RCA
2	**Boom! Shake The Room** Jazzy Jeff & Fresh Prince	Jive
3	**Moving On Up** M-People	Deconstruction
4	**She Don't Let Nobody** Chaka Demus & Pliers	Mango
5	**Relax** Frankie Goes To Hollywood	ZTT
6	**Life** Haddaway	Logic/Arista
7	**Go West** Pet Shop Boys	Parlophone
8	**I'd Do Anything For Love...** Meat Loaf	Virgin
9	**Mr. Vain** Culture Beat	Epic
10	**Stay** Eternal	EMI

us singles

1	**Dreamlover** Mariah Carey	Columbia
2	**Right Here (Human Nature)/Dow** SWV	RCA
3	**Whoomp! (There It Is)** Tag Team	Life
4	**The River Of Dreams** Billy Joel	Columbia
5	**If** Janet Jackson	Virgin
6	**Can't Help Falling In Love** UB40	Virgin
7	**Another Sad Love Song** Toni Braxton	LaFace
8	**Will You Be There** Michael Jackson	MJJ
9	**I'd Do Anything For Love...** Meat Loaf	MCA
10	**Runaway Train** Soul Asylum	Columbia

indy albums

1	**Debut** Bjork	One Little Indian
2	**The Levellers** The Levellers	China
3	**Linger Ficken' Good** Revolting Cocks	Devotion
4	**Last Splash** The Breeders	4AD
5	**Siamese Dream** Smashing Pumpkins	Hut

dance singles

1	**Relax** Frankie Goes To Hollywood	ZTT
2	**Star/I Like It** D:Ream	Magnet/East West
3	**Joy** Staxx	Champion
4	**Stay** Eternal	EMI
5	**Boom! Shake The Room** Jazzy Jeff & Fresh Prince	Jive

bjork

uk virgin Crunchie albums

1	**Bat Out Of Hell II – Back Into Hell** Meat Loaf	Virgin
2	**Construction For The Modern Idiot** Wonder Stuff	Polydor
3	**Aces And Kings – The Best Of Go West** Go West	Chrysalis
4	**Retro Active** Def Leppard	Bludgeon Riffola
5	**The Hits 2** Prince	Paisley Park/Warner
6	**The Hits 1** Symbol/Prince	Paisley Park/Warner
7	**Love Scenes** Beverley Craven	Epic
8	**Pocket Full Of Cryptonite** Spin Doctors	Epic
9	**In Utero** Nirvana	Geffen
10	**The Beatles 1962-1966** Beatles	Parlophone
11	**Promises And Lies** UB40	Virgin
12	**Wild Wood** Paul Weller	Go!
13	**The Beatles 1967-1970** Beatles	Parlophone
14	**Elements – The Best Of Mike Oldfield** Mike Oldfield	Virgin
15	**Automatic For The People** R.E.M.	Warner Bros
16	**The Singles Collection 1981-1993** Kim Wilde	MCA
17	**Laid** James	Fontana
18	**Are You Gonna Go My Way** Lenny Kravitz	Virgin
19	**Debut** Bjork	One Little Indian
20	**At Worst...The Best Of...** Boy George And Culture Club	Virgin

us albums

1	**In Pieces** Garth Brooks	Liberty
2	**In Utero** Nirvana	DGC
3	**Bat Out Of Hell II: Back Into Hell** Meat Loaf	MCA
4	**Music Box** Mariah Carey	Columbia
5	**Easy Come, Easy Go** George Strait	MCA
6	**River Of Dreams** Billy Joel	Columbia
7	**janet.** Janet Jackson	Virgin
8	**Greatest Hits Volume Two** Reba McEntire	MCA
9	**Blind Melon** Blind Melon	Capitol
10	**187 He Wrote** Spice 1	Jive
11	**Toni Braxton** Toni Braxton	LaFace
12	**Sleepless In Seattle** Soundtrack	Epic Soundtrax
13	**Black Sunday** Cypress Hill	Ruffhouse
14	**Core** Stone Temple Pilots	Atlantic
15	**Unplugged...And Seated** Rod Stewart	Warner Bros
16	**Get A Grip** Aerosmith	Geffen
17	**A lot about livin'** Alan Jackson	Arista
18	**The Bodyguard** Sountrack	Arista
19	**Barney's Favorites Vol. 1** Barney	SBK
20	**Human Wheels** John Mellencamp	Mercury

uk singles

1	**Relight My Fire** Take That/Lulu	RCA
2	**I'd Do Anything For Love...** Meat Loaf	Virgin
3	**Boom! Shake The Room** Jazzy Jeff & Fresh Prince	Jive
4	**She Don't Let Nobody** Chaka Demus & Pliers	Mango
5	**Moving On Up** M-People	Deconstruction
6	**Life** Haddaway	Logic/Arista
7	**Stay** Eternal	EMI
8	**Relax** Frankie Goes To Hollywood	ZTT
9	**Hallowed Be Thy Name** Iron Maiden	EMI
10	**Go West** Pet Shop Boys	Parlophone

us singles

1	**Dreamlover** Mariah Carey	Columbia
2	**Right Here (Human Nature)/Dow** SWV	RCA
3	**The River Of Dreams** Billy Joel	Columbia
4	**Whoomp! (There Is Is)** Tag Team	Life
5	**Just Kickin' It** Xscape	So So Def
6	**I'd Do Anything For Love (But...** Meat Loaf	MCA
7	**If** Janet Jackson	Virgin
8	**All That She Wants** Ace of Base	Arista
9	**Another Sad Love Song** Toni Braxton	LaFace
10	**Hey Mr. D.J.** Zhane	Flavor Unit

indy albums

1	**(Big Red Letter Day)** Buffalo Tom	Beggars Banquet
2	**Debut** Bjork	One Little Indian
3	**The Levellers** The Levellers	China
4	**Mezcal Head** Swervedriver	Creation
5	**Siamese Dream** Smashing Pumpkins	Hut

dance singles

1	**Say What!** X-Press 2	Junior Boy's Own
2	**Breakdown** One Dove	London
3	**Joy** Staxx	Champion
4	**Stay** Eternal	EMI
5	**One Love** Prodigy	XL Recordings

indy albums

1 **Thirteen** — Teenage Fanclub — Creation
2 **Debut** — Bjork — One Little Indian
3 **(Big Red Letter Day)** — Buffalo Tom — Beggars Banquet
4 **The Levellers** — The Levellers — China
5 **Gentlemen** — Afghan Wings — Blast First

dance singles

1 **U Got 2 Let The Music** — Cappella — Internal
2 **Gotta Get It Right** — Lena Fiagbe — Mother
3 **Carnival** — Lionrock — Arista
4 **Say What!** — X-Press 2 — Junior Boy's Own
5 **Shamrocks & Shenanigans/...** — House Of Pain — Ruffness/XL

mariah carey

indy albums

1 **Chaos A.D.** — Sepultura — Roadrunner
2 **Debut** — Bjork — One Little Indian
3 **Sabresonic** — Sabres Of Paradise — Warp
4 **Thirteen** — Teenage Fanclub — Creation
5 **The Levellers** — The Levellers — China

dance singles

1 **Give It Up** — The Goodmen — Fresh Fruit/ffrreedom
2 **U Got 2 Let The Music** — Cappella — Internal
3 **Texas Cowboys** — The Grid — Deconstruction/RCA
4 **Gotta Get It Right** — Lena Fiagbe — Mother
5 **Holding On** — Clock — Media

uk singles

1 **I'd Do Anything For Love (But...** — Meat Loaf — Virgin
2 **Relight My Fire** — Take That/Lulu — RCA
3 **Boom! Shake The Room** — Jazzy Jeff & Fresh Prince — Jive
4 **Stay** — Eternal — EMI
5 **Moving On Up** — M-People — Deconstruction
6 **She Don't Let Nobody** — Chaka Demus & Pliers — Mango
7 **U Got 2 Let The Music** — Cappella — Internal
8 **One Love** — The Prodigy — XL Recordings
9 **Life** — Haddaway — Logic/Arista
10 **Don't Be A Stranger** — Dina Carroll — A&M

us singles

1 **Dreamlover** — Mariah Carey — Columbia
2 **Just Kickin' It** — Xscape — So So Def
3 **I'd Do Anything For Love...** — Meat Loaf — MCA
4 **All That She Wants** — Ace of Base — Arista
5 **The River Of Dreams** — Billy Joel — Columbia
6 **Right Here (Human Nature)/Dow** — SWV — RCA
7 **Whoomp! (There It Is)** — Tag Team — Life
8 **Hey Mr. D.J.** — Zhane — Flavor Unit
9 **If** — Janet Jackson — Virgin
10 **Anniversary** — Tony! Toni! Tone! — Wlng

uk singles

1 **I'd Do Anything For Love...** — Meat Loaf — Virgin
2 **U Got 2 Let The Music** — Cappella — Internal
3 **Please Forgive Me** — Bryan Adams — A&M
4 **Don't Be A Stranger** — Dina Carroll — A&M
5 **Boom! Shake The Room** — Jazzy Jeff & Fresh Prince — Jive
6 **Stay** — Eternal — EMI
7 **Both Sides Of The Story** — Phil Collins — Virgin
8 **Relight My Fire** — Take That/Lulu — RCA
9 **Give It Up** — The Goodmen — Fresh Fruit/ffrreedom
10 **One Love** — The Prodigy — XL Recordings

us singles

1 **Dreamlover** — Mariah Carey — Columbia
2 **I'd Do Anything For Love...** — Meat Loaf — MCA
3 **All That She Wants** — Ace of Base — Arista
4 **Just Kickin' It** — Xscape — So So Def
5 **The River Of Dreams** — Billy Joel — Columbia
6 **Hey Mr. D.J.** — Zhane — Flavor Unit
7 **Whoomp! (There It Is)** — Tag Team — Life
8 **Right Here (Human Nature)/Dow** — SWV — RCA
9 **Again** — Janet Jackson — Virgin
10 **Anniversary** — Tony! Toni! Tone! — Wlng

us albums

1 **In Pieces** — Garth Brooks — Liberty
2 **Bat Out Of Hell II: Back Into Hell** — Meat Loaf — MCA
3 **In Utero** — Nirvana — DGC
4 **Music Box** — Mariah Carey — Columbia
5 **Greatest Hits Volume Two** — Reba McEntire — MCA
6 **janet.** — Janet Jackson — Virgin
7 **River Of Dreams** — Billy Joel — Columbia
8 **Easy Come, Easy Go** — George Strait — MCA
9 **Retro Active** — Def Leppard — Mercury
10 **Blind Melon** — Blind Melon — Capitol
11 **Toni Braxton** — Toni Braxton — LaFace
12 **Black Sunday** — Cypress Hill — Ruffhouse
13 **A lot about livin'** — Alan Jackson — Arista
14 **187 He Wrote** — Spice 1 — Jive
15 **Unplugged...And Seated** — Rod Stewart — Warner Bros
16 **Core** — Stone Temple Pilots — Atlantic
17 **Sleepless In Seattle** — Soundtrack — Epic Soundtrax
18 **Get A Grip** — Aerosmith — Geffen
19 **The Bodyguard** — Soundtrack — Arista
20 **Very** — Pet Shop Boys — EMI

us albums

1 **Bat Out Of Hell II: Back Into Hell** — Meat Loaf — MCA
2 **In Pieces** — Garth Brooks — Liberty
3 **In Utero** — Nirvana — DGC
4 **River Of Dreams** — Billy Joel — Columbia
5 **Music Box** — Mariah Carey — Columbia
6 **janet.** — Janet Jackson — Virgin
7 **Greatest Hits Volume Two** — Reba McEntire — MCA
8 **Easy Come, Easy Go** — George Strait — MCA
9 **Blind Melon** — Blind Melon — Capitol
10 **Common Thread...** — Various Artists — Giant
11 **Toni Braxton** — Toni Braxton — LaFace
12 **Retro Active** — Def Leppard — Mercury
13 **Core** — Stone Temple Pilots — Atlantic
14 **Black Sunday** — Cypress Hill — Ruffhouse
15 **A lot about livin'** — Alan Jackson — Arista
16 **Unplugged...And Seated** — Rod Stewart — Warner Bros
17 **Judgment Night** — Soundtrack — Immortal
18 **Sleepless In Seattle** — Soundtrack — Epic Soundtrax
19 **Get A Grip** — Aerosmith — Geffen
20 **Human Wheels** — John Mellencamp — Mercury

uk virgin Crunchie albums

1 **Vs** — Pearl Jam — Epic
2 **Bat Out Of Hell II – Back Into Hell** — Meat Loaf — Virgin
3 **Together Alone** — Crowded House — Capitol
4 **Com On Feel The Lemonheads** — Lemonheads — Atlantic/East West
5 **Aces And Kings – The Best Of Go West** — Go West — Chrysalis
6 **Real** — Belinda Carlisle — Virgin
7 **The Hits 2** — Symbol/Prince — Paisley Park/Warner
8 **The Hits 1** — Symbol/Prince — Paisley Park/Warner
9 **Construction For The Modern Idiot** — Wonder Stuff — Polydor
10 **Love Scenes** — Beverley Craven — Epic
11 **Pocket Full Of Kryptonite** — Spin Doctors — Epic
12 **Promises And Lies** — UB40 — Virgin
13 **Retro Active** — Def Leppard — Bludgeon Riffola
14 **Automatic For The People** — R.E.M. — Warner Bros
15 **Debut** — Bjork — One Little Indian
16 **Wild Wood** — Paul Weller — Go!
17 **The Beatles 1962-1966** — Beatles — Parlophone
18 **In Utero** — Nirvana — Geffen
19 **The Beatles 1967-1970** — Beatles — Parlophone
20 **The Crossing** — Paul Young — Columbia

uk virgin Crunchie albums

1 **Bat Out Of Hell II – Back Into Hell** — Meat Loaf — Virgin
2 **Bang! – Greatest Hits Of F.G.T.H.** — Frankie Goes To Hollywood — ZTT
3 **Vs** — Pearl Jam — Epic
4 **Together Alone** — Crowded House — Capitol
5 **Aces And Kings – The Best Of Go West** — Go West — Chrysalis
6 **Come On Feel The Lemonheads** — Lemonheads — Atlantic/East West
7 **Four-Calendar Cafe** — Cocteau Twins — Fontana
8 **Counterparts** — Rush — Atlantic/East West
9 **The Hits 2** — Symbol/Prince — Paisley Park/Warner
10 **Debut** — Bjork — One Little Indian
11 **Real** — Belinda Carlisle — Virgin
12 **Automatic For The People** — R.E.M. — Warner Bros
13 **The Hits 1** — Symbol/Prince — Paisley Park/Warner
14 **In Utero** — Nirvana — Geffen
15 **Promises And Lies** — UB40 — Virgin
16 **Pocket Full Of Kryptonite** — Spin Doctors — Epic
17 **The Beatles 1962-1966** — Beatles — Parlophone
18 **Wild Wood** — Paul Weller — Go!
19 **Retro Active** — Def Leppard — Bludgeon Riffola
20 **Love Scenes** — Beverley Craven — Epic

107

indy albums

1	**Debut** Bjork	One Little Indian
2	**Chaos A.D.** Sepultura	Roadrunner
3	**Dream Of 100 Nations** Transglobal Underground	Nation
4	**The Levellers** The Levellers	China
5	**Sabresonic** Sabres Of Paradise	Warp

dance singles

1	**Got To Get It** Culture Beat	Epic
2	**Free Love** Juliet Roberts	Cooltempo
3	**Give It Up** The Goodmen	Fresh Fruit/ffrreedom
4	**Feel Like Making Love** Pauline Henry	Sony
5	**Drop The Rock (EP)** D-Tek	Positiva

uk singles

1	**I'd Do Anything For Love...** Meat Loaf	Virgin
2	**Please Forgive Me** Bryan Adams	A&M
3	**U Got 2 Let The Music** Cappella	Internal
4	**Don't Be A Stranger** Dina Carroll	A&M
5	**Give It Up** The Goodmen	Fresh Fruit/ffrreedom
6	**Boom! Shake The Room** Jazzy Jeff & Fresh Prince	Jive
7	**Got To Get It** Culture Beat	EPic
8	**Hero** Mariah Carey	Columbia
9	**Stay** Eternal	EMI
10	**Both Sides Of The Story** Phil Collins	Virgin

us singles

1	**I'd Do Anything For Love...** Meat Loaf	MCA
2	**All That She Wants** Ace of Base	Arista
3	**Just Kickin' It** Xscape	So So Def
4	**Again** Janet Jackson	Virgin
5	**Dreamlover** Mariah Carey	Columbia
6	**Hey Mr. D.J.** Zhane	Flavor Unit
7	**Gangsta Lean** DRS	Capitol
8	**The River Of Dreams** Billy Joel	Columbia
9	**Whoomp! (There It Is)** Tag Team	Life
10	**Anniversary** Tony! Toni! Tone!	WIng

us albums

1	**Vs** Pearl Jam	Epic
2	**Counterparts** Rush	Atlantic
3	**Bat Out Of Hell II: Back Into Hell** Meat Loaf	MCA
4	**In Utero** Nirvana	DGC
5	**It's On (Dr. Dre 187um) Killa** Eazy-E	Ruthless
6	**Common Thread...** Various Artists	Giant
7	**Music Box** Mariah Carey	Columbia
8	**River Of Dreams** Billy Joel	Columbia
9	**In Pieces** Garth Brooks	Liberty
10	**janet.** Janet Jackson	Virgin
11	**Greatest Hits Volume Two** Reba McEntire	MCA
12	**Toni Braxton** Toni Braxton	LaFace
13	**Blind Melon** Blind Melon	Capitol
14	**Easy Come, Easy Go** George Strait	MCA
15	**Retro Active** Def Leppard	Mercury
16	**No Pressure** Erick Sermon	RAL
17	**Judgment Night** Sountrack	Immortal
18	**Unplugged...And Seated** Rod Stewart	Warner Bros
19	**Black Sunday** Cypress Hill	Ruffhouse
20	**A lot about livin'** Alan Jackson	Arista

uk virgin Crunchie albums

1	**Bat Out Of Hell II – Back Into Hell** Meat Loaf	Virgin
2	**Bang! – Greatest Hits Of F.G.T.H.** Frankie Goes To Hollywood	ZTT
3	**Vs** Pearl Jam	Epic
4	**Together Alone** Crowded House	Capitol
5	**Aces And Kings – The Best Of Go West** Go West	Chrysalis
6	**Come On Feel The Lemonheads** Lemonheads	Atlantic/East West
7	**Debut** Bjork	One Little Indian
8	**Pocket Full Of Kryptonite** Spin Doctors	Epic
9	**The Hits 2** Symbol/Prince	Paisley Park/Warner
10	**Automatic For The People** R.E.M.	Warner Bros
11	**Bat Out Of Hell** Meat Loaf	Epic
12	**Promises And Lies** UB40	Virgin
13	**In Utero** Nirvana	Geffen
14	**What's Love Got To Do With It** Tina Turner	Parlophone
15	**The Hits 1** Symbol/Prince	Paisley Park/Warner
16	**Live Jam** Jam	Polydor
17	**Counterparts** Rush	Atlantic/East West
18	**Four-Calendar Cafe** Cocteau Twins	Fontana
19	**The Beatles 1967-1970** Beatles	Parlophone
20	**Time Machine** Joe Satriani	Relativity

uk singles

1	**I'd Do Anything For Love...** Meat Loaf	Virgin
2	**Please Forgive Me** Bryan Adams	A&M
3	**Don't Be A Stranger** Dina Carroll	A&M
4	**Got To Get It** Culture Beat	Epic
5	**U Got 2 Let The Music** Cappella	Internal
6	**Give It Up** The Goodmen	Fresh Fruit/ffrreedom
7	**Hero** Mariah Carey	Columbia
8	**Real Love '93** Time Frequency	Internal Affairs
9	**Feels Like Heaven** Urban Cookie Collective	Pulse 8
10	**Little Fluffy Clouds** The Orb	Big Life

us singles

1	**I'd Do Anything For Love...** Meat Loaf	MCA
2	**All That She Wants** Ace of Base	Arista
3	**Again** Janet Jackson	Virgin
4	**Just Kickin' It** Xscape	So So Def
5	**Gangsta Lean** DRS	Capitol
6	**Dreamlover** Mariah Carey	Columbia
7	**Shoop** Salt-N-Pepa	Next Plateau
8	**Hey Mr. D.J.** Zhane	Flavor Unit
9	**Whoomp! (There It is)** Tag Team	Life
10	**Anniversary** Tony! Toni! Tone!	Wing

indy albums

1	**Debut** Bjork	One Little Indian
2	**The Levellers** The Levellers	China
3	**Chaos A.D.** Sepultura	Roadrunner
4	**Heartwork** Carcass	Earache
5	**King Puck** Christy Moore	Equator

dance singles

1	**Open Up** Leftfield Lydon	Hard Hands
2	**So In Love (The Real Deal)** Judy Cheeks	Positiva
3	**Feels Like Heaven** Urban Cookie Collective	Pulse 8
4	**Never** Jomanda	Big Beat/Atlantic
5	**Little Fluffy Clouds** The Orb	Big Life

us albums

1	**Vs** Pearl Jam	Epic
2	**Bat Out Of Hell II: Back Into Hell** Meat Loaf	MCA
3	**Common Thread...** Various Artists	Giant
4	**Get In Where You Fit In** Too Short	Jive
5	**Music Box** Mariah Carey	Columbia
6	**River Of Dreams** Billy Joel	Columbia
7	**It's On (Dr. Dre 187um) Killa** Eazy-E	Ruthless
8	**janet.** Janet Jackson	Virgin
9	**Greatest Hits Volume Two** Reba McEntire	MCA
10	**In Utero** Nirvana	DGC
11	**In Pieces** Garth Brooks	Liberty
12	**Toni Braxton** Toni Braxton	LaFace
13	**MTV Unplugged** 10,000 Maniacs	Elektra
14	**Counterparts** Rush	Atlantic
15	**Easy Come, Easy Go** George Strait	MCA
16	**Blind Melon** Blind Melon	Capitol
17	**Unplugged...And Seated** Rod Stewart	Warner Bros
18	**I'm Ready** Tevin Campbell	Qwest
19	**A lot about livin'** Alan Jackson	Arista
20	**Siamese Dream** Smashing Pumpkins	Virgin

uk virgin Crunchie albums

1	**Bat Out Of Hell II – Back Into Hell** Meat Loaf	Virgin
2	**The Red Shoes** Kate Bush	EMI
3	**Full Moon, Dirty Hearts** INXS	Mercury
4	**Espresso Logic** Chris Rea	East West
5	**Greatest Hits** Tom Petty & The Heartbreakers	MCA
6	**Bang! Greatest Hits Of F.G.T.H.** Frankie Goes To Hollywood	ZTT
7	**Together Alone** Crowded House	Capitol
8	**Vs** Pearl Jam	Epic
9	**Aces And Kings – The Best Of Go West** Go West	Chrysalis
10	**Ricks Road** Texas	Vertigo
11	**Bat Out Of Hell** Meat Loaf	Epic
12	**Pocket Full Of Kryptonite** Spin Doctors	Epic
13	**The Hits 2** Symbol/Prince	Paisley Park/Warner
14	**Automatic For The People** R.E.M.	Warner Bros
15	**Come On Feel The Lemonheads** Lemonheads	Atlantic/East West
16	**The Best Of Nanci Griffith** Nanci Griffith	MCA
17	**What's Love Got To Do With It** Tina Turner	Parlophone
18	**Promises And Lies** UB40	Virgin
19	**Debut** Bjork	One Little Indian
20	**The Beatles 1962-1966** Beatles	Parlophone

us albums

1	**Vs** Pearl Jam	Epic
2	**Duets** Frank Sinatra	Capitol
3	**Bat Out Of Hell II: Back Into Hell** Meat Loaf	MCA
4	**Common Thread...** Various Artists	Giant
5	**Music Box** Mariah Carey	Columbia
6	**janet.** Janet Jackson	Virgin
7	**River Of Dreams** Billy Joel	Columbia
8	**It's On (Dr. Dre 187um) Killa** Eazy-E	Ruthless
9	**Get In Where You Fit In** Too Short	Jive
10	**Toni Braxton** Toni Braxton	LaFace
11	**In Utero** Nirvana	DGC
12	**Greatest Hits Volume Two** Reba McEntire	MCA
13	**In Pieces** Garth Brooks	Liberty
14	**MTV Unplugged** 10,000 Maniacs	Elektra
15	**Siamese Dream** Smashing Pumpkins	Virgin
16	**Blind Melon** Blind Melon	Capitol
17	**Hummin' Comin' At 'Cha** Xscape	So So Def
18	**Everybody Else Is Doing It...** The Cranberries	Island
19	**Unplugged...And Seated** Rod Stewart	Warner Bros
20	**I'm Ready** Tevin Campbell	Qwest

uk singles

1	**I'd Do Anything For Love...** Meat Loaf	Virgin
2	**Please Forgive Me** Bryan Adams	A&M
3	**Don't Be A Stranger** Dina Carroll	A&M
4	**Got To Get It** Culture Beat	Epic
5	**Feels Like Heaven** Urban Cookie Collective	Pulse 8
6	**U Got 2 Let The Music** Cappella	Internal
7	**Runaway Train** Soul Asylum	Columbia
8	**True Love** Elton John & Kiki Dee	Rocket
9	**Ain't It Fun** Guns N' Roses	Geffen
10	**Give It Up** The Goodmen	Fresh Fruit/ffrreedom

us singles

1	**I'd Do Anything For Love...** Meat Loaf	MCA
2	**Again** Janet Jackson	Virgin
3	**All That She Wants** Ace of Base	Arista
4	**Gangsta Lean** DRS	Capitol
5	**Just Kickin' It** Xscape	So So Def
6	**Shoop** Salt-N-Pepa	Next Plateau
7	**Please Forgive Me** Bryan Adams	A&M
8	**Hero** Mariah Carey	Columbia
9	**Hey Mr. D.J.** Zhane	Flavor Unit
10	**Dreamlover** Mariah Carey	Columbia

indy albums

1	**Debut** Bjork	One Little Indian
2	**The Levellers** The Levellers	China
3	**King Puck** Christy Moore	Equator
4	**Chaos A.D.** Sepultura	Roadrunner
5	**Dream Of 100 Nations** Transglobal Underground	Nation

dance singles

1	**I'll Be There For You (Doya...)** House Of Virginism	ffrr
2	**Open Up** Leftfield Lydon	Hard Hands
3	**Welcome To The Pleasuredome** Frankie Goes To Hollywood	ZTT
4	**As I Am** Sound Of One	Cooltempo
5	**Little Fluffy Clouds** The Orb	Big Life

the shamen

indy albums

1	**On Air** The Shamen	Band Of Joy
2	**The Levellers** The Levellers	China
3	**Debut** Bjork	One Little Indian
4	**Kitchen** Sun Electric	R&S
5	**Chaos A.D.** Sepultura	Roadrunner

dance singles

1	**Long Train Runnin'** The Doobie Brothers	Warner Bros
2	**Let Me Show You** K-Klass	Deconstruction/EMI
3	**On** The Aphex Twin	Warp
4	**Backstab (EP)** Direct 2 Disc	Cleveland City
5	**Hip Hop Hooray** Naughty By Nature	Big Life

uk virgin Crunchie albums

1	**Both Sides** Phil Collins	Virgin
2	**So Far So Good** Bryan Adams	A&M
3	**Bat Out Of Hell II – Back Into Hell** Meat Loaf	Virgin
4	**The Red Shoes** Kate Bush	EMI
5	**The Singles Collection** David Bowie	EMI
6	**Espresso Logic** Chris Rea	East West
7	**Greatest Hits** Tom Petty & The Heartbreakers	MCA
8	**Full Moon, Dirty Hearts** INXS	Mercury
9	**The Hits 2** Symbol/Prince	Paisley Park/Warner
10	**Bang! Greatest Hits Of F.G.T.H.** Frankie Goes To Hollywood	ZTT
11	**The Best Of The Christians** Christians	Island
12	**Aces And Kings – The Best Of Go West** Go West	Chrysalis
13	**Together Alone** Crowded House	Capitol
14	**The Hits 1** Symbol/Prince	Paisley Park/Warner
15	**Bat Out Of Hell** Meat Loaf	Epic
16	**Vs** Pearl Jam	Epic
17	**Automatic For The People** R.E.M.	Warner Bros
18	**Pocket Full Of Kryptonite** Spin Doctors	Epic
19	**What's Love Got To Do With It** Tina Turner	Parlophone
20	**Paul Is Live!** Paul McCartney	Parlophone

us albums

1	**Vs** Pearl Jam	Epic
2	**Duets** Frank Sinatra	Capitol
3	**Bat Out Of Hell II: Back Into Hell** Meat Loaf	MCA
4	**Common Thread...** Various Artists	Giant
5	**Music Box** Mariah Carey	Columbia
6	**janet.** Janet Jackson	Virgin
7	**River Of Dreams** Billy Joel	Columbia
8	**Midnight Marauders** A Tribe Called Quest	Jive
9	**So Far So Good** Bryan Adams	A&M
10	**Greatest Hits Volume Two** Reba McEntire	MCA
11	**Toni Braxton** Toni Braxton	LaFace
12	**In Pieces** Garth Brooks	Liberty
13	**Both Sides** Phil Collins	Atlantic
14	**It's On (Dr. Dre 187um) Killa** Eazy-E	Ruthless
15	**In Utero** Nirvana	DGC
16	**MTV Unplugged** 10,000 Maniacs	Elektra
17	**Get In Where You Fit In** Too Short	Jive
18	**A lot about livin'** Alan Jackson	Arista
19	**Blind Melon** Blind Melon	Capitol
20	**Siamese Dream** Smashing Pumpkins	Virgin

uk singles

1	**I'd Do Anything For Love...** Meat Loaf	Virgin
2	**True Love** Elton John & Kiki Dee	Rocket
3	**Please Forgive Me** Bryan Adams	A&M
4	**Don't Be A Stranger** Dina Carroll	A&M
5	**Got To Get It** Culture Beat	Epic
6	**Again** Janet Jackson	Virgin
7	**Runaway Train** Soul Asylum	Columbia
8	**Feels Like Heaven** Urban Cookie Collective	Pulse 8
9	**Hero** Mariah Carey	Columbia
10	**Long Train Runnin'** The Doobie Brothers	Warner Bros

us singles

1	**I'd Do Anything For Love...** Meat Loaf	MCA
2	**Again** Janet Jackson	Virgin
3	**All That She Wants** Ace of Base	Arista
4	**Gangsta Lean** DRS	Capitol
5	**Shoop** Salt-N-Pepa	Next Plateau
6	**Just Kickin' It** Xscape	So So Def
7	**Hero** Mariah Carey	Columbia
8	**Please Forgive Me** Bryan Adams	A&M
9	**Whoomp! (There It Is)** Tag Team	Life
10	**Hey Mr. D.J.** Zhane	Flavor Unit

uk virgin Crunchie albums

1	**Bat Out Of Hell II – Back Into Hell** Meat Loaf	Virgin
2	**So Far So Good** Bryan Adams	A&M
3	**Both Sides** Phil Collins	Virgin
4	**The One Thing** Michael Bolton	Columbia
5	**The Singles Collection** David Bowie	EMI
6	**The Red Shoes** Kate Bush	EMI
7	**Debut** Bjork	One Little Indian
8	**Espresso Logic** Chris Rea	East West
9	**Bang! Greatest Hits Of F.G.T.H.** Frankie Goes To Hollywood	ZTT
10	**Live 1983-1989** Eurythmics	RCA
11	**Greatest Hits** Tom Petty & The Heartbreakers	MCA
12	**The Best Of The Christians** Christians	Island
13	**The Hits 2** Symbol/Prince	Paisley Park/Warner
14	**River Of Dreams** Billy Joel	Columbia
15	**Together Alone** Crowded House	Capitol
16	**Full Moon, Dirty Hearts** INXS	Mercury
17	**Vs** Pearl Jam	Epic
18	**Pocket Full Of Kryptonite** Spin Doctors	Epic
19	**Aces And Kings – The Best Of Go West** Go West	Chrysalis
20	**What's Love Got To Do With It** Tina Turner	Parlophone

uk virgin Crunchie albums

#	Title / Artist	Label
1	**Bat Out Of Hell II – Back Into Hell** Meat Loaf	Virgin
2	**The Spaghetti Incident?** Guns N' Roses	Geffen
3	**So Far So Good** Bryan Adams	A&M
4	**Both Sides** Phil Collins	Virgin
5	**Duets** Elton John/Various	Rocket
6	**The One Thing** Michael Bolton	Columbia
7	**The Red Shoes** Kate Bush	EMI
8	**The Singles Collection** David Bowie	EMI
9	**Jump Back – The Best Of...1971-93** Rolling Stones	Virgin
10	**Bang! Greatest Hits Of F.G.T.H.** Frankie Goes To Hollywood	ZTT
11	**Live 93** ORB	Island
12	**Debut** Bjork	One Little Indian
13	**Espresso Logic** Chris Rea	East West
14	**River Of Dreams** Billy Joel	Columbia
15	**Together Alone** Crowded House	Capitol
16	**Greatest Hits** Tom Petty & The Heartbreakers	MCA
17	**Live 1983-1989** Eurythmics	RCA
18	**The Hits 2** Symbol/Prince	Paisley Park/Warner
19	**The Best Of The Christians** Christians	Island
20	**Bat Out Of Hell** Meat Loaf	Epic

us albums

#	Title / Artist	Label
1	**Vs** Pearl Jam	Epic
2	**Duets** Frank Sinatra	Capitol
3	**The One Thing** Michael Bolton	Columbia
4	**Bat Out Of Hell II: Back Into Hell** Meat Loaf	MCA
5	**Common Thread...** Various Artists	Giant
6	**Music Box** Mariah Carey	Columbia
7	**So Far So Good** Bryan Adams	A&M
8	**Greatest Hits** Tom Petty & The Heartbreakers	MCA
9	**janet.** Janet Jackson	Virgin
10	**River Of Dreams** Billy Joel	Columbia
11	**Toni Braxton** Toni Braxton	LaFace
12	**In Pieces** Garth Brooks	Liberty
13	**Greatest Hits Volume Two** Reba McEntire	MCA
14	**It's On (Dr. Dre 187um) Killa** Eazy-E	Ruthless
15	**In Utero** Nirvana	DGC
16	**Midnight Marauders** A Tribe Called Quest	Jive
17	**MTV Unplugged** 10,000 Maniacs	Elektra
18	**Both Sides** Phil Collins	Atlantic
19	**Siamese Dream** Smashing Pumpkins	Virgin
20	**Straight Up Sewaside** Das EFX	EastWest

uk singles

#	Title / Artist	Label
1	**I'd Do Anything For Love...** Meat Loaf	Virgin
2	**True Love** Elton John & Kiki Dee	Rocket
3	**Mr Blobby** Mr Blobby	Destiny Music
4	**Please Forgive Me** Bryan Adams	A&M
5	**Don't Be A Stranger** Dina Carroll	A&M
6	**Stay/Under My Skin** U2:Frank Sinatra with Bono	Island
7	**Long Train Runnin'** The Doobie Brothers	Warner Bros
8	**Again** Janet Jackson	Virgin
9	**Don't Look Any Further** M-People	Decon/RCA
10	**Runaway Train** Soul Asylum	Columbia

us singles

#	Title / Artist	Label
1	**I'd Do Anything For Love...** Meat Loaf	MCA
2	**Again** Janet Jackson	Virgin
3	**All That She Wants** Ace of Base	Arista
4	**Shoop** Salt-N-Pepa	Next Plateau
5	**Gangsta Lean** DRS	Capitol
6	**Hero** Mariah Carey	Columbia
7	**Just Kickin' It** Xscape	So So Def
8	**Please Forgive Me** Bryan Adams	A&M
9	**Breathe Again** Toni Braxton	LaFace
10	**Can We Talk** Tevin Campbell	Qwest

indy albums

#	Title / Artist	Label
1	**Debut** Bjork	One Little Indian
2	**The Levellers** The Levellers	China
3	**On Air** The Shamen	Band Of Joy
4	**Levelling The Land** The Levellers	China
5	**Siamese Dream** Smashing Pumpkins	Hut

dance singles

#	Title / Artist	Label
1	**Long Train Runnin'** The Doobie Brothers	Warner Bros
2	**What's My Name** Snoop Doggy Dogg	Interscope/East West
3	**Don't Look Any Further** M-People	Deconstruction/RCA
4	**Let Me Show You** K-Klass	Deconstruction/EMI
5	**Big Time Sensuality** Bjork	One Little Indian

janet jackson

---

uk virgin Crunchie albums

#	Title / Artist	Label
1	**Bat Out Of Hell II – Back Into Hell** Meat Loaf	Virgin
2	**So Far So Good** Bryan Adams	A&M
3	**Both Sides** Phil Collins	Virgin
4	**Duets** Elton John/Various	Rocket
5	**The One Thing** Michael Bolton	Columbia
6	**The Spaghetti Incident?** Guns N' Roses	Geffen
7	**Jump Back – The Best Of...** The Rolling Stones	Virgin
8	**The Red Shoes** Kate Bush	EMI
9	**The Singles Collection** David Bowie	EMI
10	**Debut** Bjork	One Little Indian
11	**River Of Dreams** Billy Joel	Columbia
12	**Bang! – Greatest Hits Of F.G.T.H.** Frankie Goes To Hollywood	ZTT
13	**Together Alone** Crowded House	Capitol
14	**The Best Of The Christians** The Christians	Island
15	**Espresso Logic** Chris Rea	East West
16	**Desire Walks On** Heart	Capitol
17	**Greatest Hits** Tom Petty & The Heartbreakers	MCA
18	**The Hits 2** Symbol/Prince	Paisley Park/Warner
19	**Live 1983-1989** Eurythmics	RCA
20	**Promises And Lies** UB40	Virgin

us albums

#	Title / Artist	Label
1	**Doggy Style** Snoop Doggy Dogg	Death Row
2	**Vs** Pearl Jam	Epic
3	**Music Box** Mariah Carey	Columbia
4	**The Spaghetti Incident?** Guns N' Roses	Geffen
5	**The Beavis & Butt-Head Experience** Beavis & Butt-Head	Geffen
6	**Duets** Frank Sinatra	Capitol
7	**Bat Out Of Hell II: Back Into Hell** Meat Loaf	MCA
8	**The One Thing** Michael Bolton	Columbia
9	**Common Thread...** Various Artists	Giant
10	**janet.** Janet Jackson	Virgin
11	**So Far So Good** Bryan Adams	A&M
12	**River Of Dreams** Billy Joel	Columbia
13	**Toni Braxton** Toni Braxton	LaFace
14	**Greatest Hits** Tom Petty & The Heartbreakers	MCA
15	**In Pieces** Garth Brooks	Liberty
16	**Greatest Hits Volume Two** Reba McEntire	MCA
17	**Let There Be Peace On Earth** Vince Gill	MCA
18	**Siamese Dream** Smashing Pumpkins	Virgin
19	**MTV Unplugged** 10,000 Maniacs	Elektra
20	**In Utero** Nirvana	DGC

uk singles

#	Title / Artist	Label
1	**Mr Blobby** Mr Blobby	Destiny Music
2	**I'd Do Anything For Love...** Meat Loaf	Virgin
3	**True Love** Elton John & Kiki Dee	Rocket
4	**Stay/Under My Skin** U2:Frank Sinatra with Bono	Island
5	**Controversy** Symbol/Prince	Paisley Park
6	**For Whom The Bell Tolls** Bee Gees	Polydor
7	**Please Forgive Me** Bryan Adams	A&M
8	**Don't Be A Stranger** Dina Carroll	A&M
9	**It's Alright** East 17	London
10	**Again** Janet Jackson	Virgin

us singles

#	Title / Artist	Label
1	**Again** Janet Jackson	Virgin
2	**I'd Do Anything For Love...** Meat Loaf	MCA
3	**All That She Wants** Ace of Base	Arista
4	**Hero** Mariah Carey	Columbia
5	**Shoop** Salt-N-Pepa	Next Plateau
6	**Gangsta Lean** DRS	Capitol
7	**Just Kickin' It** Xscape	So So Def
8	**Breathe Again** Toni Braxton	LaFace
9	**Please Forgive Me** Bryan Adams	A&M
10	**All For Love** Bryan Adams/Rod Stewart/Sting	A&M

indy albums

#	Title / Artist	Label
1	**Debut** Bjork	One Little Indian
2	**You Need A Mess Of Help...** Saint Etienne	Heavenly
3	**The Levellers** The Levellers	China
4	**Vitamin Enhanced** Ozric Tentacles	Dovetail
5	**Levelling The Land** The Levellers	China

dance singles

#	Title / Artist	Label
1	**I Ain't Goin' Out Like That** Cypress Hill	Columbia
2	**Wopbabalubop** Funkdoobiest	Epic
3	**Big Time Sensuality** Bjork	One Little Indian
4	**I Wish** Gabrielle	Go.Beat
5	**Funk Dat** Sagat	ffrr

indy albums

1	**Debut** Bjork	One Little Indian
2	**The Levellers** The Levellers	China
3	**(Incunabula)** Autechre	Warp
4	**Floored Genius 2** Julian Cope	Nighttacks
5	**You Need A Mess Of Help** Saint Etienne	Heavenly

dance singles

1	**Alex Party (Saturday Night...)** Alex Party	Cleveland City Imports
2	**Twist And Shout** Chaka Demus/Pliers/Jack Radics	Mango
3	**I Am The Music, Hear Me!** The Millionaire Hippies	Decon./RCA
4	**Spikee/Dogman Go Wolf** Underworld	Junior Boy's Own
5	**I Ain't Going Out Like That** Cypress Hill	Columbia

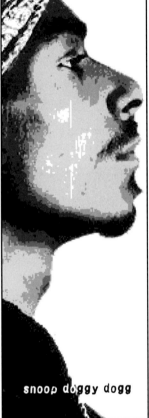

snoop doggy dogg

indy albums

1	**Debut** Bjork	One Little Indian
2	**Songs Of Faith And Devotion** Depeche Mode	Mute
3	**Boss Drum** The Shamen	One Little Indian
4	**The Levellers** The Levellers	China
5	**Levelling The Land** The Levellers	China

dance singles

1	**Twist And Shout** Chaka Demus/Pliers/Jack Radics	Mango
2	**Alex Party (Saturday Night...)** Alex Party	Cleveland City Imports
3	**My Time** Jeanie Tracy	3 Beat
4	**That's How I'm Livin'** Ice-T	Virgin
5	**Tri-Ply** B-Line	Cleveland City Imports

uk singles

1	**Babe** Take That	RCA
2	**Mr Blobby** Mr Blobby	Destiny Music
3	**I'd Do Anything For Love...** Meat Loaf	Virgin
4	**Twist And Shout** Chaka Demus & Pliers	Mango
5	**For Whom The Bell Tolls** Bee Gees	Polydor
6	**True Love** Elton John & Kiki Dee	Rocket
7	**It's Alright** East 17	London
8	**Don't Be A Stranger** Dina Carroll	A&M
9	**Please Forgive Me** Bryan Adams	A&M
10	**The Perfect Year** Dina Carroll	A&M

us singles

1	**Again** Janet Jackson	Virgin
2	**All That She Wants** Ace of Base	Arista
3	**Hero** Mariah Carey	Columbia
4	**I'd Do Anything For Love...** Meat Loaf	MCA
5	**Shoop** Salt-N-Pepa	Next Plateau
6	**Gangsta Lean** DRS	Capitol
7	**All For Love** Bryan Adams/Rod Stewart/Sting	A&M
8	**Breathe Again** Toni Braxton	LaFace
9	**Please Forgive Me** Bryan Adams	A&M
10	**Said I Loved You...But I Lied** Michael Bolton	Columbia

uk singles

1	**Mr Blobby** Mr Blobby	Destiny Music
2	**Babe** Take That	RCA
3	**Twist And Shout** Chaka Demus & Pliers	Mango
4	**For Whom The Bell Tolls** Bee Gees	Polydor
5	**It's Alright** East 17	London
6	**I'd Do Anything For Love...** Meat Loaf	Virgin
7	**The Perfect Year** Dina Carroll	A&M
8	**Bat Out Of Hell** Meat Loaf	Epic
9	**True Love** Elton John & Kiki Dee	Rocket
10	**The Power Of Love** Frankie Goes To Hollywood	ZTT

us singles

1	**Hero** Mariah Carey	Columbia
2	**Again** Janet Jackson	Virgin
3	**All That She Wants** Ace of Base	Arista
4	**I'd Do Anything For Love...** Meat Loaf	MCA
5	**All For Love** Bryan Adams/Rod Stewart/Sting	A&M
6	**Gangsta Lean** DRS	Capitol
7	**Shoop** Salt-N-Pepa	Next Plateau
8	**Breathe Again** Toni Braxton	LaFace
9	**What's My Name?** Snoop Doggy Dogg	Death Row
10	**Said I Loved You...But I Lied** Michael Bolton	Columbia

us albums

1	**Doggy Style** Snoop Doggy Dogg	Death Row
2	**Music Box** Mariah Carey	Columbia
3	**Vs** Pearl Jam	Epic
4	**The One Thing** Michael Bolton	Columbia
5	**Bat Out Of Hell II: Back Into Hell** Meat Loaf	MCA
6	**Duets** Frank Sinatra	Capitol
7	**The Beavis & Butt-Head Experience** Beavis & Butt-Head	Geffen
8	**janet.** Janet Jackson	Virgin
9	**Common Thread...** Various Artists	Giant
10	**The Spaghetti Incident?** Guns N' Roses	Geffen
11	**So Far So Good** Bryan Adams	A&M
12	**River Of Dreams** Billy Joel	Columbia
13	**In Pieces** Garth Brooks	Liberty
14	**Let There Be Peace On Earth** Vince Gill	MCA
15	**Greatest Hits Volume Two** Reba McEntire	MCA
16	**When My Heart Finds Christmas** Harry Connick, Jr.	Columbia
17	**Toni Braxton** Toni Braxton	LaFace
18	**Greatest Hits** Tom Petty & The Heartbreakers	MCA
19	**Christmas Interpretations** Boyz II Men	Motown
20	**A lot about livin'** Alan Jackson	Arista

us albums

1	**Music Box** Mariah Carey	Columbia
2	**Doggy Style** Snoop Doggy Dogg	Death Row
3	**Vs** Pearl Jam	Epic
4	**Bat Out Of Hell II: Back Into Hell** Meat Loaf	MCA
5	**Lethal Injection** Ice Cube	Priority
6	**The One Thing** Michael Bolton	Columbia
7	**Duets** Frank Sinatra	Capitol
8	**janet.** Janet Jackson	Virgin
9	**Common Thread...** Various Artists	Giant
10	**River Of Dreams** Billy Joel	Columbia
11	**So Far So Good** Bryan Adams	A&M
12	**The Beavis & Butt-Head Experience** Beavis & Butt-Head	Geffen
13	**In Pieces** Garth Brooks	Liberty
14	**When My Heart Finds Christmas** Harry Connick, Jr.	Columbia
15	**The Spaghetti Incident?** Guns N' Roses	Geffen
16	**Greatest Hits Volume Two** Reba McEntire	MCA
17	**Let There Be Peace On Earth** Vince Gill	MCA
18	**Toni Braxton** Toni Braxton	LaFace
19	**Greatest Hits** Tom Petty & The Heartbreakers	MCA
20	**Christmas Interpretations** Boyz II Men	Motown

uk virgin Crunchie albums

1	**Bat Out Of Hell II – Back Into Hell** Meat Loaf	Virgin
2	**So Far So Good** Bryan Adams	A&M
3	**Both Sides** Phil Collins	Virgin
4	**Duets** Elton John/Various	Rocket
5	**The One Thing** Michael Bolton	Columbia
6	**The Spaghetti Incident?** Guns N' Roses	Geffen
7	**The Red Shoes** Kate Bush	EMI
8	**Jump Back – The Best Of...** The Rolling Stones	Virgin
9	**Debut** Bjork	One Little Indian
10	**The Singles Collection** David Bowie	EMI
11	**River Of Dreams** Billy Joel	Columbia
12	**Aces And Kings – The Best Of Go West** Go West	Chrysalis
13	**Bang! – Greatest Hits Of F.G.T.H.** Frankie Goes To Hollywood	ZTT
14	**Promises And Lies** UB40	Virgin
15	**Espresso Logic** Chris Rea	East West
16	**Together Alone** Crowded House	Capitol
17	**The Hits 2** Symbol/Prince	Paisley Park/Warner
18	**The Best Of The Christians** The Christians	Island
19	**The Beatles 1962-1966** Beatles	Parlophone
20	**Bat Out Of Hell** Meat Loaf	Epic

uk virgin Crunchie albums

1	**Bat Out Of Hell II – Back Into Hell** Meat Loaf	Virgin
2	**So Far So Good** Bryan Adams	A&M
3	**Duets** Elton John/Various	Rocket
4	**Both Sides** Phil Collins	Virgin
5	**The One Thing** Michael Bolton	Columbia
6	**Promises And Lies** UB40	Virgin
7	**Debut** Bjork	One Little Indian
8	**Jump Back – The Best Of...** The Rolling Stones	Virgin
9	**The Red Shoes** Kate Bush	EMI
10	**The Spaghetti Incident?** Guns N' Roses	Geffen
11	**The Singles Collection** David Bowie	EMI
12	**River Of Dreams** Billy Joel	Columbia
13	**The Hits 2** Symbol/Prince	Paisley Park/Warner
14	**Bat Out Of Hell** Meat Loaf	Epic
15	**Bang! – Greatest Hits Of F.G.T.H.** Frankie Goes To Hollywood	ZTT
16	**The Hits 1** Symbol/Prince	Paisley Park/Warner
17	**Espresso Logic** Chris Rea	East West
18	**Aces And Kings – The Best Of Go West** Go West	Chrysalis
19	**Together Alone** Crowded House	Capitol
20	**The Beatles 1962-1966** Beatles	Parlophone

uk singles

#	Title	Artist	Label
1	Mr Blobby	Mr Blobby	Destiny Music
2	Babe	Take That	RCA
3	Twist And Shout	Chaka Demus & Pliers	Mango
4	For Whom The Bell Tolls	Bee Gees	Polydor
5	It's Alright	East 17	London
6	The Perfect Year	Dina Carroll	A&M
7	I'd Do Anything For Love...	Meat Loaf	Virgin
8	Bat Out Of Hell	Meat Loaf	Epic
9	True Love	Elton John & Kiki Dee	Rocket
10	Come Baby Come	K7	Tommy Boy/Big Life

us singles

#	Title	Artist	Label
1	Hero	Mariah Carey	Columbia
2	Again	Janet Jackson	Virgin
3	All That She Wants	Ace of Base	Arista
4	All For Love	Bryan Adams/Rod Stewart/Sting	A&M
5	I'd Do Anything For Love...	Meat Loaf	MCA
6	Breathe Again	Toni Braxton	LaFace
7	Gangsta Lean	DRS	Capitol
8	What's My Name?	Snoop Doggy Dogg	Death Row
9	Said I Loved You...But I Lied	Michael Bolton	Columbia
10	Shoop	Salt-N-Pepa	Next Plateau

us albums

#	Title	Artist	Label
1	Music Box	Mariah Carey	Columbia
2	Vs	Pearl Jam	Epic
3	Doggy Style	Snoop Doggy Dogg	Death Row
4	Duets	Frank Sinatra	Capitol
5	Bat Out Of Hell II: Back Into Hell	Meat Loaf	MCA
6	The One Thing	Michael Bolton	Columbia
7	janet.	Janet Jackson	Virgin
8	Common Thread...	Various Artists	Giant
9	River Of Dreams	Billy Joel	Columbia
10	The Beavis & Butt-Head Experience	Beavis & Butt-Head	Geffen
11	So Far So Good	Bryan Adams	A&M
12	In Pieces	Garth Brooks	Liberty
13	When My Heart Finds Christmas	Harry Connick, Jr.	Columbia
14	Lethal Injection	Ice Cube	Priority
15	Greatest Hits Volume Two	Reba McEntire	MCA
16	Greatest Hits	Tom Petty & The Heartbreakers	MCA
17	The Spaghetti Incident?	Guns N' Roses	Geffen
18	MTV Unplugged	10,000 Maniacs	Elektra
19	Get A Grip	Aerosmith	Geffen
20	Toni Braxton	Toni Braxton	LaFace

uk virgin Crunchie albums

#	Title	Artist	Label
1	Bat Out Of Hell II – Back Into Hell	Meat Loaf	Virgin
2	So Far So Good	Bryan Adams	A&M
3	Duets	Elton John/Various	Rocket
4	The One Thing	Michael Bolton	Columbia
5	Both Sides	Phil Collins	Virgin
6	Promises And Lies	UB40	Virgin
7	Debut	Bjork	One Little Indian
8	The Red Shoes	Kate Bush	EMI
9	Jump Back – The Best Of...	The Rolling Stones	Virgin
10	The Spaghetti Incident?	Guns N' Roses	Geffen
11	The Singles Collection	David Bowie	EMI
12	Bat Out Of Hell	Meat Loaf	Epic
13	The Hits 2	Symbol/Prince	Paisley Park/Warner
14	The Hits 1	Symbol/Prince	Paisley Park/Warner
15	Bang! – Greatest Hits Of F.G.T.H.	Frankie Goes To Hollywood	ZTT
16	River Of Dreams	Billy Joel	Columbia
17	Automatic For The People	R.E.M.	Warner Bros
18	What's Love Got To Do With It	Tina Turner	Parlophone
19	The Beatles 1962-1966	Beatles	Parlophone
20	Espresso Logic	Chris Rea	East West

uk singles

#	Title	Artist	Label
1	Twist And Shout	Chaka Demus & Pliers	Mango
2	Babe	Take That	RCA
3	Mr Blobby	Mr Blobby	Destiny Music
4	It's Alright	East 17	London
5	The Perfect Year	Dina Carroll	A&M
6	For Whom The Bell Tolls	Bee Gees	Polydor
7	Come Baby Come	K7	Tommy Boy/Big Life
8	I'd Do Anything For Love...	Meat Loaf	Virgin
9	Bat Out Of Hell	Meat Loaf	Epic
10	Things Can Only Get Better	D:Ream	FXU/Magnet

us singles

#	Title	Artist	Label
1	Hero	Mariah Carey	Columbia
2	All For Love	Bryan Adams/Rod Stewart/Sting	A&M
3	All That She Wants	Ace of Base	Arista
4	Again	Janet Jackson	Virgin
5	Gangsta Lean	DRS	Capitol
6	Breathe Again	Toni Braxton	LaFace
7	Whoomp! (There It Is)	Tag Team	Life
8	What's My Name?	Snoop Doggy Dogg	Death Row
9	I'd Do Anything For Love...	Meat Loaf	MCA
10	Said I Loved You...But I Lied	Michael Bolton	Columbia

us albums

#	Title	Artist	Label
1	Music Box	Mariah Carey	Columbia
2	Vs	Pearl Jam	Epic
3	Doggy Style	Snoop Doggy Dogg	Death Row
4	The One Thing	Michael Bolton	Columbia
5	Duets	Frank Sinatra	Capitol
6	Bat Out Of Hell II: Back Into Hell	Meat Loaf	MCA
7	janet.	Janet Jackson	Virgin
8	The Beavis & Butt-Head Experience	Beavis & Butt-Head	Geffen
9	Common Thread...	Various Artists	Giant
10	River Of Dreams	Billy Joel	Columbia
11	So Far So Good	Bryan Adams	A&M
12	In Pieces	Garth Brooks	Liberty
13	Greatest Hits	Tom Petty & The Heartbreakers	MCA
14	MTV Unplugged	10,000 Maniacs	Elektra
15	When My Heart Finds Christmas	Harry Connick, Jr.	Columbia
16	Toni Braxton	Toni Braxton	LaFace
17	Get A Grip	Aerosmith	Geffen
18	Greatest Hits Volume Two	Reba McEntire	MCA
19	Christmas Interpretations	Boyz II Men	Motown
20	The Spaghetti Incident?	Guns N' Roses	Geffen

uk virgin Crunchie albums

#	Title	Artist	Label
1	So Far So Good	Bryan Adams	A&M
2	Bat Out Of Hell II – Back Into Hell	Meat Loaf	Virgin
3	Debut	Bjork	One Little Indian
4	Both Sides	Phil Collins	Virgin
5	The One Thing	Michael Bolton	Columbia
6	Duets	Elton John/Various	Rocket
7	The Spaghetti Incident?	Guns N' Roses	Geffen
8	Promises And Lies	UB40	Virgin
9	Bat Out Of Hell	Meat Loaf	Epic
10	Automatic For The People	R.E.M.	Warner Bros
11	The Hits 2	Symbol/Prince	Paisley Park/Warner
12	The Red Shoes	Kate Bush	EMI
13	Vs	Pearl Jam	Epic
14	The Singles Collection	David Bowie	EMI
15	Jump Back – The Best Of...	The Rolling Stones	Virgin
16	Bang! – Greatest Hits Of F.G.T.H.	Frankie Goes To Hollywood	ZTT
17	Pocket Full Of Kryptonite	Spin Doctors	Epic
18	The Hits 1	Symbol/Prince	Paisley Park/Warner
19	Together Alone	Crowded House	Capitol
20	Aces And Kings – The Best Of Go West	Go West	Chrysalis

indy albums

#	Title	Artist	Label
1	Debut	Bjork	One Little Indian
2	Boss Drum	The Shamen	One Little Indian
3	Songs Of Faith And Devotion	Depeche Mode	Mute
4	The Levellers	The Levellers	China
5	Levelling The Land	The Levellers	China

dance singles

#	Title	Artist	Label
1	Things Can Only Get Better	D:Ream	FXU/Magnet
2	Blow Your Whistle	DJ Duke	ffrr
3	Time Of Our Lives	Alison Limerick	Arista
4	Evolutiondance Part 1	Evolution	Deconstruction/RCA
5	Alex Party (Saturday Night...)	Alex Party	Cleveland City Imports

us albums

1. **Doggy Style**
Snoop Doggy Dogg — Death Row
2. **Music Box**
Mariah Carey — Columbia
3. **Vs**
Pearl Jam — Epic
4. **janet.**
Janet Jackson — Virgin
5. **The One Thing**
Michael Bolton — Columbia
6. **Bat Out Of Hell II: Back Into Hell**
Meat Loaf — MCA
7. **So Far So Good**
Bryan Adams — A&M
8. **Diary Of A Mad Band**
Jodeci — Uptown
9. **Greatest Hits**
Tom Petty & The Heartbreakers — MCA
10. **Get A Grip**
Aerosmith — Geffen
11. **Common Thread...**
Various Artists — Giant
12. **In Pieces**
Garth Brooks — Liberty
13. **Toni Braxton**
Toni Braxton — LaFace
14. **The Beavis & Butt-Head Experience**
Beavis & Butt-Head — Geffen
15. **Greatest Hits Volume Two**
Reba McEntire — MCA
16. **MTV Unplugged**
10,000 Maniacs — Elektra
17. **Siamese Dream**
Smashing Pumpkins — Virgin
18. **Lethal Injection**
Ice Cube — Priority
19. **In Utero**
Nirvana — DGC
20. **Duets**
Frank Sinatra — Capitol

uk singles

1. **Twist And Shout**
Chaka Demus & Pliers — Mango
2. **Things Can Only Get Better**
D:Ream — FXU
3. **It's Alright**
East 17 — London
4. **Come Baby Come**
K7 — Tommy Boy
5. **Anything**
Culture Beat — Epic
6. **The Perfect Year**
Dina Carroll — A&M
7. **All For Love**
Bryan Adams/Rod Stewart/Sting — A&M
8. **For Whom The Bell Tolls**
Bee Gees — Polydor
9. **Mr Blobby**
Mr Blobby — Destiny Music
10. **Babe**
Take That — RCA

us singles

1. **Hero**
Mariah Carey — Columbia
2. **All For Love**
Bryan Adams/Rod Stewart/Sting — A&M
3. **All That She Wants**
Ace Of Base — Arista
4. **Again**
Janet Jackson — Virgin
5. **Breathe Again**
Toni Braxton — LaFace
6. **Gangsta Lean**
DRS — Capitol
7. **Said I Loved You...But I Lied**
Michael Bolton — Columbia
8. **Whoomp! (There It Is)**
Tag Team — Life
9. **Can We Talk**
Tevin Campbell — Qwest
10. **What's My Name?**
Snoop Doggy Dogg — Death Row

indy albums

1. **Debut**
Bjork — One Little Indian
2. **Boss Drum**
The Shamen — One Little Indian
3. **Songs Of Faith And Devotion**
Depeche Mode — Mute
4. **Levelling The Land**
The Levellers — China
5. **The Levellers**
The Levellers — China

dance singles

1. **Things Can Only Get Better**
D:Ream — FXU/Magnet
2. **Anything**
Culture Beat — Epic
3. **Blow Your Whistle**
DJ Duke — ffrr
4. **I'm In The Mood**
Ce Ce Peniston — A&M
5. **Time Of Our Lives**
Alison Limerick — Arista

d:ream

uk virgin Crunchie albums

1. **So Far So Good**
Bryan Adams — A&M
2. **Debut**
Bjork — One Little Indian
3. **Bat Out Of Hell II – Back Into Hell**
Meat Loaf — Virgin
4. **Both Sides**
Phil Collins — Virgin
5. **Duets**
Elton John/Various — Rocket
6. **Bat Out Of Hell**
Meat Loaf — Epic
7. **Promises And Lies**
UB40 — Virgin
8. **The One Thing**
Michael Bolton — Columbia
9. **Automatic For The People**
R.E.M — Warner Bros
10. **The Spaghetti Incident?**
Guns N' Roses — Geffen
11. **The Red Shoes**
Kate Bush — EMI
12. **The Hits 2**
Symbol/Prince — Paisley Park/Warner
13. **Vs**
Pearl Jam — Epic
14. **Bang! – Greatest Hits Of F.G.T.H.**
Frankie Goes To Hollywood — ZTT
15. **The Singles Collection**
David Bowie — EMI
16. **Jump Back – The Best Of...**
The Rolling Stones — Virgin
17. **Zooropa**
U2 — Island
18. **Pocket Full Of Kryptonite**
Spin Doctors — Epic
19. **Stars**
Simply Red — East West
20. **The Hits 1**
Symbol/Prince — Paisley Park/Warner

---

us albums

1. **Music Box**
Mariah Carey — Columbia
2. **Vs**
Pearl Jam — Epic
3. **The One Thing**
Michael Bolton — Columbia
4. **Doggy Style**
Snoop Doggy Dogg — Death Row
5. **Bat Out Of Hell II: Back Into Hell**
Meat Loaf — MCA
6. **janet.**
Janet Jackson — Virgin
7. **So Far So Good**
Bryan Adams — A&M
8. **Diary Of A Mad Band**
Jodeci — Uptown
9. **Greatest Hits Volume Two**
Reba McEntire — MCA
10. **Greatest Hits**
Tom Petty & The Heartbreakers — MCA
11. **Common Thread...**
Various Artists — Giant
12. **Toni Braxton**
Toni Braxton — LaFace
13. **In Pieces**
Garth Brooks — Liberty
14. **Get A Grip**
Aerosmith — Geffen
15. **MTV Unplugged**
10,000 Maniacs — Elektra
16. **Duets**
Frank Sinatra — Capitol
17. **River Of Dreams**
Billy Joel — Columbia
18. **The Bodyguard**
Soundtrack — Arista
19. **Lethal Injection**
Ice Cube — Priority
20. **Siamese Dream**
Smashing Pumpkins — Virgin

uk singles

1. **Things Can Only Get Better**
D:Ream — FXU
2. **Twist And Shout**
Chaka Demus & Pliers — Mango
3. **Come Baby Come**
K7 — Tommy Boy
4. **All For Love**
Bryan Adams/Rod Stewart/Sting — A&M
5. **Anything**
Culture Beat — Epic
6. **It's Alright**
East 17 — London
7. **Cornflake Girl**
Tori Amos — East West
8. **Save Our Love**
Eternal — EMI
9. **I Miss You**
Haddaway — Logic/Arista
10. **Here I Stand**
Bitty McLean — Brilliant Recordings

us singles

1. **All For Love**
Bryan Adams/Rod Stewart/Sting — A&M
2. **Hero**
Mariah Carey — Columbia
3. **Breathe Again**
Toni Braxton — LaFace
4. **Again**
Janet Jackson — Virgin
5. **All That She Wants**
Ace Of Base — Arista
6. **Said I Loved You...But I Lied**
Michael Bolton — Columbia
7. **Please Forgive Me**
Bryan Adams — A&M
8. **Shoop**
Salt-N-Pepa — Next Plateau
9. **Can We Talk**
Tevin Campbell — Qwest
10. **The Power Of Love**
Celine Dion — 550 Music

indy albums

1. **Debut**
Bjork — One Little Indian
2. **Suede**
Suede — Nude
3. **Boss Drum**
The Shamen — One Little Indian
4. **The Levellers**
The Levellers — China
5. **Levelling The Land**
The Levellers — China

dance singles

1. **Things Can Only Get Better**
D:Ream — FXU
2. **U**
Loni Clark — A&M
3. **I'm In Luv**
Joe — Mercury
4. **Anything**
Culture Beat — Epic
5. **Nuthin' But A 'G' Thang/Let Me Ride**
Dr Dre — Interscope

uk virgin Crunchie albums

1. **So Far So Good**
Bryan Adams — A&M
2. **Debut**
Bjork — One Little Indian
3. **Both Sides**
Phil Collins — Virgin
4. **Bat Out Of Hell II – Back Into Hell**
Meat Loaf — Virgin
5. **Promises And Lies**
UB40 — Virgin
6. **Duets**
Elton John/Various — Rocket
7. **Bat Out Of Hell**
Meat Loaf — Epic
8. **The One Thing**
Michael Bolton — Columbia
9. **Automatic For The People**
R.E.M — Warner Bros
10. **Vs**
Pearl Jam — Epic
11. **Jump Back – The Best Of...**
The Rolling Stones — Virgin
12. **The Red Shoes**
Kate Bush — EMI
13. **The Spaghetti Incident?**
Guns N' Roses — Geffen
14. **The Singles Collection**
David Bowie — EMI
15. **The Hits 2**
Symbol/Prince — Paisley Park/Warner
16. **Ten Summoner'sTales**
Sting — A&M
17. **Stars**
Simply Red — East West
18. **Zooropa**
U2 — Island
19. **Ingénue**
kd lang — Sire/Warner Bros
20. **Bang! – Greatest Hits Of F.G.T.H.**
Frankie Goes To Hollywood — ZTT

113

uk virgin Cadbury's Crunchie albums

1	**So Far So Good** Bryan Adams	A&M
2	**Debut** Bjork	One Little Indian
3	**Both Sides** Phil Collins	Virgin
4	**Bat Out Of Hell II – Back Into Hell** Meat Loaf	Virgin
5	**Ingénue** kd lang	Sire/Warner Bros
6	**Bat Out Of Hell** Meat Loaf	Epic
7	**The One Thing** Michael Bolton	Columbia
8	**Promises And Lies** UB40	Virgin
9	**Duets** Elton John/Various	Rocket
10	**Automatic For The People** R.E.M.	Warner Bros
11	**Vs** Pearl Jam	Epic
12	**The Red Shoes** Kate Bush	EMI
13	**Mirror Blue** Richard Thompson	Capitol
14	**The Spaghetti Incident?** Guns N' Roses	Geffen
15	**Jump Back – The Best Of...** The Rolling Stones	Virgin
16	**Grave Dancers Union** Soul Asylum	Columbia
17	**Ten Summoner's Tales** Sting	A&M
18	**The Beatles 1962-1966** Beatles	Parlophone
19	**The Hits 2** Symbol/Prince	Paisley Park/Warner
20	**Together Alone** Crowded House	Capitol

us albums

1	**Music Box** Mariah Carey	Columbia
2	**Doggy Style** Snoop Doggy Dogg	Death Row
3	**Vs** Pearl Jam	Epic
4	**The One Thing** Michael Bolton	Columbia
5	**Diary Of A Mad Band** Jodeci	Uptown
6	**So Far So Good** Bryan Adams	A&M
7	**janet.** Janet Jackson	Virgin
8	**Bat Out Of Hell II: Back Into Hell** Meat Loaf	MCA
9	**Greatest Hits** Tom Petty & The Heartbreakers	MCA
10	**Toni Braxton** Toni Braxton	LaFace
11	**12 Play** R. Kelly	Jive
12	**Very Necessary** Salt-N-Pepa	Next Plateau
13	**MTV Unplugged** 10,000 Maniacs	Elektra
14	**Get A Grip** Aerosmith	Geffen
15	**Common Thread...** Various Artists	Giant
16	**The Sign** Ace Of Base	Arista
17	**Greatest Hits Volume Two** Reba McEntire	MCA
18	**Siamese Dream** Smashing Pumpkins	Virgin
19	**The Bodyguard** Soundtrack	Arista
20	**Everybody Else Is Doing It...** The Cranberries	Island

uk singles

1	**Things Can Only Get Better** D:Ream	FXU
2	**All For Love** Bryan Adams/Rod Stewart/Sting	A&M
3	**Come Baby Come** K7	Tommy Boy
4	**Cornflake Girl** Tori Amos	East West
5	**Twist And Shout** Chaka Demus & Pliers	Mango
6	**Anything** Culture Beat	Epic
7	**Breathe Again** Toni Braxton	Arista/La Face
8	**In Your Room** Depeche Mode	Mute
9	**Return To Innocence** Enigma	Virgin
10	**I Miss You** Haddaway	Logic/Arista

us singles

1	**All For Love** Bryan Adams/Rod Stewart/Sting	A&M
2	**Hero** Mariah Carey	Columbia
3	**Breathe Again** Toni Braxton	LaFace
4	**The Power Of Love** Celine Dion	550 Music
5	**Again** Janet Jackson	Virgin
6	**Said I Loved You...But I Lied** Michael Bolton	Columbia
7	**All That She Wants** Ace Of Base	Arista
8	**Please Forgive Me** Bryan Adams	A&M
9	**Shoop** Salt-N-Pepa	Next Plateau
10	**Can We Talk** Tevin Campbell	Qwest

indy albums

1	**Debut** Bjork	One Little Indian
2	**Songs Of Faith And Devotion** Depeche Mode	Mute
3	**Giant Steps** The Boo Radleys	Creation
4	**Last Splash** The Breeders	4AD
5	**Selected Ambient Works** Aphex Twin	Apollo

dance singles

1	**Things Can Only Get Better** D:Ream	FXU
2	**Get Off Your High Horse** Rollo Goes Camping	Cheeky
3	**Can't Take Your Love** Pauline Henry	Sony
4	**U** Loni Clark	A&M
5	**Hyperactive!** Thomas Dolby	Parlophone

uk virgin Cadbury's Crunchie albums

1	**Antenna** ZZ Top	RCA
2	**Jar Of Flies/Sap** Alice In Chains	Columbia
3	**Both Sides** Phil Collins	Virgin
4	**Hips & Makers** Kristin Hersh	4AD
5	**Debut** Bjork	One Little Indian
6	**So Far So Good** Bryan Adams	A&M
7	**Promises And Lies** UB40	Virgin
8	**Bat Out Of Hell II – Back Into Hell** Meat Loaf	Virgin
9	**Ingénue** kd lang	Sire/Warner
10	**Bat Out Of Hell** Meat Loaf	Virgin
11	**The One Thing** Michael Bolton	Columbia
12	**Duets** Elton John/Various	Rocket
13	**Automatic For The People** R.E.M.	Warner Bros
14	**Vs** Pearl Jam	Epic
15	**Grave Dancers Union** Soul Asylum	Columbia
16	**The Red Shoes** Kate Bush	EMI
17	**Mirror Blue** Richard Thompson	Capitol
18	**Jump Back – The Best Of...** The Rolling Stones	Virgin
19	**Together Alone** Crowded House	Capitol
20	**The Spaghetti Incident?** Guns N' Roses	Geffen

us albums

1	**Music Box** Mariah Carey	Columbia
2	**Doggy Style** Snoop Doggy Dogg	Death Row
3	**Diary Of A Mad Band** Jodeci	Uptown
4	**janet.** Janet Jackson	Virgin
5	**Greatest Hits** Tom Petty & The Heartbreakers	MCA
6	**So Far So Good** Bryan Adams	A&M
7	**Vs** Pearl Jam	Epic
8	**The One Thing** Michael Bolton	Columbia
9	**Bat Out Of Hell II: Back Into Hell** Meat Loaf	MCA
10	**Very Necessary** Salt-N-Pepa	Next Plateau
11	**Toni Braxton** Toni Braxton	LaFace
12	**12 Play** R. Kelly	Jive
13	**August & Everything After** Counting Crows	DGC
14	**Antenna** ZZ Top	RCA
15	**Get A Grip** Aerosmith	Geffen
16	**The Sign** Ace Of Base	Arista
17	**Philadelphia** Soundtrack	Epic Soundtrax
18	**Siamese Dream** Smashing Pumpkins	Virgin
19	**MTV Unplugged** 10,000 Maniacs	Elektra
20	**The Colour Of My Love** Celine Dion	550 Music

uk singles

1	**Things Can Only Get Better** D:Ream	FXU
2	**Breathe Again** Toni Braxton	Arista/La Face
3	**All For Love** Bryan Adams/Rod Stewart/Sting	A&M
4	**Return To Innocence** Enigma	Virgin
5	**Come Baby Come** K7	Tommy Boy
6	**Cornflake Girl** Tori Amos	East West
7	**The Power Of Love** Celine Dion	Epic
8	**Anything** Culture Beat	Epic
9	**Give It Away** Red Hot Chili Peppers	Warner Bros
10	**I Miss You** Haddaway	Logic/Arista

us singles

1	**All For Love** Bryan Adams/Rod Stewart/Sting	A&M
2	**Hero** Mariah Carey	Columbia
3	**The Power Of Love** Celine Dion	550 Music
4	**Breathe Again** Toni Braxton	LaFace
5	**The Sign** Ace Of Base	Arista
6	**All That She Wants** Ace Of Base	Arista
7	**Said I Loved You...But I Lied** Michael Bolton	Columbia
8	**Again** Janet Jackson	Virgin
9	**Please Forgive Me** Bryan Adams	A&M
10	**Shoop** Salt-N-Pepa	Next Plateau

indy albums

1	**Hips And Makers** Kristin Hersh	4AD
2	**Dubnobasswithmyheadman** Underworld	Junior Boy's Own
3	**Debut** Bjork	One Little Indian
4	**Songs Of Faith And Devotion** Depeche Mode	Mute
5	**Chocolate Revenge** Voodoo Queens	Too Pure

dance singles

1	**Bells Of NY** Slo-Moshun	SIX6
2	**Raise** Hyper Go-Go	Positiva
3	**Sweet Lullaby** Deep Forest	Columbia
4	**The Music's Got Me** Bass Bumpers	Vertigo
5	**Things Can Only Get Better** D:Ream	FXU/Magnet

indy albums

1	**Debut** Bjork	One Little Indian
2	**Hips And Makers** Kristin Hersh	4AD
3	**Dubnobasswithmyheadman** Underworld	Junior Boy's Own
4	**Giant Steps** The Boo Radleys	Creation
5	**Songs Of Faith And Devotion** Depeche Mode	Mute

dance singles

1	**A Deeper Love** Aretha Franklin	Arista
2	**I Like To Move It** Reel 2 Real/The Mad Stuntman	Positiva
3	**Bells Of NY** Slo Moshun	Six6
4	**Raise** Hyper Go-Go	Positiva
5	**Gonna Make You Move** Boomshanka	Slip'N'Slide

uk singles

1	**Things Can Only Get Better** D:Ream	FXU/Magnet
2	**Breathe Again** Toni Braxton	Arista/LaFace
3	**Return To Innocence** Enigma	Virgin
4	**The Power Of Love** Celine Dion	Epic
5	**A Deeper Love** Aretha Franklin	Arista
6	**All For Love** Bryan Adams/Rod Stewart/Sting	A&M
7	**Come Baby Come** K7	Tommy Boy/Big Life
8	**Come In Out Of The Rain** Wendy Moten	EMI
9	**I Like To Move It** Reel 2 Real/The Mad Stuntman	Positiva
10	**Sweet Lullaby** Deep Forest	Columbia

us singles

1	**The Power Of Love** Celine Dion	550 Music
2	**All For Love** Bryan Adams/Rod Stewart/Sting	A&M
3	**Breathe Again** Toni Braxton	LaFace
4	**Hero** Mariah Carey	Columbia
5	**The Sign** Ace Of Base	Arista
6	**Whatta Man** Salt-N-Pepa/En Vogue	Next Plateau
7	**Getto Jam** Domino	Outburst
8	**Linger** The Cranberries	Island
9	**Said I Loved You...But I Lied** Michael Bolton	Columbia
10	**All That She Wants** Ace Of Base	Arista

us albums

1	**Jar Of Flies (EP)** Alice In Chains	Columbia
2	**Music Box** Mariah Carey	Columbia
3	**Kickin' It Up** John Michael Monto	Atlantic
4	**Doggy Style** Snoop Doggy Dogg	Death Row
5	**Greatest Hits** Tom Petty & The Heartbreakers	MCA
6	**Diary Of A Mad Band** Jodeci	Uptown
7	**Very Necessary** Salt-N-Pepa	Next Plateau
8	**So Far So Good** Bryan Adams	A&M
9	**12 Play** R. Kelly	Jive
10	**Toni Braxton** Toni Braxton	LaFace
11	**The One Thing** Michael Bolton	Columbia
12	**Bat Out Of Hell II: Back Into Hell** Meat Loaf	MCA
13	**janet.** Janet Jackson	Virgin
14	**Vs** Pearl Jam	Epic
15	**August & Everything After** Counting Crows	DGC
16	**The Colour Of My Love** Celine Dion	550 Music
17	**The Sign** Ace Of Base	Arista
18	**Antenna** ZZ Top	RCA
19	**Philadelphia** Soundtrack	Epic Soundtrax
20	**Siamese Dream** Smashing Pumpkins	Virgin

uk virgin Crunchie albums

1	**Under The Pink** Tori Amos	East West
2	**So Far So Good** Bryan Adams	A&M
3	**Debut** Bjork	One LittleIndian
4	**Antenna** ZZ Top	RCA
5	**Both Sides** Phil Collins	Virgin
6	**Bat Out Of Hell II – Back Into Hell** Meat Loaf	Virgin
7	**Jar Of Flies/Sap** Alice In Chains	Columbia
8	**Ingénue** kd lang	Sire/Warner
9	**Promises And Lies** UB40	Virgin
10	**Hips & Makers** Kristin Hersh	4AD
11	**Bat Out Of Hell** Meat Loaf	Virgin
12	**Duets** Elton John/Various	Rocket
13	**Grave Dancers Union** Soul Asylum	Columbia
14	**The One Thing** Michael Bolton	Columbia
15	**Automatic For The People** R.E.M.	Warner Bros
16	**Together Alone** Crowded House	Capitol
17	**Vs** Pearl Jam	Epic
18	**Ten Summoner's Tales** Sting	A&M
19	**Blood Sugar Sex Magik** Red Hot Chili Peppers	Warner Bros
20	**Jump Back – The Best Of...** The Rolling Stones	Virgin

alice in chains

indy albums

1	**Debut** Bjork	One Little Indian
2	**Hips And Makers** Kristin Hersh	4AD
3	**Dubnobasswithmyheadman** Underworld	Junior Boy's Own
4	**Suede** Suede	Nude
5	**Giant Steps** The Boo Radleys	Creation

dance singles

1	**Higher Ground** Sasha	Deconstruction/RCA
2	**I Like To Move It** Reel 2 Real/The Mad Stuntman	Positiva
3	**A Deeper Love** Aretha Franklin	Arista
4	**Move On Baby** Cappella	Internal Dance
5	**Waterfall** Atlantic Ocean	Eastern Bloc

uk singles

1	**Things Can Only Get Better** D:Ream	FXu/Magnet
2	**Breathe Again** Toni Braxton	Arista/LaFace
3	**Return To Innocence** Enigma	Virgin
4	**The Power Of Love** Celine Dion	Epic
5	**A Deeper Love** Aretha Franklin	Arista
6	**All For Love** Bryan Adams/Rod Stewart/Sting	A&M
7	**Come Baby Come** K7	Tommy Boy/Big LIfe
8	**Come In Out Of The Rain** Wendy Moten	EMI
9	**I Like To Move It** Reel 2 Real/The Mad Stuntman	Positiva
10	**Sweet Lullaby** Deep Forest	Columbia

us singles

1	**The Power Of Love** Celine Dion	550 Music
2	**All For Love** Bryan Adams/Rod Stewart/Sting	A&M
3	**The Sign** Ace Of Base	Arista
4	**Breathe Again** Toni Braxton	LaFace
5	**Whatta Man** Salt-N-Pepa/En Vogue	Next Plateau
6	**Hero** Mariah Carey	Columbia
7	**Without You/Never Forget You** Mariah Carey	Columbia
8	**Understanding** Xscape	So So Def
9	**Getto Jam** Domino	Outburst
10	**So Much In Love** All-4-One	Blitzz

us albums

1	**Kickin' It Up** John Michael Montgo	Atlantic
2	**Music Box** Mariah Carey	Columbia
3	**Doggy Style** Snoop Doggy Dogg	Death Row
4	**Jar Of Flies (EP)** Alice In Chains	Columbia
5	**12 Play** R. Kelly	Jive
6	**Very Necessary** Salt-N-Pepa	Next Plateau
7	**Toni Braxton** Toni Braxton	LaFace
8	**Diary Of A Mad Band** Jodeci	Uptown
9	**Greatest Hits** Tom Petty & The Heartbreakers	MCA
10	**August & Everything After** Counting Crows	DGC
11	**The One Thing** Michael Bolton	Columbia
12	**Under The Pink** Tori Amos	Atlantic
13	**The Sign** Ace Of Base	Arista
14	**The Colour Of My Love** Celine Dion	550 Music
15	**So Far So Good** Bryan Adams	A&M
16	**Bat Out Of Hell II: Back Into Hell** Meat Loaf	MCA
17	**janet.** Janet Jackson	Virgin
18	**Philadelphia** Soundtrack	Epic Soundtrax
19	**Vs** Pearl Jam	Epic
20	**Siamese Dream** Smashing Pumpkins	Virgin

uk virgin Crunchie albums

1	**Under The Pink** Tori Amos	East West
2	**Troublegum** Therapy?	A&M
3	**Softly With These Songs** Roberta Flack	Atlantic
4	**The Heart Of Chicago** Chicago	Warner Bros
5	**Brave** Marillion	EMI
6	**Paid Vacation** Richard Marx	Capitol
7	**Bat Out Of Hell II: Back Into Hell** Meat Loaf	Virgin
8	**Debut** Bjork	One Little Indian
9	**So Far So Good** Bryan Adams	A&M
10	**Both Sides** Phil Collins	Virgin
11	**Live At Brixton Academy** Brian May	Parlophone
12	**Antenna** ZZ Top	RCA
13	**Promises And Lies** UB40	Virgin
14	**The One Thing** Michael Bolton	Columbia
15	**Bat Out Of Hell** Meat Loaf	Epic
16	**Automatic For The People** R.E.M.	Warner Bros
17	**Ingénue** kd lang	Sire/Warner
18	**Duets** Elton John	Rocket
19	**Jar Of Flies/Sap** Alice In Chains	Columbia
20	**Ten Summoner's Tales** Sting	A&M

indy albums

1	**Debut** Bjork	One Little Indian
2	**Crooked Rain Crooked Rain** Pavement	Big Cat
3	**Suede** Suede	Nude
4	**Hips And Makers** Kristin Hersh	4AD
5	**Dubnobasswithmyheadman** Underworld	Junior Boy's Own

dance singles

1	**I Like To Move It** Reel 2 Real/The Mad Stuntman	Positiva
2	**Downtown** SWV	RCA
3	**Insane In The Brain** Cypress Hill	Columbia
4	**Higher Ground** Sasha	Deconstruction/RCA
5	**Right In The Night** Jam & Spoon/Plavka	Epic

uk singles

1	**Without You** Mariah Carey	Columbia
2	**Things Can Only Get Better** D:Ream	FXU/Magnet
3	**Breathe Again** Toni Braxton	Arista/LaFace
4	**Return To Innocence** Enigma	Virgin
5	**The Power Of Love** Celine Dion	Epic
6	**A Deeper Love** Aretha Franklin	Arista
7	**Move On Baby** Cappella	Internal
8	**All For Love** Bryan Adams/Rod Stewart/Sting	A&M
9	**Let The Beat Control Your Body** 2 Unlimited	PWL Continental
10	**I Like To Move It** Reel 2 Real/The Mad Stuntman	Positiva

us singles

1	**The Power Of Love** Celine Dion	550 Music
2	**The Sign** Ace Of Base	Arista
3	**Whatta Man** Salt-N-Pepa/En Vogue	Next Plateau
4	**All For Love** Bryan Adams/Rod Stewart/Sting	A&M
5	**Breathe Again** Toni Braxton	LaFace
6	**Without You/Never Forget You** Mariah Carey	Columbia
7	**Hero** Mariah Carey	Columbia
8	**So Much In Love** All-4-One	Blitzz
9	**Understanding** Xscape	So So Def
10	**Now And Forever** Richard Marx	Capitol

us albums

1	**Toni Braxton** Toni Braxton	LaFace
2	**Music Box** Mariah Carey	Columbia
3	**Doggy Style** Snoop Doggy Dogg	Death Row
4	**Kickin' It Up** John Michael Montgo	Atlantic
5	**12 Play** R. Kelly	Jive
6	**Very Necessary** Salt-N-Pepa	Next Plateau
7	**August & Everything After** Counting Crows	DGC
8	**Greatest Hits** Tom Petty & The Heartbreakers	MCA
9	**Jar Of Flies (EP)** Alice In Chains	Columbia
10	**The Colour Of My Love** Celine Dion	550 Music
11	**The Bodyguard** Soundtrack	Arista
12	**The Cross Of Changes** Enigma	Charisma
13	**The Sign** Ace Of Base	Arista
14	**Diary Of A Mad Band** Jodeci	Uptown
15	**The One Thing** Michael Bolton	Columbia
16	**Bat Out Of Hell II: Back Into Hell** Meat Loaf	MCA
17	**So Far So Good** Bryan Adams	A&M
18	**janet.** Janet Jackson	Virgin
19	**Philadelphia** Soundtrack	Epic Soundtrax
20	**Vs** Pearl Jam	Epic

uk virgin Crunchie albums

1	**Debut** Bjork	One Little Indian
2	**Bat Out Of Hell II: Back Into Hell** Meat Loaf	Virgin
3	**Under The Pink** Tori Amos	East West
4	**Softly With These Songs** Roberta Flack	Atlantic
5	**The Heart Of Chicago** Chicago	Warner Bros
6	**Ten Summoner's Tales** Sting	A&M
7	**Connected** Stereo MCs	4th+Bway
8	**So Far So Good** Bryan Adams	A&M
9	**Troublegum** Therapy?	A&M
10	**Paid Vacation** Richard Marx	Capitol
11	**The Best Of...** Van Morrison	Polydor
12	**Both Sides** Phil Collins	Virgin
13	**Together Alone** Crowded House	Capitol
14	**Bat Out Of Hell** Meat Loaf	Epic
15	**Ingénue** kd lang	Sire/Warner
16	**Automatic For The People** R.E.M.	Warner Bros
17	**Suede** Suede	Nude
18	**Promises And Lies** UB40	Virgin
19	**Brave** Marillion	EMI
20	**Duets** Elton John	Rocket

kristin hersh

indy albums

1	**Patashnik** Biosphere	Apollo
2	**Debut** Bjork	One Little Indian
3	**The People Tree** Mother Earth	Acid Jazz
4	**Dubnobasswithmyheadman** Underworld	Junior Boy's Own
5	**Hips And Makers** Kristin Hersh	4AD

dance singles

1	**Beautiful People** Barbara Tucker	Positiva
2	**Saxy Lady** Quivver	A&M
3	**Downtown** SWV	RCA
4	**Love And Happiness** River Ocean	Cooltempo
5	**I Like To Move It** Reel 2 Real/The Mad Stuntman	Positiva

uk singles

1	**Without You** Mariah Carey	Columbia
2	**Things Can Only Get Better** D:Ream	FXU/Magnet
3	**Stay Together** Suede	Nude
4	**Return To Innocence** Enigma	Virgin
5	**Breathe Again** Toni Braxton	Arista/LaFace
6	**All For Love** Bryan Adams/Rod Stewart/Sting	A&M
7	**The Sign** Ace Of Base	Metronome/London
8	**Let The Beat Control Your Body** 2 Unlimited	PWL Continental
9	**The Power Of Love** Celine Dion	Epic
10	**Move On Baby** Cappella	Internal

us singles

1	**The Power Of Love** Celine Dion	550 Music
2	**The Sign** Ace Of Base	Arista
3	**Whatta Man** Salt-N-Pepa/En Vogue	Next Plateau
4	**Without You/Never Forget You** Mariah Carey	Columbia
5	**Breathe Again** Toni Braxton	LaFace
6	**All For Love** Bryan Adams/Rod Stewart/Sting	A&M
7	**So Much In Love** All-4-One	Blitz
8	**Now And Forever** Richard Marx	Capitol
9	**Cantaloop (Flip Fantasia)** US3	Blue Note
10	**Hero** Mariah Carey	Columbia

us albums

1	**Music Box** Mariah Carey	Columbia
2	**Toni Braxton** Toni Braxton	LaFace
3	**12 Play** R. Kelly	Jive
4	**Very Necessary** Salt-N-Pepa	Next Plateau
5	**Doggy Style** Snoop Doggy Dogg	Death Row
6	**Kickin' It Up** John Michael Montgo	Atlantic
7	**August & Everything After** Counting Crows	DGC
8	**The Colour Of My Love** Celine Dion	550 Music
9	**The Sign** Ace Of Base	Arista
10	**Greatest Hits** Tom Petty & The Heartbreakers	MCA
11	**So Far So Good** Bryan Adams	A&M
12	**The One Thing** Michael Bolton	Columbia
13	**The Bodyguard** Soundtrack	Arista
14	**Jar Of Flies (EP)** Alice In Chains	Columbia
15	**Bat Out Of Hell II: Back Into Hell** Meat Loaf	MCA
16	**The Cross Of Changes** Enigman	Charisma
17	**Diary Of A Mad Band** Jodeci	Uptown
18	**janet.** Janet Jackson	Virgin
19	**Vs** Pearl Jam	Epic
20	**Siamese Dream** Smashing Pumpkins	Virgin

uk virgin Crunchie albums

1	**Debut** Bjork	One Little Indian
2	**Ten Summoner's Tales** Sting	A&M
3	**Bat Out Of Hell II: Back Into Hell** Meat Loaf	Virgin
4	**Under The Pink** Tori Amos	East West
5	**Connected** Stereo MCs	4th+Bway
6	**The Heart Of Chicago** Chicago	Warner Bros
7	**Together Alone** Crowded House	Capitol
8	**The Best Of...** Van Morrison	Polydor
9	**Softly With These Songs** Roberta Flack	Atlantic
10	**So Far So Good** Bryan Adams	A&M
11	**Paid Vacation** Richard Marx	Capitol
12	**Troublegum** Therapy?	A&M
13	**Both Sides** Phil Collins	Virgin
14	**Suede** Suede	Nude
15	**Bat Out Of Hell** Meat Loaf	Epic
16	**Woodface** Crowded House	Capitol
17	**The One Thing** Michael Bolton	Columbia
18	**Ingénue** kd lang	Sire/Warner
19	**Automatic For The People** R.E.M.	Warner Bros
20	**Brave** Marillion	EMI

us albums

1. **Music Box** — Mariah Carey — Columbia
2. **12 Play** — R. Kelly — Jive
3. **The Sign** — Ace Of Base — Arista
4. **Doggy Style** — Snoop Doggy Dogg — Death Row
5. **Very Necessary** — Salt-N-Pepa — Next Plateau
6. **The Colour Of My Love** — Celine Dion — 550 Music
7. **August & Everything After** — Counting Crows — DGC
8. **Toni Braxton** — Toni Braxton — LaFace
9. **Greatest Hits** — Tom Petty & The Heartbreakers — MCA
10. **The Cross Of Changes** — Enigma — Charisma
11. **Jar Of Flies (EP)** — Alice In Chains — Columbia
12. **Kickin' It Up** — John Michael Montgo — Atlantic
13. **So Far So Good** — Bryan Adams — A&M
14. **Diary Of A Mad Band** — Jodeci — Uptown
15. **Bat Out Of Hell II: Back Into Hell** — Meat Loaf — MCA
16. **The Bodyguard** — Soundtrack — Arista
17. **Reality Bites** — Soundtrack — RCA
18. **janet.** — Janet Jackson — Virgin
19. **The One Thing** — Michael Bolton — Columbia
20. **Siamese Dream** — Smashing Pumpkins — Virgin

uk singles

1. **Without You** — Mariah Carey — Columbia
2. **The Sign** — Ace Of Base — Metronome/London
3. **Return To Innocence** — Enigma — Virgin
4. **Breathe Again** — Toni Braxton — Arista
5. **Things Can Only Get Better** — D:ream — FXU/Magnet
6. **Let The Beat Control Your Body** — 2 Unlimited — PWL Continental
7. **Don't Go Breaking My Heart** — Elton John with RuPaul — Rocket
8. **Move On Baby** — Cappella — Internal
9. **All For Love** — Bryan Adams/Rod Stewart/Sting — A&M
10. **Stay Together** — Suede — Nude

us singles

1. **The Sign** — Ace Of Base — Arista
2. **The Power Of Love** — Celine Dion — 550 Music
3. **Whatta Man** — Salt-N-Pepa/En Vogue — Next Plateau
4. **Without You/Never Forget You** — Mariah Carey — Columbia
5. **So Much In Love** — All-4-One — Blitzz
6. **Bump N' Grind** — R. Kelly — Jive
7. **Breathe Again** — Toni Braxton — LaFace
8. **Now And Forever** — Richard Marx — Capitol
9. **Cantaloop (Flip Fantasia)** — US3 — Blue Note
10. **All For Love** — Bryan Adams/Rod Stewart/Sting — A&M

indy albums

1. **Tiger Bay** — Saint Etienne — Heavenly
2. **Maya** — Banco De Gaia — Ultimate
3. **Debut** — Bjork — One Little Indian
4. **Crooked Rain Crooked Rain** — Pavement — Big Cat
5. **Hips And Makers** — Kristin Hersh — 4AD

dance singles

1. **Doop** — Doop — Citybeat
2. **Renaissance** — M-People — Deconstruction
3. **There But For The Grace Of God** — Fire Island — Junior Boy's Own
4. **Pieces Of A Dream** — Incognito — Talkin Loud
5. **Because Of Love** — Janet Jackson — Virgin

ace of base

uk virgin Crunchie albums

1. **Everybody Else Is Doing It...** — The Cranberries — Island
2. **Ten Summoner's Tales** — Sting — A&M
3. **Debut** — Bjork — One Little Indian
4. **Tiger Bay** — Saint Etienne — Heavenly
5. **Bat Out Of Hell II: Back Into Hell** — Meat Loaf — Virgin
6. **Under The Pink** — Tori Amos — East West
7. **Connected** — Stereo MCs — 4th+Bway
8. **August & Everything After** — Counting Crows — Geffen
9. **The Best Of...** — Van Morrison — Poldor
10. **So Far So Good** — Bryan Adams — A&M
11. **Together Alone** — Crowded House — Capitol
12. **The Heart Of Chicago** — Chicago — Warner Bros
13. **Softly Within These Songs** — Roberta Flack — Atlantic
14. **The One Thing** — Michael Bolton — Columbia
15. **Troublegum** — Therapy? — A&M
16. **Paid Vacation** — Richard Marx — Capitol
17. **Both Sides** — Phil Collins — Virgin
18. **Automatic For The People** — R.E.M. — Warner Bros
19. **Bat Out Of Hell** — Meat Loaf — Epic
20. **Titanic Days** — Kirsty Maccoll — ZTT

---

us albums

1. **Toni Braxton** — Toni Braxton — LaFace
2. **The Sign** — Ace Of Base — Arista
3. **12 Play** — R. Kelly — Jive
4. **The Colour Of My Love** — Celine Dion — 550 Music
5. **Music Box** — Mariah Carey — Columbia
6. **The Bodyguard** — Soundtrack — Arista
7. **August & Everything After** — Counting Crows — DGC
8. **Doggy Style** — Snoop Doggy Dogg — Death Row
9. **Very Necessary** — Salt-N-Pepa — Next Plateau
10. **The Cross Of Changes** — Enigma — Charisma
11. **Greatest Hits** — Tom Petty & The Heartbreakers — MCA
12. **The Funky Headhunter** — Hammer — Giant
13. **Reality Bites** — Soundtrack — RCA
14. **Kickin' It Up** — John Michael Montgo — Atlantic
15. **Mellow Gold** — Beck — DGC
16. **Jar Of Flies (EP)** — Alice In Chains — Columbia
17. **Diary Of A Mad Band** — Jodeci — Uptown
18. **Bat Out Of Hell II: Back Into Hell** — Meat Loaf — MCA
19. **Siamese Dream** — Smashing Pumpkins — Virgin
20. **janet.** — Janet Jackson — Virgin

uk singles

1. **Without You** — Mariah Carey — Columbia
2. **The Sign** — Ace Of Base — Metronome/London
3. **Doop** — Doop — Citybeat
4. **Breathe Again** — Toni Braxton — Arista
5. **Renaissance** — M-People — Deconstruction/RCA
6. **Return To Innocence** — Enigma — Virgin
7. **Rocks/Funky Jam** — Primal Scream — Creation
8. **The More You Ignore Me...** — Morrissey — Parlophone
9. **Let The Beat Control Your Body** — 2 Unlimited — PWL Continental
10. **I Like To Move It** — Reel 2 Real/The Mad Stuntman — Positiva

us singles

1. **The Sign** — Ace Of Base — Arista
2. **The Power Of Love** — Celine Dion — 550 Music
3. **With You/Never Forget You** — Mariah Carey — Columbia
4. **Whatta Man** — Salt-N-Pepa/En Vogue — Next Plateau
5. **Bump N' Grind** — R. Kelly — Jive
6. **So Much In Love** — All-4-One — Blitzz
7. **Now And Forever** — Richard Marx — Capitol
8. **Breathe Again** — Toni Braxton — LaFace
9. **Gin And Juice** — Snoop Doggy Dogg — Death Row
10. **Because Of Love** — Janet Jackson — Virgin

indy albums

1. **Selected Ambient Works Vol II** — Aphex Twin — Warp
2. **Devil Hopping** — Inspiral Carpets — Mute
3. **Peel Sessions** — Orbital
4. **Tiger Bay** — Saint Etienne — Heavenly
5. **Debut** — Bjork — One Little Indian

dance singles

1. **Shine On** — Degrees Of Motion/Biti
2. **Doop** — Doop — Citybeat
3. **Again/I Want You** — Juliet Roberts — Cooltempo
4. **There But For The Grace Of God** — Fire Island — Junior Boy's Own
5. **Groove Thang** — Zhane — Motown

uk virgin Crunchie albums

1. **Brutal Youth** — Elvis Costello — Warner Bros
2. **Superunknown** — Soundgarden — A&M
3. **The Heart Of Chicago** — Chicago — Warner Bros
4. **Everybody Else Is Doing...** — The Cranberries — Island
5. **Hit The Highway** — The Proclaimers — Chrysalis
6. **Devil Hopping** — Inspiral Carpets — Cow/Mute
7. **Ten Summoner's Tales** — Sting — A&M
8. **Debut** — Bjork — One Little Indian
9. **Bat Out Of Hell II: Back Into Hell** — Meat Loaf — Virgin
10. **Softly With These Songs...** — Roberta Flack — Atlantic
11. **The One Thing** — Michael Bolton — Columbia
12. **Under The Pink** — Tori Amos — East West
13. **So Far So Good** — Bryan Adams — A&M
14. **Greatest Hits 1980-1994** — Aretha Franklin — Arista
15. **Your Filthy Little Mouth** — David Lee Roth — Reprise
16. **Connected** — Stereo MCs — 4th+Bway
17. **Tiger Bay** — Saint Etienne — Heavenly
18. **August & Everything After** — Counting Crows — Geffen
19. **Together Alone** — Crowded House — Capitol
20. **Both Sides** — Phil Collins — Virgin

uk virgin Crunchie albums

1	**Vauxhall And I** Morrissey	Parlophone
2	**Everybody Else Is Doing It...** The Cranberries	Island
3	**Debut** Bjork	One Little Indian
4	**Forever Now** Level 42	RCA
5	**Brutal Youth** Elvis Costello	Warner Bros
6	**Softly With Those Songs...** Roberta Flack	Atlantic
7	**The Heart Of Chicago** Chicago	Warner Bros
8	**Under The Pink** Tori Amos	East West
9	**Ten Summoner's Tales** Sting	A&M
10	**Superunknown** Soundgarden	A&M
11	**Motley Crue** Motley Crue	Elektra
12	**Bat Out Of Hell II: Back Into Hell** Meat Loaf	Virgin
13	**Hit The Highway** The Proclaimers	Chrysalis
14	**Devil Hopping** Inspiral Carpets	Cow/Mute
15	**Antmusic – The Very Best Of** Adam Ant	Arcade
16	**So Far So Good** Bryan Adams	A&M
17	**The One Thing** Michael Bolton	Columbia
18	**Connected** Stereo MCs	4th+Bway
19	**Together Alone** Crowded House	Capitol
20	**Greatest Hits 1980-1994** Aretha Franklin	Arista

us albums

1	**Superunknown** Soundgarden	A&M
2	**The Downward Spiral** Nine Inch Nails	Nothing
3	**The Sign** Ace Of Base	Arista
4	**12 Play** R. Kelly	Jive
5	**Toni Braxton** Toni Braxton	LaFace
6	**Music Box** Mariah Carey	Columbia
7	**August & Everything After** Counting Crows	DGC
8	**The Colour Of My Love** Celine Dion	550 Music
9	**Doggy Style** Snoop Doggy Dogg	Death Row
10	**The Cross Of Changes** Enigma	Charisma
11	**The Bodyguard** Soundtrack	Arista
12	**Very Necessary** Salt-N-Pepa	Next Plateau
13	**Mellow Gold** Beck	DGC
14	**Greatest Hits** Tom Petty & The Heartbreakers	MCA
15	**Reality Bites** Soundtrack	RCA
16	**Jar Of Flies (EP)** Alice In Chains	Columbia
17	**God Shuffled His Feet** Crash Test Dummies	Arista
18	**Rhythm Country & Blues** Various Artists	MCA
19	**Siamese Dream** Smashing Pumpkins	Virgin
20	**Bat Out Of Hell II: Back Into Hell** Meat Loaf	MCA

uk singles

1	**Doop** Doop	Citybeat
2	**Without You** Mariah Carey	Columbia
3	**The Sign** Ace Of Base	Metronome/London
4	**Streets Of Philadelphia** Bruce Springsteen	Columbia
5	**Girls And Boys** Blur	Food/Parlophone
6	**Renaissance** M-People	Deconstruction/RCA
7	**Pretty Good Year** Tori Amos	East West
8	**Return To Innocence** Enigma	Virgin
9	**I Like To Move It** Reel 2 Real/The Mad Stuntman	Positiva
10	**Breathe Again** Toni Braxton	Arista

us singles

1	**The Sign** Ace Of Base	Arista
2	**Bump N' Grind** R. Kelly	Jive
3	**Without You/Never Forget You** Mariah Carey	Columbia
4	**The Power Of Love** Celine Dion	550 Music
5	**Whatta Man** Salt-N-Pepa/En Vogue	Next Plateau
6	**So Much In Love** All-4-One	Blitzz
7	**Now And Forever** Richard Marx	Capitol
8	**Gin And Juice** Snoop Doggy Dogg	Death Row
9	**Cantaloop (Flip Fantasia)** US3	Blue Note
10	**Breathe Again** Toni Braxton	LaFace

indy albums

1	**U Got 2 Know** Cappella	Internal
2	**Selcted Ambient Works Vol II** Aphex Twin	Warp
3	**Devil Hopping** Inspiral Carpets	Mute
4	**Debut** Bjork	One Little Indian
5	**Maya** Banco De Gaia	Ultimate

dance singles

1	**I Believe** Sounds Of Blackness	A&M
2	**Dream On Dreamer** Brand New Heavies	ffrr
3	**Shine On** Degrees Of Motion/Biti	ffrr
4	**Again/I Want You** Juliet Roberts	Cooltempo
5	**Skip To My Lu** Lisa Lisa	Pendulum

---

uk virgin Crunchie albums

1	**Vauxhall And I** Morrissey	Parlophone
2	**Up To Our Hips** Charlatans	Beggars Ban
3	**Everybody Else Is Doing It...** The Cranberries	Island
4	**Debut** Bjork	One Little Indian
5	**Ten Summoner's Tales** Sting	A&M
6	**Under The Pink** Tori Amos	East West
7	**Bat Out Of Hell II: Back Into Hell** Meat Loaf	Virgin
8	**Softly With These Songs...** Roberta Flack	Atlantic
9	**The Heart Of Chicago** Chicago	Warner Bros
10	**Talk** Yes	Victory
11	**Superunknown** Soundgarden	A&M
12	**Brutal Youth** Elvis Costello	Warner Bros
13	**Essex** Alison Moyet	Columbia
14	**Hit The Highway** The Proclaimers	Chrysalis
15	**Forever Now** Level 42	RCA
16	**Antmusic – The Very Best Of** Adam Ant	Arcade
17	**So Far So Good** Bryan Adams	A&M
18	**Tracy Chapman** Tracy Chapman	Elektra
19	**Together Alone** Crowded House	Capitol
20	**Let's Go Round Again – Best Of** Average White Band	Hit Label

us albums

1	**The Sign** Ace Of Base	Arista
2	**Superunknown** Soundgarden	A&M
3	**12 Play** R. Kelly	Jive
4	**August & Everything After** Counting Crows	DGC
5	**Music Box** Mariah Carey	Columbia
6	**Toni Braxton** Toni Braxton	LaFace
7	**Motley Crue** Motley Crue	Elektra
8	**The Colour Of My Love** Celine Dion	550 Music
9	**Doggy Style** Snoop Doggy Dogg	Death Row
10	**Very Necessary** Salt-N-Pepa	Next Plateau
11	**Live At The Acropolis** Yanni	Private Music
12	**The Downward Spiral** Nine Inch Nails	Nothing
13	**The Cross Of Changes** Enigma	Charisma
14	**Mellow Gold** Beck	DGC
15	**God Shuffled His Feet** Crash Test Dummies	Arista
16	**Reality Bites** Soundtrack	RCA
17	**Greatest Hits** Tom Petty & The Heartbreakers	MCA
18	**The Bodyguard** Soundtrack	Arista
19	**Rhythm Country & Blues** Various Artists	MCA
20	**Siamese Dream** Smashing Pumpkins	Virgin

uk singles

1	**Doop** Doop	Citybeat
2	**The Sign** Ace Of Base	Metronome/London
3	**Return To Innocence** Enigma	Virgin
4	**Breathe Again** Toni Braxton	Arista
5	**Things Can Only Get Better** D:ream	FXU/Magnet
6	**Let The Beat Control Your Body** 2 Unlimited	PWL Continental
7	**Don't Go Breaking My Heart** Elton John with RuPaul	Rocket
8	**Move On Baby** Cappella	Internal
9	**All For Love** Bryan Adams/Rod Stewart/Sting	A&M
10	**Stay Together** Suede	Nude

us singles

1	**The Sign** Ace Of Base	Arista
2	**Bump N' Grind** R. Kelly	Jive
3	**Without You/Never Forget You** Mariah Carey	Columbia
4	**The Power Of Love** Celine Dion	550 Music
5	**Whatta Man** Salt-N-Pepa/En Vogue	Next Plateau
6	**So Much In Love** All-4-One	Blitzz
7	**Now And Forever** Richard Marx	Capitol
8	**Mmm Mmm Mmm Mmm** Crash Test Dummies	Arista
9	**Gin And Juice** Snoop Doggy Dogg	Death Row
10	**Cantaloop (Flip Fantasia)** US3	Blue Note

indy albums

1	**Up To Our Hips** Charlatans	Beggars Banquet
2	**S*M*A*S*H** S*M*A*S*H	Hi-Rise Recordings
3	**Point Blank** Nailbomb	Roadrunner
4	**Selected Ambient Works Vol II** Aphex Twin	Warp
5	**Debut** Bjork	One Little Indian

dance singles

1	**Son Of A Gun** JX	Internal Dance
2	**I Believe** Sounds Of Blackness	A&M
3	**Dream On Dreamer** Brand New Heavies	ffrr
4	**Shine On** Degress Of Motion/Biti	ffrr
5	**House Of Love (In The House)** Smooth Touch	Six6

indy albums

1	**Give Out But Don't Give Up**	
	Primal Scream	Creation
2	**Take Dis**	
	Credit To The Nation	One Little Indian
3	**Up To Our Hips**	
	Charlatans	Beggars Banquet
4	**S*M*A*S*H**	
	S*M*A*S*H	Hi-Rise Recordings
5	**Comforter**	
	Compulsion	One Little Indian

dance singles

1	**The Real Thing**	
	Tony Di Bart	Cleveland City Blues
2	**Son Of A Gun**	
	JX	Internal Dance
3	**How Gee**	
	Black Machine	London
4	**Tap The Bottle**	
	Young Black Teenagers	MCA
5	**Theme**	
	Sabres Of Paradise	Sabres Of Paradise

uk singles

1	**Doop**	
	Doop	Citybeat
2	**Streets Of Philadelphia**	
	Bruce Springsteen	Columbia
3	**The Sign**	
	Ace Of Base	Metronome/London
4	**U R The Best Thing**	
	D:ream	FXU/Magnet
5	**I Like To Move It**	
	Reel 2 Real/The Mad Stuntman	Positiva
6	**Without You**	
	Maria Carey	Columbia
7	**Whatta Man**	
	Salt-N-Pepa with En Vogue	ffrr
8	**Shine On**	
	Degrees Of Motion/Biti	ffrr
9	**Dry Country**	
	Bon Jovi	Vertigo
10	**I'll Remember**	
	Madonna	Maverick/Sire

us singles

1	**Bump 'N' Grind**	
	R. Kelly	Jive
2	**The Sign**	
	Ace Of Base	Arista
3	**Without You/Never Forget You**	
	Mariah Carey	Columbia
4	**The Power Of Love**	
	Celine Dion	550 Music
5	**So Much In Love**	
	All-4-One	Blitzz
6	**Whatta Man**	
	Salt-N-Pepa/En Vogue	Next Plateau
7	**Mmm Mmm Mmm Mmm**	
	Crash Test Dummies	Arista
8	**Now And Forever**	
	Richard Marx	Capitol
9	**The Most Beautiful Girl In The World**	
	Symbol/Prince	NPG
10	**Streets Of Philadelphia**	
	Bruce Springsteen	Columbia

us albums

1	**Far Beyond Driven**	
	Pantera	East West
2	**Longing In Their Hearts**	
	Bonnie Raitt	Capitol
3	**The Sign**	
	Ace Of Base	Arista
4	**Above The Rim**	
	Soundtrack	Death Row
5	**Live At The Acropolis**	
	Yanni	Private Music
6	**12 Play**	
	R. Kelly	Jive
7	**August & Everything After**	
	Counting Crows	DGC
8	**Superunknown**	
	Soundgarden	A&M
9	**Music Box**	
	Mariah Carey	Columbia
10	**The Colour Of Love**	
	Celine Dion	550 Music
11	**Toni Braxton**	
	Toni Braxton	LaFace
12	**Philadelphia**	
	Soundtrack	Epic Soundtrax
13	**Doggy Style**	
	Snoop Doggy Dogg	Death Row
14	**Very Necessary**	
	Salt-N-Pepa	Next Plateau
15	**God Shuffled His Feet**	
	Crash Test Dummies	Arista
16	**The Cross Of Changes**	
	Enigma	Charisma
17	**Mellow Gold**	
	Beck	DGC
18	**Vauxhall And I**	
	Morrissey	Sire
19	**Not A Moment Too Soon**	
	Tim McGraw	Curb
20	**Rhythm Country & Blues**	
	Various Artists	MCA

uk virgin Cadbury's Crunchie albums

1	**The Division Bell**	
	Pink Floyd	EMI
2	**Give Out But Don't Give Up**	
	Primal Scream	Creation
3	**The Very Best Of**	
	Marvin Gaye	Motown
4	**Miaow**	
	Beautiful South	Go! Discs
5	**Debut**	
	Bjork	One Little Indian
6	**Vauxhall And I**	
	Morrissey	Parlophone
7	**Everybody Else Is Doing It...**	
	The Cranberries	Island
8	**Jewel**	
	Marcella Detroit	London
9	**The Heart Of Chicago**	
	Chicago	Warner Bros
10	**Under The Pink**	
	Tori Amos	East West
11	**Ten Summoner's Tales**	
	Sting	A&M
12	**Bat Out Of Hell II: Back Into Hell**	
	Meat Loaf	Virgin
13	**Up To Our Hips**	
	Charlatans	Beggars Banquet
14	**Softly With These Songs...**	
	Roberta Flack	Atlantic
15	**Superunknown**	
	Soundgarden	A&M
16	**So Far So Good**	
	Bryan Adams	A&M
17	**Tracy Chapman**	
	Tracy Chapman	Elektra
18	**Hit The Highway**	
	The Proclaimers	Chrysalis
19	**Essex**	
	Alison Moyet	Columbia
20	**Talk**	
	Yes	Victory

primal scream

indy albums

1	**Give Out But Don't Give Up**	
	Primal Scream	Creation
2	**Take Dis**	
	Credit To The Nation	One Little Indian
3	**Debut**	
	Bjork	One Little Indian
4	**S*M*A*S*H**	
	S*M*A*S*H	Hi-Rise Recordings
5	**Up To Our Hips**	
	Charlatans	Beggars Banquet

dance singles

1	**Let The Music (Lift You Up)**	
	Loveland Vs Darlene Lewis	KMS
2	**The Real Thing**	
	Tony Di Bart	Cleveland City Blues
3	**Son Of A Gun**	
	JX	Internal Dance
4	**Theme**	
	Sabres Of Paradise	Sabres Of Paradise
5	**I'll Wait**	
	Taylor Dayne	Arista

uk singles

1	**Everything Changes**	
	Take That	RCA
2	**Doop**	
	Doop	Citybeat
3	**Streets Of Philadelphia**	
	Bruce Springsteen	Columbia
4	**The Most Beautiful Girl In The World**	
	Symbol/Prince	NPG
5	**The Sign**	
	Ace Of Base	Metronome/London
6	**U R The Best Thing**	
	D:ream	FXU/Magnet
7	**I'll Remember**	
	Madonna	Maverick/Sire
8	**I Like To Move It**	
	Reel 2 Real/The Mad Stuntman	Positiva
9	**Without You**	
	Mariah Carey	Columbia
10	**Whatta Man**	
	Salt-N-Pepa with En Vogue	ffrr

us singles

1	**Bump 'N' Grind**	
	R. Kelly	Jive
2	**The Sign**	
	Ace Of Base	Arista
3	**Without You/Never Forget You**	
	Mariah Carey	Columbia
4	**Mmm Mmm Mmm Mmm**	
	Crash Test Dummies	Arista
5	**The Power Of Love**	
	Celine Dion	550 Music
6	**So Much In Love**	
	All-4-One	Blitzz
7	**Whatta Man**	
	Salt-N-Pepa/En Vogue	Next Plateau
8	**The Most Beautiful Girl In The World**	
	Symbol/Prince	NPG
9	**Now And Forever**	
	Richard Marx	Capitol
10	**Streets Of Philadelphia**	
	Bruce Springsteen	Columbia

us albums

1	**Longing In Their Hearts**	
	Bonnie Raitt	Capitol
2	**The Sign**	
	Ace Of Base	Arista
3	**Above The Rim**	
	Soundtrack	Death Row
4	**August & Everything After**	
	Counting Crows	DGC
5	**12 Play**	
	R. Kelly	Jive
6	**Music Box**	
	Mariah Carey	Columbia
7	**The Colour Of My Love**	
	Celine Dion	550 Music
8	**Not A Moment Too Soon**	
	Tim McGraw	Curb
9	**Far Beyond Driven**	
	Pantera	EastWest
10	**Live At The Acropolis**	
	Yanni	Private Music
11	**Toni Braxton**	
	Toni Braxton	LaFace
12	**God Shuffled His Feet**	
	Crash Test Dummies	Arista
13	**Chant**	
	Benedictine Monks	Angel
14	**Superunknown**	
	Soundgarden	A&M
15	**Very Necessary**	
	Salt-N-Pepa	Next Plateau
16	**The Cross Of Changes**	
	Enigma	Charisma
17	**Doggy Style**	
	Snoop Doggy Dogg	Death Row
18	**Philadelphia**	
	Soundtrack	Epic Soundtrax
19	**Mellow Gold**	
	Beck	DGC
20	**Rhythm Country & Blues**	
	Various Artists	MCA

uk virgin Cadbury's Crunchie albums

1	**The Division Bell**	
	Pink Floyd	EMI
2	**Our Town – The Greatest Hits**	
	Deacon Blue	Columbia
3	**The Very Best Of**	
	Marvin Gaye	Motown
4	**Give Out But Don't Give Up**	
	Primal Scream	Creation
5	**Miaow**	
	Beautiful South	Go! Discs
6	**Everybody Else Is Doing It...**	
	The Cranberries	Island
7	**Debut**	
	Bjork	One Little Indian
8	**Under The Pink**	
	Tori Amos	East West
9	**The Heart Of Chicago**	
	Chicago	Warner Bros
10	**Jewel**	
	Marcella Detroit	London
11	**Vauxhall And I**	
	Morrissey	Parlophone
12	**Permanent Shade Of Blue**	
	Roachford	Columbia
13	**Longing In Their Hearts**	
	Bonnie Raitt	Capitol
14	**Bat Out Of Hell II: Back Into Hell**	
	Meat Loaf	Virgin
15	**Ten Summoner's Tales**	
	Sting	A&M
16	**Superunknown**	
	Soundgarden	A&M
17	**August & Everything After**	
	Counting Crows	Geffen
18	**Keep The Faith**	
	Bon Jovi	Jambco/Mercury
19	**Hit The Highway**	
	The Proclaimers	Chrysalis
20	**So Far So Good**	
	Bryan Adams	A&M

119

indy albums

1	**Live Through This** Hole	City Slang
2	**Give Out But Don't Give Up** Primal Scream	Creation
3	**Take Dis** Credit To The Nation	One Little Indian
4	**S*M*A*S*H** S*M*A*S*H	Hi-Rise Recordings
5	**Debut** Bjork	One Little Indian

dance singles

1	**100% Pure Love** Crystal Waters	A&M
2	**Let The Music (Lift You Up)** Loveland Vs Darlene Lewis	KMS
3	**The Real Thing** Tony Di Bart	Cleveland City Blues
4	**Pressure** Drizabone	4th+Bway
5	**Bubble** Fluke	Circa

uk singles

1	**Everything Changes** Take That	RCA
2	**The Most Beautiful Girl In The World** Symbol /Prince	NPG
3	**Streets Of Philadelphia** Bruce Springsteen	Columbia
4	**Doop** Doop	Citybeat
5	**The Sign** Ace Of Base	Metronome/London
6	**The Real Thing** Toni Di Bart	Cleveland City
7	**I Like To Move It** Reel 2 Real/The Mad Stuntman	Positiva
8	**I'll Remember** Madonna	Maverick/Sire
9	**Rock My Heart** Haddaway	Logic/Arista
10	**U R The Best Thing** D:ream	FXU/Magnet

us singles

1	**Bump 'N' Grind** R. Kelly	Jive
2	**The Sign** Ace Of Base	Arista
3	**Without You/Never Forget You** Mariah Carey	Columbia
4	**Mmm Mmm Mmm Mmm** Crash Test Dummies	Arista
5	**So Much In Love** All-4-One	Blitzz
6	**The Most Beautiful Girl In The World** Symbol/Prince	NPG
7	**The Power Of Love** Celine Dion	550 Music
8	**Whatta Man** Salt-N-Pepa/En Vogue	Next Plateau
9	**Streets Of Philadelphia** Bruce Springsteen	Columbia
10	**Now And Forever** Richard Marx	Capitol

us albums

1	**The Division Bell** Pink Floyd	Columbia
2	**Above The Rim** Soundtrack	Death Row
3	**The Sign** Ace Of Base	Arista
4	**Longing In Their Hearts** Bonnie Raitt	Capitol
5	**August & Everything After** Counting Crows	DGC
6	**12 Play** R. Kelly	Jive
7	**Not A Moment Too Soon** Tim McGraw	Curb
8	**Live At The Acropolis** Yanni	Private Music
9	**Music Box** Mariah Carey	Columbia
10	**The Colour Of My Love** Celine Dion	550 Music
11	**God Shuffled His Feet** Crash Test Dummies	Arista
12	**Chant** Benedictine Monks	Angel
13	**The Cross Of Changes** Enigma	Charisma
14	**Toni Braxton** Toni Braxton	LaFace
15	**Superunknown** Soundgarden	A&M
16	**Very Necessary** Salt-N-Pepa	Next Plateau
17	**Doggy Style** Snoop Doggy Dogg	Death Row
18	**Siamese Dream** Smashing Pumpkins	Virgin
19	**Far Beyond Driven** Pantera	EastWest
20	**Mellow Gold** Beck	DGC

uk virgin Crunchie albums

1	**The Division Bell** Pink Floyd	EMI
2	**Our Town – The Greatest Hits** Deacon Blue	Columbia
3	**Crash! Boom! Bang!** Roxette	EMI
4	**The Very Best Of** Marvin Gaye	Motown
5	**Give Out But Don't Give Up** Primal Scream	Creation
6	**Miaow** Beautiful South	Go! Discs
7	**Everybody Else Is Doing It...** The Cranberries	Island
8	**Little Of The Past** Little Angels	Polydor
9	**Debut** Bjork	One Little Indian
10	**Nevermind** Nirvana	Geffen
11	**Under The Pink** Tori Amos	East West
12	**In Utero** Nirvana	Geffen
13	**Bat Out Of Hell II: Back Into Hell** Meat Loaf	Virgin
14	**Permanent Shade Of Blue** Roachford	Columbia
15	**Longing In Their Hearts** Bonnie Raitt	Capitol
16	**Jewel** Marcella Detroit	London
17	**In The Heart Of Chicago** Chicago	Warner Bros
18	**In Pieces** Garth Brooks	Liberty
19	**Vauxhall And I** Morrissey	Parlophone
20	**August & Everything After** Counting Crows	Geffen

uk singles

1	**The Most Beautiful Girl In The World** Symbol/Prince	NPG
2	**Everything Changes** Take That	RCA
3	**The Real Thing** Tony Di Bart	Cleveland City
4	**Always** Erasure	Mute
5	**Mmm Mmm Mmm Mmm** Crash Test Dummies	RCA
6	**Streets Of Philadelphia** Bruce Springsteen	Columbia
7	**I Like To Move It** Reel 2 Real/The Mad Stuntman	Positiva
8	**Dedicated To The One I Love** Bitty McLean	Brilliant Recordings
9	**Rock My Heart** Haddaway	Logic/Arista
10	**The Sign** Ace Of Base	Metronome/London

us singles

1	**Bump 'N' Grind** R. Kelly	Jive
2	**The Sign** Ace Of Base	Arista
3	**The Most Beautiful Girl In The World** *Prince*	NPG
4	**Without You/Never Forget You** Mariah Carey	Columbia
5	**Mmm Mmm Mmm Mmm** Crash Test Dummies	Arista
6	**The Power Of Love** Celine Dion	550 Music
7	**So Much In Love** All-4-One	Blitzz
8	**Now And Forever** Richard Marx	Capitol
9	**Return To Innocence** Enigma	Virgin
10	**Loser** Beck	DGC

indy albums

1	**Let Love In** Nick Cave & The Bad Seeds	Mute
2	**Live Through This** Hole	City Slang
3	**Give Out But Don't Give Up** Primal Scream	Creation
4	**Dun-Ya** Loop Guru	Nation
5	**Funalogue EP** Hardfloor	Harthouse

dance singles

1	**Hold That Sucker Down** O.T. Quartet	Cheeky
2	**100% Pure Love** Crystal Waters	A&M
3	**Forever And A Day** Brothers In Rhythm/Charvoni	Stress
4	**Light My Fire** Clubhouse	PWL Continental
5	**The Real Thing** Tony Di Bart	Cleveland City Blues

us albums

1	**The Division Bell** Pink Floyd	Columbia
2	**The Sign** Ace Of Base	Arista
3	**Above The Rim** Soundtrack	Death Row
4	**Not A Moment Too Soon** Tim McGraw	Curb
5	**August & Everything After** Counting Crows	DGC
6	**Chant** Benedictine Monks	Angel
7	**Longing In Their Hearts** Bonnie Raitt	Capitol
8	**12 Play** R. Kelly	Jive
9	**Music Box** Mariah Carey	Columbia
10	**The Colour Of My Love** Celine Dion	550 Music
11	**In Utero** Nirvana	DGC
12	**God Shuffled His Feet** Crash Test Dummies	Arista
13	**Toni Braxton** Toni Braxton	LaFace
14	**Live At The Acropolis** Yanni	Private Music
15	**The Cross Of Changes** Enigma	Charisma
16	**Superunknown** Soundgarden	A&M
17	**Siamese Dream** Smashing Pumpkins	Virgin
18	**Very Necessary** Salt-N-Pepa	Next Plateau
19	**Doggy Style** Snoop Doggy Dogg	Death Row
20	**Rhythm Country & Blues** Various Artists	MCA

uk virgin Crunchie albums

1	**The Division Bell** Pink Floyd	EMI
2	**Our Town – The Greatest Hits** Deacon Blue	Columbia
3	**The Very Best Of** Marvin Gaye	Motown
4	**Crash! Boom! Bang!** Roxette	EMI
5	**A Night In San Francisco** Van Morrison	Polydor
6	**His 'N' Hers** Pulp	Island
7	**Blues** Jimi Hendrix	Polydor
8	**Let Love In** Nick Cave & The Bad Seeds	Mute
9	**Everybody Else Is Doing It...** The Cranberries	Island
10	**How To Make Friends...** Terrorvision	Total Vegas
11	**Give Out But Don't Give Up** Primal Scream	Creation
12	**Automatic For The People** R.E.M.	Warner Bros
13	**Legend** Bob Marley & The Wailers	Tuff Gong
14	**Greatest Hits** Queen	Parlophone
15	**Nevermind** Nirvana	Geffen
16	**Miaow** Beautiful South	Go! Discs
17	**Stars** Simply Red	East West
18	**The Definitive...** Simon & Garfunkel	Columbia
19	**The Hits 2** Symbol/Prince	Paisley Park/Warner
20	**The Best Of Rod Stewart** Rod Stewart	Warner Bros

us albums

1	The Division Bell	Pink Floyd	Columbia
2	The Sign	Ace Of Base	Arista
3	Not A Moment Too Soon	Tim McGraw	Curb
4	Above The Rim	Soundtrack	Death Row
5	Chant	Benedictine Monks	Angel
6	August & Everything After	Counting Crows	DGC
7	12 Play	R. Kelly	Jive
8	Longing In Their Hearts	Bonnie Raitt	Capitol
9	God Shuffled His Feet	Crash Test Dummies	Arista
10	The Colour Of My Love	Celine Dion	550 Music
11	Music Box	Mariah Carey	Columbia
12	Illmatic	NAS	Columbia
13	Toni Braxton	Toni Braxton	LaFace
14	The Cross Of Changes	Enigma	Charisma
15	In Utero	Nirvana	DGC
16	Superunknown	Soundgarden	A&M
17	Siamese Dream	Smashing Pumpkins	Virgin
18	Live At The Acropolis	Yanni	Private Music
19	Doggy Style	Snoop Doggy Dogg	Death Row
20	Rhythm Country & Blues	Various Artists	MCA

uk singles

1	The Most Beautiful Girl In The World	Symbol/Prince	NPG
2	Mmm Mmm Mmm Mmm	Crash Test Dummies	RCA
3	The Real Thing	Tony Di Bart	Cleveland City
4	Always	Erasure	Mute
5	Sweets For My Sweet	CJ Lewis	Blackmarket/MCA
6	Dedicated To The One I Love	Bitty McLean	Brilliant Recordings
7	Everything Changes	Take That	RCA
8	I Like To Move It	Reel 2 Real/The Mad Stuntman	Positiva
9	Streets Of Philadelphia	Bruce Springsteen	Columbia
10	I'll Stand By You	The Pretenders	WEA

us singles

1	The Sign	Ace Of Base	Arista
2	Bump 'N' Grind	R. Kelly	Jive
3	The Most Beautiful Girl In The World	Symbol/Prince	NPG
4	Return To Innocence	Enigma	Virgin
5	Without You/Never Forget You	Mariah Carey	Columbia
6	Mmm Mmm Mmm Mmm	Crash Test Dummies	Arista
7	I'll Remember	Madonna	Maverick
8	Baby I Love Your Way	Big Mountain	RCA
9	The Power Of Love	Celine Dion	550 Music
10	Now And Forever	Richard Marx	Capitol

indy albums

1	Stacked Up	Senser	Ultimate
2	Anarchy	Chumbawamba	One Little Indian
3	Let Love In	Nick Cave & The Bad Seeds	Mute
4	Give Out But Don't Give Up	Primal Scream	Creation
5	Live Through This	Hole	City Slang

dance singles

1	Saturday Night Sunday Morning	T-Empo	Out On Vinyl
2	Reach	Judy Cheeks	Positiva
3	Rockin' For Myself	Motiv 8	WEA
4	Bass Cadet EP	Autechre	Warp
5	Hold That Sucker Down	O.T. Quartet	Cheeky

blur

uk virgin Crunchie albums

1	Parklife	Blur	Food
2	The Division Bell	Pink Floyd	EMI
3	Our Town – The Greatest Hits	Deacon Blue	Columbia
4	The Very Best Of	Marvin Gaye	Motown
5	Everybody Else Is Doing It...	The Cranberries	Island
6	Automatic For The People	R.E.M.	Warner Bros
7	Legend	Bob Marley & The Wailers	Tuff Gong
8	Crash! Boom! Bang!	Roxette	EMI
9	Stars	Simply Red	East West
10	Greatest Hits	Queen	Parlophone
11	The Immaculate Collection	Madonna	Sire
12	The Best Of Rod Stewart	Rod Stewart	Warner Bros
13	Wild Wood	Paul Weller	Go! Discs
14	The Definitive...	Simon & Garfunkel	Columbia
15	A Night In San Francisco	Van Morrison	Polydor
16	Anarchy	Chumbawumba	One Little Indian
17	Shepherd Moons	Enya	WEA
18	Blues	Jimi Hendrix	Polydor
19	Nevermind	Nirvana	Geffen
20	Give Out But Don't Give Up	Primal Scream	Creation

us albums

1	The Division Bell	Pink Floyd	Columbia
2	Not A Moment Too Soon	Tim McGraw	Curb
3	The Sign	Ace Of Base	Arista
4	Chant	Benedictine Monks	Angel
5	Read My Mind	Reba McEntire	MCA
6	August & Everything After	Counting Crows	DGC
7	Above The Rim	Soundtrack	Death Row
8	12 Play	R. Kelly	Jive
9	The Cross Of Changes	Enigma	Charisma
10	Longing In Their Hearts	Bonnie Raitt	Capitol
11	Toni Braxton	Toni Braxton	LaFace
12	The Colour Of My Love	Celine Dion	550 Music
13	Music Box	Mariah Carey	Columbia
14	God Shuffled His Feet	Crash Test Dummies	Arista
15	Siamese Dream	Smashing Pumpkins	Virgin
16	Superunknown	Soundgarden	A&M
17	In Utero	Nirvana	DGC
18	Live At The Acropolis	Yanni	Private Music
19	Doggy Style	Snoop Doggy Dogg	Death Row
20	Southernplayalisticadillacmuz	Outkast	LaFace

uk singles

1	The Real Thing	Tony Di Bart	Cleveland City Blues
2	The Most Beautiful Girl In The World	Symbol/Prince	NPG
3	Sweets For My Sweet	CJ Lewis	Blackmarket/MCA
4	Mmm Mmm Mmm Mmm	Crash Test Dummies	RCA
5	Inside	Stiltskin	White Water
6	Always	Erasure	Mute
7	Light My Fire	Clubhouse/Carl	PWL
8	Come On You Reds	Manchester Utd Football Squad	PolyGram TV
9	Dedicated To The One I Love	Bitty McLean	Brilliant Recordings
10	I Like To Move It	Reel 2 Real/The Mad Stuntman	Positiva

us singles

1	The Sign	Ace Of Base	Arista
2	Bump N' Grind	R. Kelly	Jive
3	The Most Beautiful Girl In The World	Symbol/Prince	NPG
4	I'll Remember	Madonna	Maverick
5	Return To Innocence	Enigma	Virgin
6	Baby I Love Your Way	Big Mountain	RCA
7	Mmm Mmm Mmm Mmm	Crash Test Dummies	Arista
8	I Swear	All-4-One	Blitzz
9	Without You/Never Forget You	Mariah Carey	Columbia
10	I'm Ready	Tevin Campbell	Qwest

indy albums

1	Stacked Up	Senser	Ultimate
2	Anarchy	Chumbawamba	One Little Indian
3	Give Out But Don't Give Up	Primal Scream	Creation
4	XC-NN 4	XC-NN	Transglobal
5	Let Love In	Nick Cave & The Bad Seeds	Mute

dance singles

1	Rockin' For Myself	Motiv 8	WEA
2	Carry Me Home	Gloworm	Go.Beat
3	My Love/Reminisce	Mary J. Blige	MCA
4	Saturday Night Sunday Morning	T-Empo	Out On Vinyl/ffrr
5	Reach	Judy Cheeks	Positiva

uk virgin Crunchie albums

1	Our Town – The Greatest Hits	Deacon Blue	Columbia
2	God Shuffled His Feet	Crash Test Dummies	RCA
3	Parklife	Blur	Food
4	The Division Bell	Pink Floyd	EMI
5	Everybody Else Is Doing It...	The Cranberries	Island
6	Skin	Skin	Parlophone
7	The Very Best Of...	Marvin Gaye	Motown
8	Automatic For The People	R.E.M.	Warner Bros
9	Greatest Hits	Queen	Parlophone
10	Legend	Bob Marley & The Wailers	Tuff Gong
11	The Best Of Rod Stewart	Rod Stewart	Warner Bros
12	Stars	Simply Red	East West
13	The Definitive...	Simon And Garfunkel	Columbia
14	The Immaculate Collection	Madonna	Sire
15	Nevermind	Nirvana	Geffen
16	Shepherd Moons	Enya	WEA
17	The Hits 2	Symbol/Prince	Paisley Park/Warner
18	End Of Part 1 – Greatest Hits	Wet Wet Wet	Precious Organisation
19	Crash! Boom! Bang!	Roxette	EMI
20	The Hits 1	Symbol/Prince	Paisley Park/Warner

May'94

uk virgin Crunchie albums

1	**Our Town – The Greatest Hits** Deacon Blue	Columbia
2	**God Shuffled His Feet** Crash Test Dummies	RCA
3	**The Division Bell** Pink Floyd	EMI
4	**Everybody Else Is Doing It...** The Cranberries	Island
5	**Parklife** Blur	Food
6	**Last Of The Independents** The Pretenders	WEA
7	**I Ain't Movin'** Des'ree	Sony S2
8	**The Best Of The Eagles** The Eagles	Elektra
9	**Legend** Bob Marley & The Wailers	Tuff Gong
10	**Nevermind** Nirvana	Geffen
11	**The Very Best Of** Marvin Gaye	Motown
12	**Falling Forward** Julia Fordham	Circa
13	**Greatest Hits** Queen	Parlophone
14	**The Definitive...** Simon And Garfunkel	Columbia
15	**Automatic For The People** R.E.M.	Warner Bros
16	**Now I'm A Cowboy** Auteurs	Virgin
17	**August & Everything After** Counting Crows	Geffen
18	**Far From Home** Traffic	Virgin
19	**Crash! Boom! Bang!** Roxette	EMI
20	**End Of Par 1 – Greatest Hits** Wet Wet Wet	Precious Organisation

us albums

1	**Not A Moment Too Soon** Tim McGraw	Curb
2	**Read My Mind** Reba McEntire	MCA
3	**The Sign** Ace Of Base	Arista
4	**The Division Bell** Pink Floyd	Columbia
5	**Chant** Benedictine Monks	Angel
6	**August & Everything After** Counting Crows	DGC
7	**Above The Rim** Soundtrack	Death Row
8	**12 Play** R. Kelly	Jive
9	**Longing In Their Hearts** Bonnie Raitt	Capitol
10	**Toni Braxton** Toni Braxton	LaFace
11	**The Colour Of My Love** Celine Dion	550 Music
12	**The Cross Of Changes** Enigma	Charisma
13	**Music Box** Mariah Carey	Columbia
14	**Live At The Acropolis** Yanni	Private Music
15	**The Crow** Soundtrack	Interscope
16	**Siamese Dream** Smashing Pumpkins	Virgin
17	**God Shuffled His Feet** Crash Test Dummies	Arista
18	**Superunknown** Soundgarden	A&M
19	**Kickin' It Up** John Michael Montgo	Atlantic
20	**All-4-One** All-4-One	Blitzz

uk singles

1	**Inside** Stiltskin	White Water
2	**Come On You Reds** Manchester Utd Football Squad	PolyGram TV
3	**The Real Thing** Tony Di Bart	Cleveland City Blues
4	**Sweets For My Sweet** CJ Lewis	Blackmarket/MCA
5	**Mmm Mmm Mmm Mmm** Crash Test Dummies	RCA
6	**The Most Beautiful Girl In The World** Symbol/Prince	NPG
7	**Around The World** East 17	London
8	**Light My Fire** Clubhouse/Carl	PWL
9	**Just A Step From Heaven** Eternal	EMI
10	**Always** Erasure	Mute

us singles

1	**I Swear** All-4-One	Blitzz
2	**The Sign** Ace Of Base	Arista
3	**I'll Remember** Madonna	Maverick
4	**The Most Beautiful Girl In The World** Symbol/Prince	NPG
5	**Bump N' Grind** R. Kelly	Jive
6	**Baby I Love Your Way** Big Mountain	RCA
7	**Return To Innocence** Enigma	Virgin
8	**Mmm Mmm Mmm Mmm** Crash Test Dummies	Arista
9	**I'm Ready** Tevin Campbell	Qwest
10	**You Mean The World To Me** Toni Braxton	LaPlace

indy albums

1	**Stacked Up** Senser	Ultimate
2	**Fear, Emptiness, Despair** Napalm Death	Earache
3	**Anarchy** Chumbawamba	One Little Indian
4	**The White Birch** Codeine	Sub Pop
5	**Give Out But Don't Give Up** Primal Scream	Creation

dance singles

1	**The Rhythm** Clock	Media/MCA
2	**When A Man Loves A Woman** Jody Watley	MCA
3	**My Love/Reminisce** Mary J. Blige	MCA
4	**Back In My Life** Joe Roberts	ffrr
5	**Get-A-Way** Maxx	Pulse 8

erasure

uk virgin Crunchie albums

1	**Our Town – The Greatest Hits** Deacon Blue	Columbia
2	**Everybody Else Is Doing It...** The Cranberries	Island
3	**This Way Up** Chris De Burgh	A&M
4	**The Division Bell** Pink Floyd	EMI
5	**God Shuffled His Feet** Crash Test Dummies	RCA
6	**Parklife** Blur	Food
7	**Last Of The Independents** The Pretenders	WEA
8	**Take Me To God** Jah Wobble's Invaders	Island
9	**The Very Best Of** Marvin Gaye	Motown
10	**Legend** Bob Marley & The Wailers	Tuff Gong
11	**End Of Part 1 – Greatest Hits** Wet Wet Wet	Precious Organisation
12	**I Ain't Movin'** Des'ree	Sony S2
13	**The Best Of The Eagles** The Eagles	Elektra
14	**Automatic For The People** R.E.M.	Warner Bros
15	**The Definitive...** Simon And Garfunkel	Columbia
16	**Greatest Hits** Queen	Parlophone
17	**Nevermind** Nirvana	Geffen
18	**The Hits 2** Symbol/Prince	Paisley Park/Warner
19	**Stars** Simply Red	East West
20	**Crash! Boom! Bang!** Roxette	EMI

us albums

1	**Not A Moment Too Soon** Tim McGraw	Curb
2	**Read My Mind** Reba McEntire	MCA
3	**The Sign** Ace Of Base	Arista
4	**The Division Bell** Pink Floyd	Columbia
5	**Chant** Benedictine Monks	Angel
6	**August & Everything After** Counting Crows	DGC
7	**Above The Rim** Soundtrack	Death Row
8	**12 Play** R. Kelly	Jive
9	**Longing In Their Hearts** Bonnie Raitt	Capitol
10	**Toni Braxton** Toni Braxton	LaFace
11	**The Colour Of My Love** Celine Dion	550 Music
12	**The Cross Of Changes** Enigma	Charisma
13	**Music Box** Mariah Carey	Columbia
14	**Live At The Acropolis** Yanni	Private Music
15	**The Crow** Soundtrack	Interscope
16	**Siamese Dream** Smashing Pumpkins	Virgin
17	**God Shuffled His Feet** Crash Test Dummies	Arista
18	**Superunknown** Soundgarden	A&M
19	**Kickin' It Up** John Michael Montgo	Atlantic
20	**All-4-One** All-4-One	Blitzz

uk singles

1	**Come On You Reds** Manchester Utd Football Squad	PolyGram TV
2	**Inside** Stiltskin	White Water
3	**Around The World** East 17	London
4	**Love Is All Around** Wet Wet Wet	Precious Organisation
5	**Sweets For My Sweet** CJ Lewis	Blackmarket/MCA
6	**The Real Thing** Tony Di Bart	Cleveland City Blues
7	**Mmm Mmm Mmm Mmm** Crash Test Dummies	RCA
8	**Just A Step From Heaven** Eternal	EMI
9	**The Real Thing** 2 Unlimited	PWL Continental
10	**More To This World** Bad Boys Inc	A&M

us singles

1	**I Swear** All-4-One	Blitzz
2	**I'll Remember** Madonna	Maverick
3	**The Sign** Ace Of Base	Arista
4	**The Most Beautiful Girl In The World** Symbol/Prince	NPG
5	**Return To Innocence** Enigma	Virgin
6	**Baby I Love Your Way** Big Mountain	RCA
7	**You Mean The World To Me** Toni Braxton	LaPlace
8	**Bump N' Grind** R. Kelly	Jive
9	**I'm Ready** Tevin Campbell	Qwest
10	**Back & Forth** Aaliyah	Background

indy albums

1	**I Say I Say I Say** Erasure	Mute
2	**Stacked Up** Senser	Ultimate
3	**Give Out But Don't Give Up** Primal Scream	Creation
4	**Let Love In** Nick Cave & The Bad Seeds	Mute
5	**Anarchy** Chumbawamba	One Little Indian

dance singles

1	**What You're Missing** K-Klass	Parlophone/Decon.
2	**Mama Said** Carleen Anderson	Circa
3	**Long Time Gone** Galliano	Talkin Loud
4	**Saturday Night Party** Alex Party	Cleveland City Imports
5	**The Rhythm** Clock	Media/MCA

indy albums

1	**Teenager Of The Year** Frank Black	4AD
2	**I Say I Say I Say** Erasure	Mute
3	**Stacked Up** Senser	Ultimate
4	**Anarchy** Chumbawamba	One Little Indian
5	**Debut** Bjork	One Little Indian

dance singles

1	**Swamp Thing** The Grid	Deconstruction
2	**Testament 4** Chubby Chunks Volume 2	Cleveland City
3	**Don't Go '94** Awesome 3	Citybeat
4	**Shoop** Salt 'N' Pepa	ffrr
4	**No Good (Start The Dance)** The Prodigy	XL Recordings

uk singles

1	**Come On You Reds** Manchester Utd Football Squad	PolyGram TV
2	**Love Is All Around** Wet Wet Wet	Precious Organisation
3	**Around The World** East 17	London
4	**Inside** Stiltskin	White Water
5	**Get-A-Way** Maxx	Pulse-8
6	**The Real Thing** 2 Unlimited	PWL Continental
7	**Sweets For My Sweet** CJ Lewis	Blackmarket/MCA
8	**More To This World** Bad Boys Inc	A&M
9	**No Good (Start The Dance)** The Prodigy	XL Recordings
10	**Just A Step From Heaven** Eternal	EMI

us singles

1	**I Swear** All-4-One	Blitzz
2	**I'll Remember** Madonna	Maverick
3	**The Sign** Ace Of Base	Arista
4	**Return To Innocence** Enigma	Virgin
5	**The Most Beautiful Girl In The World** Symbol/Prince	NPG
6	**Baby I Love Your Way** Big Mountain	RCA
7	**Don't Turn Around** Ace Of Base	Arista
8	**Regulate** Warren G /Nate Dogg	Death Row
9	**You Mean The World To Me** Toni Braxton	LaPlace
10	**Back & Forth** Aaliyah	Blackground

us albums

1	**The Crow** Soundtrack	Interscope
2	**Not A Moment Too Soon** Tim McGraw	Curb
3	**The Sign** Ace Of Base	Arista
4	**Chant** Benedictine Monks	Angel
5	**Above The Rim** Soundtrack	Death Row
6	**August & Everything After** Counting Crows	DGC
7	**The Division Bell** Pink Floyd	Columbia
8	**12 Play** R. Kelly	Jive
9	**Read My Mind** Reba McEntire	MCA
10	**All-4-One** All-4-One	Blitzz
11	**Swamp Ophelia** Indigo Girls	Epic
12	**Toni Braxton** Toni Braxton	LaFace
13	**Music Box** Mariah Carey	Columbia
14	**The Cross Of Changes** Enigma	Charisma
15	**Live At The Acropolis** Yanni	Private Music
16	**The Colour Of My Love** Celine Dion	550 Music
17	**Siamese Dream** Smashing Pumpkins	Virgin
18	**I Say, I Say, I Say** Erasure	Mute
19	**Superunknown** Soundgarden	A&M
20	**Ten Feet Tall & Bulletproof** Travis Tritt	Warner Bros

uk virgin Crunchie albums

1	**Seal** Seal	ZTT
2	**Our Town – The Greatest Hits** Deacon Blue	Columbia
3	**Everybody Else Is Doing It...** The Cranberries	Island
4	**The Division Bell** Pink Floyd	EMI
5	**Parklife** Blur	Food
6	**This Way Up** Chris De Burgh	A&M
7	**God Shuffled His Feet** Crash Test Dummies	RCA
8	**Street Angel** Stevie Nicks	EMI
9	**End Of Part One – Their Greatest Hits** Wet Wet Wet	Precious Organisation
10	**The Very Best Of** Marvin Gaye	Motown
11	**Teenager Of The Year** Frank Black	4AD
12	**Legend** Bob Marley & The Wailers	Tuff Gong
13	**Last Of The Independents** The Pretenders	WEA
14	**The Eagles** The Eagles	Asylum
15	**Automatic For The People** R.E.M.	Warner Bros
16	**The Definitive...** Simon And Garfunkel	Columbia
17	**Take Me To God** Jah Wobble's Invaders Of Heart	Island
18	**Nevermind** Nirvana	Geffen
19	**Crash! Boom! Bang!** Roxette	EMI
20	**Miaow** Beautiful South	Go! Discs

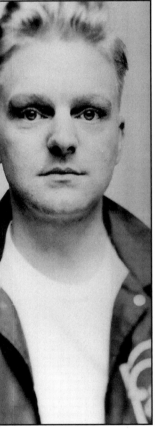

indy albums

1	**Suits** Fish	Dick Bros
2	**Teenager Of The Year** Frank Black	4AD
3	**I Say I Say I Say** Erasure	Mute
4	**Stacked Up** Senser	Ultimate
5	**Give Out But Don't Give Up** Primal Scream	Creation

dance singles

1	**You Don't Love Me (No, No, No)** Dawn Penn	Big Beat
2	**Swamp Thing** The Grid	Deconstruction
3	**Back To Love** Brand New Heavies	ffrr
4	**Anything** SWV	RCA
5	**No More Tears (Enough Is Enough)** Kym Mazelle & Jocelyn Brown	Bell

uk singles

1	**Love Is All Around** Wet Wet Wet	Precious Organisation
2	**Come On You Reds** Manchester Utd Football Squad	PolyGram TV
3	**Around The World** East 17	London
4	**Get-A-Way** Maxx	Pulse-8
5	**No Good (Start The Dance)** The Prodigy	XL Recordings
6	**Inside** Stiltskin	White Water
7	**Baby, I Love Your Way** Big Mountain	RCA
8	**Sweets For My Sweet** CJ Lewis	Blackmarket/MCA
9	**Carry Me Home** Gloworm	Go.Beat
10	**The Real Thing** 2 Unlimited	PWL Continental

us singles

1	**I Swear** All-4-One	Blitzz
2	**I'll Remember** Madonna	Maverick
3	**Any Time, Any Place** Janet Jackson	Virgin
4	**Regulate** Warren G /Nate Dogg	Death Row
5	**The Sign** Ace Of Base	Arista
6	**Don' Turn Around** Ace Of Base	Arista
7	**Baby I Love Your Way** Big Mountain	RCA
8	**The Most Beautiful Girl In The World** Symbol/Prince	NPG
9	**You Mean The World To Me** Toni Braxton	LaFace
10	**Back & Forth** Aaliyah	Blackground

us albums

1	**The Sign** Ace Of Base	Arista
2	**The Crow** Soundtrack	Interscope
3	**Not A Moment Too Soon** Tim McGraw	Curb
4	**Chant** Benedictine Monks	Angel
5	**Fruitcakes** Jimmy Buffett	Margaritaville
6	**August & Everything After** Counting Crows	DGC
7	**Above The Rim** Soundtrack	Death Row
8	**The Division Bell** Pink Floyd	Columbia
9	**12 Play** R. Kelly	Jive
10	**All-4-One** All-4-One	Blitzz
11	**Nuttin' But Love** Heavy D &The Boyz	Uptown
12	**Toni Braxton** Toni Braxton	LaFace
13	**Music Box** Mariah Carey	Columbia
14	**Swamp Ophelia** Indigo Girls	Epic
15	**The Cross Of Changes** Enigma	Charisma
16	**Superunknown** Soundgarden	A&M
17	**The Colour Of My Love** Celine Dion	550 Music
18	**Read My Mind** Reba McEntire	MCA
19	**Siamese Dream** Smashing Pumpkins	Virgin
20	**Live At The Acropolis** Yanni	Private Music

uk virgin Crunchie albums

1	**Seal** Seal	ZTT
2	**Everybody Else Is Doing It...** The Cranberries	Island
3	**Our Town – Greatest Hits** Deacon Blue	Columbia
4	**The Division Bell** Pink Floyd	EMI
5	**The Plot Thickens** Galliano	Talkin Loud
6	**Parklife** Blur	Food
7	**God Shuffled His Feet** Crash Test Dummies	RCA
8	**End Of Part One – Their Greatest Hits** Wet Wet Wet	Precious Organisation
9	**This Way Up** Chris De Burgh	A&M
10	**Suits** Fish	Dick Bros
11	**Legend** Bob Marley & The Wailers	Tuff Gong
12	**The Eagles** The Eagles	Asylum
13	**Crash! Boom! Bang!** Roxette	EMI
14	**Nevermind** Nirvana	Geffen
15	**Miaow** Beautiful South	Go! Discs
16	**Automatic For The People** R.E.M.	Warner Bros
17	**Bat Out Of Hell II: Back Into Hell** Meat Loaf	Virgin
18	**The Very Best Of** Marvin Gaye	Motown
19	**The Definitive...** Simon And Garfunkel	Columbia
20	**Stars** Simply Red	East West

June'94:29th May–4th June

indy albums

1	**Give Out But Don't Give Up** Primal Scream	Creation
2	**Suits** Fish	Dick Bros
3	**Teenager Of The Year** Frank Black	4AD
4	**I Say I Say I Say** Erasure	Mute
5	**Stacked Up** Senser	Ultimate

dance singles

1	**Crayzy Man** Blast	MCA
2	**Throb/Any Time, Any Place** Janet Jackson	Virgin
3	**Swamp Thing** The Grid	Deconstruction
4	**You Don't Love Me (No, No, No)** Dawn Penn	Big Beat
5	**Harmonica Man** Bravado	Peach/PWL

beastie boys

uk singles

1	**Love Is All Around** Wet Wet Wet	Precious Organisation
2	**Baby, I Love Your Way** Big Mountain	RCA
3	**Come On You Reds** Manchester Utd. Football Squad	PolyGram TV
4	**Get-A-Way** Maxx	Pulse-8
5	**Around The World** East 17	London
6	**No Good (Start The Dance)** The Prodigy	XL Recordings
7	**Absolutely Fabulous** Absolutely Fabulous	Spaghetti/Parlophone
8	**Inside** Stiltskin	White Water
9	**You Don't Love me (No, No, No)** Dawn Penn	Big Beat/Atlantic
10	**Since I Don't Have You** Guns N' Roses	Geffen

us singles

1	**I Swear** All-4-One	Blitzz
2	**I'll Remember** Madonna	Maverick
3	**Any Time, Any Place** Janet Jackson	Virgin
4	**Don't Turn Around** Ace Of Base	Arista
5	**Regulate** Warren G / Nate Dog	Death Row
6	**Back & Forth** Aaliyah	Blackground
7	**You Mean The World To Me** Ace Of Base	Arista
8	**The Sign** Ace Of Base	Arista
9	**Baby I Love Your Way** Big Mountain	RCA
10	**The Most Beautiful Girl In The World** Symbol/Prince	NPG

uk singles

1	**Love Is All Around** Wet Wet Wet	Precious Organisation
2	**Baby, I Love Your Way** Big Mountain	RCA
3	**You Don't Love Me (No, No, No)** Dawn Penn	Big Beat/Atlantic
4	**No Good (Start The Dance)** The Prodigy	XL Recordings
5	**Get-A-Way** Maxx	Pulse-8
6	**Absolutely Fabulous** Absolutely Fabulous	Spaghetti/Parlophone
7	**Don't Turn Around** Ace Of Base	Metronome/London
8	**Swamp Thing** The Grid	Deconstruction/RCA
9	**Anytime You Need A Friend** Mariah Carey	Columbia
10	**Come On You Reds** Manchester Utd. Football Squad	PolyGram TV

us singles

1	**I Swear** All-4-One	Blitzz
2	**Any Time, Any Place** Janet Jackson	Virgin
3	**Regulate** Warren G / Nate Dogg	Death Row
4	**Don't Turn Around** Ace Of Base	Arista
5	**I'll Remember** Madonna	Maverick
6	**Back & Forth** Aaliyah	Blackground
7	**You Mean The World To Me** Ace Of Base	Arista
8	**The Sign** Ace Of Base	Arista
9	**Baby I Love Your Way** Big Mountain	RCA
10	**Stay (I Missed You)** Lisa Loeb & Nine St	RCA

indy albums

1	**Implant** Eat Static	Planet Dog
2	**Split** Lush	4AD
3	**Give Out But Don't Give Up** Primal Scream	Creation
4	**Aaah! EP** Sun Electric	R&S
5	**Are You Satisfied?** Daou	Tribal UK

dance singles

1	**Feel What You Want** Kristine W	Champion
2	**Do You Want It Right Now** Degrees Of Motion	ffrr
3	**Two Can Play That Game** Bobby Brown	MCA
4	**Dark & Long** Underworld	Junior Boy's Own
5	**Crayzy Man** Blast/VDC	MCA

us albums

1	**III Communication** Beastie Boys	Capitol
2	**The Sign** Ace Of Base	Arista
3	**The Crow** Soundtrack	Interscope
4	**Not A Moment Too Soon** Tim McGraw	Curb
5	**Above The Rim** Soundtrack	Death Row
6	**August & Everything After** Counting Crows	DGC
7	**Chant** Benedictine Monks	Angel
8	**The Division Bell** Pink Floyd	Columbia
9	**Fruitcakes** Jimmy Buffett	Margaritaville
10	**All-4-One** All-4-One	Blitzz
11	**12 Play** R. Kelly	Jive
12	**Toni Braxton** Toni Braxton	LaFace
13	**The Lion King** Soundtrack	Walt Disney
14	**Nuttin' But Love** Heavy D &The Boyz	Uptown
15	**Superunknown** Soundgarden	A&M
16	**Music Box** Mariah Carey	Columbia
17	**Live At The Acropolis** Yanni	Private Music
18	**Age Ain't Nothing But A Number** Aaliyah	Blackground
19	**Hints, Allegations & Things...** Collective Soul	Atlantic
20	**Seal** Seal	ZTT

us albums

1	**Purple** Stone Temple Pilots	Atlantic
2	**Regulate** Warren G/Nate Dogg	Violator
3	**The Sign** Ace Of Base	Arista
4	**III Communication** Beastie Boys	Capitol
5	**Not A Moment Too Soon** Tim McGraw	Curb
6	**The Crow** Soundtrack	Interscope
7	**Walk On** Boston	MCA
8	**Above The Rim** Soundtrack	Death Row
9	**August & Everything After** Counting Crows	DGC
10	**When Love Finds You** Vince Gill	MCA
11	**The Division Bell** Pink Floyd	Columbia
12	**All-4-One** All-4-One	Blitzz
13	**Chant** Benedictine Monks	Angel
14	**The Lion King** Soundtrack	Walt Disney
15	**Fruitcakes** Jimmy Buffett	Margaritaville
16	**Toni Braxton** Toni Braxton	LaFace
17	**12 Play** R. Kelly	Jive
18	**Live At The Acropolis** Yanni	Private Music
19	**Hints, Allegations & Things...** Collective Soul	Atlantic
20	**Superunknown** Soundgarden	A&M

uk virgin Crunchie albums

1	**Everybody Else Is Doing It...** The Cranberries	Island
2	**Our Town – Greatest Hits** Deacon Blue	Columbia
3	**Seal** Seal	ZTT
4	**The Last Temptation** Alice Cooper	Epic
5	**The Division Bell** Pink Floyd	EMI
6	**Around The Next Dream** BBM	Virgin
7	**Purple** Stone Temple Pilots	Atlantic
8	**Parklife** Blur	Food
9	**The Plot Thickens** Galliano	Talkin Loud
10	**Balls To Picasso** Bruce Dickinson	EMI
11	**God Shuffled His Feet** Crash Test Dummies	RCA
12	**End Of Part One – Their Greatest Hits** Wet Wet Wet	Precious Organisation
13	**Miaow** Beautiful South	Go! Discs
14	**This Way Up** Chris De Burgh	A&M
15	**Legend** Bob Marley & The Wailers	Tuff Gong
16	**Woodface** Crowded House	Capitol
17	**Crash! Boom! Bang!** Roxette	EMI
18	**Without The Aid Of A Safety Net (Live)** Big Country	Compulsion
19	**The Eagles** The Eagles	Asylum
20	**The Very Best Of** Marvin Gaye	Motown

uk virgin Crunchie albums

1	**Everybody Else Is Doing It...** The Cranberries	Island
2	**Our Town – Greatest Hits** Deacon Blue	Columbia
3	**The Division Bell** Pink Floyd	EMI
4	**Seal** Seal	ZTT
5	**Parklife** Blur	Food
6	**Miaow** Beautiful South	Go! Discs
7	**Around The Next Dream** BBM	Virgin
8	**Crash! Boom! Bang!** Roxette	EMI
9	**The Last Temptation** Alice Cooper	Epic
10	**Split** Lush	4AD
11	**Amplified Heart** Everything But The Girl	Blanco Y Negro
12	**Purple** Stone Temple Pilots	Atlantic
13	**Woodface** Crowded House	Capitol
14	**God Shuffled His Feet** Crash Test Dummies	RCA
15	**This Way Up** Chris De Burgh	A&M
16	**The Plot Thickens** Galliano	Talkin Loud
17	**Bat Out Of Hell II: Back Into Hell** Meat Loaf	Virgin
18	**End Of Part One – Their Greatest Hits** Wet Wet Wet	Precious Organisation
19	**Nevermind** Nirvana	Geffen
20	**Together Alone** Crowded House	Capitol

us albums

1. **Purple** — Stone Temple Pilots — Atlantic
2. **The Sign** — Ace Of Base — Arista
3. **Regulate** — Warren G/Nate Dogg — Violator
4. **Not A Moment Too Soon** — Tim McGraw — Curb
5. **The Lion King** — Soundtrack — Walt Disney
6. **When Love Finds You** — Vince Gill — MCA
7. **August & Everything After** — Counting Crows — DGC
8. **The Crow** — Soundtrack — Interscope
9. **Above The Rim** — Soundtrack — Death Row
10. **Ill Communication** — Beastie Boys — Capitol
11. **All-4-One** — All-4-One — Blitzz
12. **Chant** — Benedictine Monks — Angel
13. **Walk On** — Boston — MCA
14. **The Division Bell** — Pink Floyd — Columbia
15. **Superunknown** — Soundgarden — A&M
16. **Live At The Acropolis** — Yanni — Private Music
17. **Fruitcakes** — Jimmy Buffett — Margaritaville
18. **Toni Braxton** — Toni Braxton — LaFace
19. **12 Play** — R. Kelly — Jive
20. **Hints, Allegations & Things...** — Collective Soul — Atlantic

uk singles

1. **Love Is All Around** — Wet Wet Wet — Precious Organisation
2. **Baby, I Love Your Way** — Big Mountain — RCA
3. **You Don't Love Me (No, No, No)** — Dawn Penn — Big Beat/Atlantic
4. **Swamp Thing** — The Grid — Deconstruction/RCA
5. **Don't Turn Around** — Ace Of Base — Metronome/London
6. **No Good (Start The Dance)** — The Prodigy — XL Recordings
7. **I Swear** — All-4-One — Atlantic
8. **Anytime You Need A Friend** — Mariah Carey — Columbia
9. **Get-A-Way** — Maxx — Pulse-8
10. **Absolutely Fabulous** — Absolutely Fabulous — Spaghetti/Parlophone

us singles

1. **I Swear** — All-4-One — Blitzz
2. **Regulate** — Warren G / Nate Dog — Death Row
3. **Any Time, Any Place** — Janet Jackson — Virgin
4. **Don't Turn Around** — Ace Of Base — Arista
5. **Back & Forth** — Aaliyah — Blackground
6. **I'll Remember** — Madonna — Maverick
7. **You Mean The World To Me** — Ace Of Base — Arista
8. **Stay (I Missed You)** — Lisa Loeb & Nine St — RCA
9. **Baby I Love Your Way** — Big Mountain — RCA
10. **If You Go** — Jon Secada — SBK

indy albums

1. **Carnival Of Light** — Ride — Creation
2. **Too Sussed** — These Animal Men — Hi-Rise Recordings
3. **Implant** — Eat Static — Planet Dog
4. **The Very Best Of** — Electric Light Orchestra — Dino
5. **Split** — Lush — 4AD

dance singles

1. **Caught In The Middle** — Juliet Roberts — Cooltempo
2. **Go On Move** — Reel 2 Real/The Mad Stuntman — Positiva
3. **Ain't Nobody (Loves Me Better)** — KWS and Gwen Dickey — X-clusive
4. **Body In Motion** — Atlantic Ocean — Eastern Bloc
5. **Swamp Thing** — The Grid — Deconstruction

spin doctors

uk virgin Crunchie albums

1. **Everybody Else Is Doing It...** — The Cranberries — Island
2. **Eddi Reader** — Eddi Reader — Blanco Y Negro
3. **Carnival Of Light** — Ride — Creation
4. **Our Town – Greatest Hits** — Deacon Blue — Columbia
5. **Parklife** — Blur — Food
6. **The Division Bell** — Pink Floyd — EMI
7. **The Very Best Of** — Electric Light Orchestra — Dino
8. **Seal** — Seal — ZTT
9. **Miaow** — Beautiful South — Go! Discs
10. **God Shuffled His Feet** — Crash Test Dummies — RCA
11. **Too Posh To Nosh, Too Good To Last!** — Little Angels — Essential
12. **The Last Temptation** — Alice Cooper — Epic
13. **Crash! Boom! Bang!** — Roxette — EMI
14. **Purple** — Stone Temple Pilots — Atlantic
15. **Nevermind** — Nirvana — Geffen
16. **Around The Next Dream** — BBM — Virgin
17. **Woodface** — Crowded House — Capitol
18. **Get A Grip** — Aerosmith — Geffen
19. **Amplified Heart** — Everything But The Girl — Blanco Y Negro
20. **Slippery When Wet** — Bon Jovi — Vertigo

us albums

1. **Purple** — Stone Temple Pilots — Atlantic
2. **The Lion King** — Soundtrack — Walt Disney
3. **The Sign** — Ace Of Base — Arista
4. **Regulate** — Warren G/Nate Dogg — Violator
5. **Not A Moment Too Soon** — Tim McGraw — Curb
6. **August & Everything After** — Counting Crows — DGC
7. **All-4-One** — All-4-One — Blitzz
8. **The Crow** — Soundtrack — Interscope
9. **When Love Finds You** — Vince Gill — MCA
10. **Above The Rim** — Soundtrack — Death Row
11. **Superunknown** — Soundgarden — A&M
12. **Ill Communication** — Beastie Boys — Capitol
13. **Dance Naked** — John Mellencamp — Mercury
14. **The Division Bell** — Pink Floyd — Columbia
15. **Chant** — Benedictine Monks — Angel
16. **Walk On** — Boston — MCA
17. **Toni Braxton** — Toni Braxton — LaFace
18. **Hints, Allegations & Things...** — Collective Soul — Atlantic
19. **Kiss My Ass: Classic Kiss Reg** — Various Artists — Mercury
20. **Candlebox** — Candlebox — Maverick

uk singles

1. **Love Is All Around** — Wet Wet Wet — Precious Organisation
2. **I Swear** — All-4-One — Atlantic
3. **Swamp Thing** — The Grid — Deconstruction/RCA
4. **Baby, I Love Your Way** — Big Country — RCA
5. **You Don't Love Me (No, No, No)** — Dawn Penn — Big Beat/Atlantic
6. **Don't Turn Around** — Ace Of Base — Metronome/London
7. **Go On Move** — Reel 2 Real — Strictly Rhythm/Positiva
8. **No Good (Start The Dance)** — The Prodigy — XL Recordings
9. **Shine** — Aswad — Bubblin'
10. **U & Mr** — Cappella — Internal Dance

us singles

1. **I Swear** — All-4-One — Blitzz
2. **Regulate** — Warren G / Nate Dogg — Death Row
3. **Any Time, Any Place** — Janet Jackson — Virgin
4. **Don't Turn Around** — Ace Of Base — Arista
5. **Stay (I Missed You)** — Lisa Loeb & Nine St. — RCA
6. **Back & Forth** — Aaliyah — Blackground
7. **I'll Remember** — Madonna — Maverick
8. **You Mean The World To Me** — Toni Braxton — LaFace
9. **Can You Feel The Love Tonight** — Elton John — Hollywood
10. **If You Go** — Jon Secada — SBK

indy albums

1. **Arborescence** — OzricTentacles — Dovetail
2. **Carnival Of Light** — Ride — Creation
3. **Implant** — Eat Static — Planet Dog
4. **Too Sussed** — These Animal Men — Hi-Rise Recordings
5. **90 Degrees And Rising** — Wayne Marshall — Soul Town

dance singles

1. **Everybody Gonfi-Gon** — Two Cowboys — Ffrreedom
2. **Someday** — Eddy — Positiva
3. **Rok Da House** — Tall Paul — Effective
4. **Caught In The Middle** — Juliet Roberts — Cooltempo
5. **Share My Life** — Inner City — Six6

uk virgin Crunchie albums

1. **Turn It Upside Down** — Spin Doctors — Epic
2. **The Very Best Of** — Electric Light Orchestra — Dino
3. **End Of Part One – Their Greatest Hits** — Wet Wet Wet — Precious Organisation
4. **Everybody Else Is Doing It...** — The Cranberries — Island
5. **Parklife** — Blur — Food
6. **Eddi Reader** — Eddi Reader — Blanco Y Negro
7. **Our Town – Greatest Hits** — Deacon Blue — Columbia
8. **Loudmouth – The Best Of** — Boomtown Rats & Bob Geldof — Vertigo
9. **The Division Bell** — Pink Floyd — EMI
10. **Seal** — Seal — ZTT
11. **Carnival Of Light** — Ride — Creation
12. **Miaow** — Beautiful South — Go! Discs
13. **God Shuffled His Feet** — Crash Test Dummies — RCA
14. **The Plot Thickens** — Galliano — Talkin Loud
15. **His 'N' Hers** — Pulp — Island
16. **Nevermind** — Nirvana — Geffen
17. **Get A Grip** — Aerosmith — Geffen
18. **Crash! Boom! Bang!** — Roxette — EMI
19. **How To Make Friends And Influence People** — Terrorvision — Total Vegas
20. **Woodface** — Crowded House — Capitol

uk virgin Crunchie albums

1	**End Of Part One – Their Greatest Hits** Wet Wet Wet	Precious Organisation
2	**Greatest Hits** Whitesnake	EMI
3	**The Very Best Of** Electric Light Orchestra	Dino
4	**Turn It Upside Down** Spin Doctors	Epic
5	**Everybody Else Is Doing It...** The Cranberries	Island
6	**Our Town – Greatest Hits** Deacon Blue	Columbia
7	**Parklife** Blur	Food
8	**Eddi Reader** Eddi Reader	Blanco Y Negro
9	**God Shuffled His Feet** Crash Test Dummies	RCA
10	**The Division Bell** Pink Floyd	EMI
11	**Seal** Seal	ZTT
12	**Loudmouth – The Best Of** Boomtown Rats & Bob Geldof	Vertigo
13	**Nevermind** Nirvana	Geffen
14	**Miaow** Beautiful South	Go! Discs
15	**Greatest Hits** The Troggs	PolyGram TV
16	**Head Like A Rock** Ian McNabb	This Way Up
17	**Get A Grip** Aerosmith	Geffen
18	**The Plot Thickens** Galliano	Talkin Loud
19	**How To Make Friends And Influence People** Terrorvision	Total Vegas
20	**Carnival Of Light** Ride	Creation

us albums

1	**The Lion King** Soundtrack	Walt Disney
2	**Purple** Stone Temple Pilots	Atlantic
3	**The Sign** Ace Of Base	Arista
4	**Regulate** Warren G/Nate Dogg	Violator
5	**Not A Moment Too Soon** Tim McGraw	Curb
6	**August & Everything After** Counting Crows	DGC
7	**Who I Am** Alan Jackson	Arista
8	**Get Up On It** Keith Sweat	Elektra
9	**All-4-One** All-4-One	Blitzz
10	**Superunknown** Soundgarden	A&M
11	**Above The Rim** Soundtrack	Death Row
12	**Same As it Ever Was** House Of Pain	Tommy Boy
13	**The Crow** Soundtrack	Interscope
14	**Funkdafied** Da Brat	So So Def
15	**Ill Communication** Beastie Boys	Capitol
16	**When Love Finds You** Vince Gill	MCA
17	**Candlebox** Candlebox	Maverick
18	**Dance Naked** John Mellencamp	Mercury
19	**Chant** Benedictine Monks	Angel
20	**Toni Braxton** Toni Braxton	LaFace

uk singles

1	**Love Is All Around** Wet Wet Wet	Precious Organisation
2	**I Swear** All-4-One	Atlantic
3	**Love Ain't Here Anymore** Take That	RCA
4	**Swamp Thing** The Grid	Deconstruction/RCA
5	**(Meet) The Flintstones** BC-52s	MCA
6	**Baby, I Love Your Way** Big Mountain	RCA
7	**Go On Move** Reel 2 Real	Strictly Rhythm/Positiva
8	**Word Up** Gun	A&M
9	**Shine** Aswad	Bubblin'
10	**You Don't Love Me (No, No, No)** Dawn Penn	Big Beat/Atlantic

us singles

1	**I Swear** All-4-One	Blitzz
2	**Regulate** Warren G /Nate Dogg	Death Row
3	**Any Time, Any Place** Janet Jackson	Virgin
4	**Stay (I Missed You)** Lisa Loeb & Nine St.	RCA
5	**Don't Turn Around** Ace Of Base	Arista
6	**Back & Forth** Aaliyah	Blackground
7	**Fantastic Voyage** Coolio	Tommy Boy
8	**Can You Feel The Love Tonight** Elton John	Hollywood
9	**Funkdafied** Da Brat	So So Def
10	**If You Go** Jon Secada	SBK

indy albums

1	**Autogeddon** Julian Cope	Echo Label
2	**The Very Best Of** Electric Light Orchestra	Dino
3	**Arborescence** Ozric Tentacles	Dovetail
4	**Carnival Of Light** Ride	Creation
5	**Implant** Eat Static	Planet Dog

dance singles

1	**Feenin'** Jodeci	MCA
2	**Turn It Up** DJ Duke	ffrr
3	**Terrorist/Something I Feel** Renegade/Ray Keith	Moving Shadow
4	**Everybody Gonfi-Gon** Two Cowboys	3 Beat/Ffrreedom
5	**Rok Da House** Tall Paul	Effective

rolling stones

uk virgin Crunchie albums

1	**Voodoo Lounge** The Rolling Stones	Virgin
2	**End Of Part One – Their Greatest Hits** Wet Wet Wet	Precious Organisation
3	**Greatest Hits** Whitesnake	EMI
4	**The Very Best Of** Electric Light Orchestra	Dino
5	**The Best Of The Eagles** The Eagles	Elektra
6	**Everybody Else Is Doing It...** The Cranberries	Island
7	**God Shuffled His Feet** Crash Test Dummies	RCA
8	**Our Town – Greatest Hits** Deacon Blue	Columbia
9	**Parklife** Blur	Food
10	**Turn It Upside Down** Spin Doctors	Epic
11	**The Division Bell** Pink Floyd	EMI
12	**Seal** Seal	ZTT
13	**Eddi Reader** Eddi Reader	Blanco Y Negro
14	**Nevermind** Nirvana	Geffen
15	**Greatest Hits** The Troggs	PolyGram TV
16	**Miaow** Beautiful South	Go! Discs
17	**Get A Grip** Aerosmith	Geffen
18	**The Plot Thickens** Galliano	Talkin Loud
19	**Last Of The Independents** The Pretenders	WEA
20	**Slippery When Wet** Bon Jovi	Vertigo

us albums

1	**The Lion King** Soundtrack	Walt Disney
2	**Purple** Stone Temple Pilots	Atlantic
3	**The Sign** Ace Of Base	Arista
4	**Regulate** Warren G/Nate Dogg	Violator
5	**Who I Am** Alan Jackson	Arista
6	**August & Everything After** Counting Crows	DGC
7	**Not A Moment Too Soon** Tim McGraw	Curb
8	**All-4-One** All-4-One	Blitzz
9	**Superunknown** Soundgarden	A&M
10	**Get Up On It** Keith Sweat	Elektra
11	**Funkdafied** Da Brat	So So Def
12	**Chant** Benedictine Monks	Angel
13	**Candlebox** Candlebox	Maverick
14	**Above The Rim** Soundtrack	Death Row
15	**Hints, Allegations & Things...** Collective Soul	Atlantic
16	**The Crow** Soundtrack	Interscope
17	**When Love Finds You** Vince Gill	MCA
18	**Ill Communication** Beastie Boys	Capitol
19	**Toni Braxton** Toni Braxton	LaFace
20	**Same As It Ever Was** House Of Pain	Tommy Boy

uk singles

1	**Love Is All Around** Wet Wet Wet	Precious Organisation
2	**I Swear** All-4-One	Atlantic
3	**Love Ain't Here Anymore** Take That	RCA
4	**(Meet) The Flintstones** BC-52s	MCA
5	**Swamp Thing** The Grid	Deconstruction/RCA
6	**Shine** Aswad	Bubblin'
7	**Everybody Gonfi-Gon** Two Cowboys	3 Beat/Ffrreedom
8	**Baby, I Love Your Way** Big Mountain	RCA
9	**Word Up** Gun	A&M
10	**Crazy For You** Let Loose	Mercury

us singles

1	**I Swear** All-4-One	Blitzz
2	**Stay (I Missed You)** Lisa Loeb & Nine St	RCA
3	**Regulate** Warren G /Nate Dogg	Death Row
4	**Any Time, Any Place** Janet Jackson	Virgin
5	**Don't Turn Around** Ace Of Base	Arista
6	**Fantastic Voyage** Coolio	Tommy Boy
7	**Can You Feel The Love Tonight** Elton John	Hollywood
8	**Back & Forth** Aaliyah	Blackground
9	**Funkdafied** Da Brat	So So Def
10	**If You Go** Jon Secada	SBK

indy albums

1	**The Very Best Of** Electric Light Orchestra	Dino
2	**Autogeddon** Julian Cope	Echo Label
3	**Stacked Up** Senser	Ultimate
4	**Carnival of Light** Ride	Creation
5	**90 Degrees And Rising** Wayne Marshall	Soul Town

dance singles

1	**U Girls** Nush	Blunted Vinyl
2	**Regulate** Warren G/Nate Dogg	Interscope
3	**More To Love** Volcano	Deconstruction
4	**Nite Life** Kim English	Hi Life/Polydor
5	**Casanova** Baby D	Production House

indy albums

1. **The Very Best Of** — Electric Light Orchestra — Dino
2. **Carnival Of Light** — Ride — Creation
3. **Autogeddon** — Julian Cope — Echo Label
4. **90 Degrees And Rising** — Wayne Marshall — Soul Town
5. **Implant** — Eat Static — Planet Dog

dance singles

1. **Rock 2 House/Hip Housin'** — X-Press 2/Lo-Pro — Junior Boy's Own
2. **Help My Friend** — Slo-Moshun — Six6
3. **Reachin'** — House Of Virginism — ffrr
4. **Regulate** — Warren G /Nate Dogg — Interscope
5. **More To Love** — Volcano — Deconstruction

indy albums

1. **Pandemonium** — Killing Joke — Butterfly
2. **76:14** — Global Communication — Dedicated
3. **The Very Best Of** — Electric Light Orchestra — Dino
4. **Implant** — Eat Static — Planet Dog
5. **I Say I Say I Say** — Erasure — Mute

dance singles

1. **Girls + Boys** — Hed Boys — Deconstruction
2. **Hot** — Ideal — Cleveland City
3. **Give Me Life** — Mr. V — Cheeky
4. **Rock 2 House/Hip Housin'** — X-Press 2/Lo-Pro — Junior Boy's Own
5. **Hit By Love** — Ce Ce Peniston — A&M

uk singles

1. **Love Is All Around** — Wet Wet Wet — Precious Organisation
2. **I Swear** — All-4-One — Atlantic
3. **(Meet) The Flintstones** — BC-52s — MCA
4. **Swamp Thing** — The Grid — Deconstruction/RCA
5. **Shine** — Aswad — Bubblin'
6. **Crazy For You** — Let Loose — Mercury
7. **Love Ain't Here Anymore** — Take That — RCA
8. **Eveybody Gonfi-Gon** — Two Cowboys — 3 Beat/Freedom
9. **Regulate** — Warren G/Nate Dogg — Death Row/Interscope
10. **Everything Is Alright (Uptight)** — CJ Lewis — Blackmarket/MCA

us singles

1. **I Swear** — All-4-One — Blitzz
2. **Stay (I Missed You)** — Lisa Loeb & Nine St — RCA
3. **Fantastic Voyage** — Coolio — Tommy Boy
4. **Any Time, Any Place** — Janet Jackson — Virgin
5. **Can You Feel The Love Tonight** — Elton John — Hollywood
6. **Regulate** — Warren G/Nate Dogg — Death Row
7. **Don't Turn Around** — Ace Of Base — Arista
8. **Funkdafied** — Da Brat — So So Def
9. **Back & Forth** — Aaliyah — Blackground
10. **Wild Night** — John Mellencamp With — Mercury

uk singles

1. **Love Is All Around** — Wet Wet Wet — Precious Organisation
2. **I Swear** — All-4-One — Atlantic
3. **(Meet) The Flintstones** — BC-52s — MCA
4. **Crazy For You** — Let Loose — Mercury
5. **Regulate** — Warren G / Nate Dogg — Death Row/Interscope
6. **Run To The Sun** — Erasure — Mute
7. **Searching** — China Black — Wild Card
8. **Shine** — Aswad — Bubblin'
9. **Swamp Thing** — The Grid — Deconstruction/RCA
10. **Everything Is Alright (Uptight)** — CJ Lewis — Blackmarket/MCA

us singles

1. **Stay (I Missed You)** — Lisa Loeb & Nine St — RCA
2. **I Swear** — All-4-One — Blitzz
3. **Fantastic Voyage** — Coolio — Tommy Boy
4. **Can You Feel The Love Tonight** — Elton John — Hollywood
5. **Any Time, Any Place** — Janet Jackson — Virgin
6. **Don't Turn Around** — Ace Of Base — Arista
7. **Regulate** — Warren G /Nate Dogg — Death Row
8. **Wild Night** — John Mellencamp With — Mercury
9. **Funkdafied** — Da Brat — So So Def
10. **Back & Forth** — Aaliyah — Blackground

us albums

1. **The Lion King** — Soundtrack — Walt Disney
2. **Voodoo Lounge** — The Rolling Stones — Virgin
3. **The Sign** — Ace Of Base — Arista
4. **Purple** — Stone Temple Pilots — Atlantic
5. **August & Everything After** — Counting Crows — DGC
6. **Regulate** — Warren G/Nate Dogg — Violator
7. **Forrest Gump** — Soundtrack — Epic Soundtrax
8. **Superunknown** — Soundgarden — A&M
9. **Not A Moment Too Soon** — Tim McGraw — Curb
10. **Who I Am** — Alan Jackson — Arista
11. **All-4-One** — All-4-One — Blitzz
12. **Chant** — Benedictine Monks — Angel
13. **Candlebox** — Candlebox — Maverick
14. **Get Up On It** — Keith Sweat — Elektra
15. **Fundafied** — Da Brat — So So Def
16. **Hints, Allegations etc** — Collective Soul — Atlantic
17. **Above The Rim** — Soundtrack — Death Row
18. **Same As It Ever Was** — House Of Pain — Tommy Boy
19. **Dookie** — Green Day — Reprise
20. **Smash** — Offspring — Epitaph

us albums

1. **The Lion King** — Soundtrack — Walt Disney
2. **The Sign** — Ace Of Base — Arista
3. **Forrest Gump** — Soundtrack — Epic Soundtrax
4. **Purple** — Stone Temple Pilots — Atlantic
5. **We Come Strapped** — MC Eiht/C — Epic Street
6. **Voodoo Lounge** — The Rolling Stones — Virgin
7. **August & Everything After That** — Counting Crows — DGC
8. **It Takes A Thief** — Coolio — Tommy Boy
9. **Regulate** — Warren G/Nate Dogg — Violator
10. **Superunknown** — Soundgarden — A&M
11. **Not A Moment Too Soon** — Tim McGraw — Curb
12. **All-4-One** — All-4-One — Blitzz
13. **Candlebox** — Candlebox — Maverick
14. **Who I Am** — Alan Jackson — Arista
15. **For The Love Of Strange Medic** — Steve Perry — Columbia
16. **Smash** — Offspring — Epitaph
17. **Chant** — Benedictine Monks — Angel
18. **Reality Bites** — Soundtrack — RCA
19. **Hints, Allegations & Things...** — Collective Soul — Atlantic
20. **Dookie** — Green Day — Reprise

uk virgin Crunchie albums

1. **End Of Part One – Their Greatest Hits** — Wet Wet Wet — Precious Organisation
2. **Voodoo Lounge** — The Rolling Stones — Virgin
3. **The Best Of The Eagles** — The Eagles — Elektra
4. **God Shuffled His Feet** — Crash Test Dummies — RCA
5. **Greatest Hits** — Whitesnake — EMI
6. **The Very Best Of** — Electric Light Orchestra — Dino
7. **Everybody Else Is Doing It...** — The Cranberries — Island
8. **Seal** — Seal — ZTT
9. **Our Town – Greatest Hits** — Deacon Blue — Columbia
10. **Parklife** — Blur — Food
11. **The Division Bell** — Pink Floyd — EMI
12. **Turn It Upside Down** — Spin Doctors — Epic
13. **Eddi Reader** — Eddi Reader — Blanco Y Negro
14. **Nevermind** — Nirvana — Geffen
15. **Miaow** — Beautiful South — Go! Discs
16. **Get A Grip** — Aerosmith — Geffen
17. **The Plot Thickens** — Galliano — Talkin Loud
18. **Greatest Hits** — The Troggs — PolyGram TV
19. **So Far So Good** — Bryan Adams — A&M
20. **Last Of The Independents** — The Pretenders — WEA

uk virgin Crunchie albums

1. **End Of Part One – Their Greatest Hits** — Wet Wet Wet — Precious Organisation
2. **The Glory Of Gershwin** — Larry Adler/Various — Mercury
3. **Voodoo Lounge** — The Rolling Stones — Virgin
4. **The Best Of The Eagles** — The Eagles — Elektra
5. **God Shuffled His Feet** — Crash Test Dummies — RCA
6. **Greatest Hits** — Whitesnake — EMI
7. **Parklife** — Blur — Food
8. **The Very Best Of** — Electric Light Orchestra — Dino
9. **Seal** — Seal — ZTT
10. **Everybody Else Is Doing It...** — The Cranberries — Island
11. **Live! Live! Live!** — Bryan Adams — A&M
12. **The Division Bell** — Pink Floyd — EMI
13. **Our Town – Greatest Hits** — Deacon Blue — Columbia
14. **Turn It Upside Down** — Spin Doctors — Epic
15. **Nevermind** — Nirvana — Geffen
16. **Eddi Reader** — Eddi Reader — Blanco Y Negro
17. **Cohen Live** — Leonard Cohen — Columbia
18. **The Plot Thickens** — Galliano — Talkin Loud
19. **Pawnshop Guitars** — Gilby Clarke — Virgin
20. **Get A Grip** — Aerosmith — Geffen

July'94:24th-30th

uk virgin Crunchie albums

#	Title	Artist	Label
1	End of Part One – Their Greatest Hits	Wet Wet Wet	Precious Organisation
2	Voodoo Lounge	The Rolling Stones	Virgin
3	The Best Of The Eagles	The Eagles	Elektra
4	God Shuffled His Feet	Crash Test Dummies	RCA
5	Greatest Hits	Whitesnake	EMI
6	The Very Best Of	Electric Light Orchestra	Dino
7	Everybody Else Is Doing It...	The Cranberries	Island
8	Seal	Seal	ZTT
9	Our Town – Greatest Hits	Deacon Blue	Columbia
10	Parklife	Blur	Food
11	The Division Bell	Pink Floyd	EMI
12	Turn It Upside Down	Spin Doctors	Epic
13	Eddi Reader	Eddi Reader	Blanco Y Negro
14	Nevermind	Nirvana	Geffen
15	Miaow	The Beautiful South	Go! Discs
16	Get A Grip	Aerosmith	Geffen
17	The Plot Thickens	Galliano	Talkin Loud
18	Greatest Hits	The Troggs	Polygram TV
19	So Far So Good	Bryan Adams	A&M
20	Last Of The Independents	The Pretenders	WEA

us albums

#	Title	Artist	Label
1	The Lion King	Soundtrack	Walt Disney
2	The Sign	Ace Of Base	Arista
3	Forrest Gump	Soundtrack	Epic Soundtrax
4	Purple	Stone Temple Pilots	Atlantic
5	We Come Strapped	MC Eight /CMW	Epic Street
6	Voodoo Lounge	The Rolling Stones	Virgin
7	August & Everything After	Counting Crows	DGC
8	It Takes A Thief	Coolio	Tommy Boy
9	Regulate	Warren G/Nate Dogg	Violator
10	Superunknown	Soundgarden	A&M
11	Not A Moment Too Soon	Tim McGraw	Curb
12	All-4-One	All-4-One	Blitzz
13	Candlebox	Candlebox	Maverick
14	Who I Am	Alan Jackson	Arista
15	For The Love Of Strange Medicine	Steve Perry	Columbia
16	Smash	Offspring	Epitaph
17	Chant	Benedictine Monks	Angel
18	Reality Bites	Soundtrack	RCA
19	Hints, Allegations & Things	Collective Soul	Atlantic
20	Dookie	Green Day	Reprise

uk singles

#	Title	Artist	Label
1	Love Is All Around	Wet Wet Wet	Precious Organisation
2	I Swear	All-4-One	Atlantic
3	Crazy For You	Let Loose	Mercury
4	Searching	China Black	Wild Card
5	(Meet) The Flintstones	BC-52s	MCA
6	Regulate	Warren G/Nate Dogg	Interscope
7	Compliments on Your Kiss	Red Dragon	Mango
8	No More (I Can't Stand It)	Maxx	Pulse-8
9	Let's Get Ready to Rhumble	PJ And Duncan	Isrhythm
10	What's Up	DJ Miko	Systematic

us singles

#	Title	Artist	Label
1	Stay (I Missed You)	Lisa Loeb & Nine Stories	RCA
2	I Swear	All-4-One	Atlantic
3	Fantastic Voyage	Coolio	Tommy Boy
4	Can You Feel The Love Tonight	Elton John	Hollywood
5	Any Time, Any Place	Janet Jackson	Virgin
6	Don't Turn Around	Ace Of Base	Arista
7	Regulate	Warren G/Nate Dogg	Death Row
8	Wild Night	John Mellencamp/Me'Shell	Mercury
9	Funkdafied	Da Brat	So So Def
10	Back & Forth	Aaliyah	Blackground

indy albums

#	Title	Artist	Label
1	Pandemonium	Killing Joke	Butterfly
2	76:14	Global Communication	Dedicated
3	The Very Best Of	Electric Light Orchestra	Dino
4	Implant	Eat Static	Planet Dog
5	I Say I Say I Say	Erasure	Mute

dance singles

#	Title	Artist	Label
1	Girls & Boys	Hed Boys	Deconstruction
2	Hot	Ideal	Cleveland City
3	Give Me Life	Mr. V	Cheeky
4	Rock 2 House/Hip Housin'	X-Press 2/Lo-Pro	Junior Boy's Own
5	Hit By Love	Ce Ce Peniston	A&M

Wet Wet Wet

uk virgin Crunchie albums

#	Title	Artist	Label
1	End Of Part One – Their Greatest Hits	Wet Wet Wet	Precious Organisation
2	The Glory Of Gershwin	Larry Adler/Various	Mercury
3	Voodoo Lounge	The Rolling Stones	Virgin
4	The Best Of The Eagles	The Eagles	Elektra
5	God Shuffled His Feet	Crash Test Dummies	RCA
6	Greatest Hits	Whitesnake	EMI
7	Parklife	Blur	Food
8	The Very Best Of	Electric Light Orchestra	Dino
9	Seal	Seal	ZTT
10	Everybody Else Is Doing It...	The Cranberries	Island
11	Live! Live! Live!	Bryan Adams	A&M
12	The Division Bell	Pink Floyd	EMI
13	Our Town – Greatest Hits	Deacon Blue	Columbia
14	Turn It Upside Down	Spin Doctors	Epic
15	Nevermind	Nirvana	Geffen
16	Eddi Reader	Eddi Reader	Blanco Y Negro
17	Cohen Live	Leonard Cohen	Columbia
18	The Plot Thickens	Galliano	Talkin Loud
19	Pawnshop Guitars	Gilby Clarke	Virgin
20	Get A Grip	Aerosmith	Geffen

us albums

#	Title	Artist	Label
1	The Lion King	Soundtrack	Walt Disney
2	Forrest Gump	Soundtrack	Epic Soundtrax
3	The Sign	Ace Of Base	Arista
4	Purple	Stone Temple Pilots	Atlantic
5	August & Everything After	Counting Crows	Geffen
6	Regulate	Warren G/Nate Dogg	Violator
7	Superunknown	Soundgarden	A&M
8	Voodoo Lounge	The Rolling Stones	Virgin
9	All-4-One	All-4-One	Blitzz
10	Candlebox	Candlebox	Maverick
11	We Come Strapped	MC Eiht/CMW	Epic Stree
12	It Takes A Thief	Coolio	Tommy Boy
13	Not A Moment Too Soon	Tim McGraw	Curb
14	Smash	Offspring	Epitaph
15	Who I Am	Alan Jackson	Arista
16	Dookie	Green Day	Reprise
17	Reality Bites	Sountrack	RCA
18	Funkdafied	Da Brat	So So Def
19	Hints, Allegations & Things	Collective Soul	Atlantic
20	Age Ain't Nothing But...	Aaliyah	Blackground

uk singles

#	Title	Artist	Label
1	Live Is All Around	Wet Wet Wet	Precious Organisation
2	Crazy For You	Let Loose	Mercury
3	I Swear	All-4-One	Atlantic
4	Searching	China Black	Wild Card
5	Compliments On Your Kiss	Red Dragon	Mango
6	What's Up	DJ Miko	Systematic
7	Regulate	Warren G/Nate Dogg	Interscope
8	7 Seconds	Youssou N'Dour/Neneh Cherry	Columbia
9	(Meet) The Flintstones	BC-52s	MCA
10	Live Forever	Oasis	Creation

us singles

#	Title	Artist	Label
1	Stay (I Missed You)	Lisa Loeb & Nine Stories	RCA
2	I Swear	All-4-One	Atlantic
3	Fantastic Voyage	Coolio	Tommy Boy
4	Wild Night	John Mellencamp/Me'Shell	Mercury
5	Can You Feel The Love Tonight	Elton John	Hollywood
6	Funkdafied	Da Brat	So So Def
7	Don't Turn Around	Ace Of Base	Arista
8	Any Time, Any Place	Janet Jackson	Virgin
9	Regulate	Warren G/Nate Dogg	Death Row
10	Back & Forth	Aaliyah	Blackground

indy albums

#	Title	Artist	Label
1	Ffwd	Ffwd	Inter
2	Pandemonium	Killing Joke	Butterfly
3	Animatters	Bandulu	Infonet
4	The Very Best Of	Electric Light Orchestra	Dino
5	I Say I Say I Say	Erasure	Mute

dance singles

#	Title	Artist	Label
1	Two Fatt Guitars (Revisited)	Direckt	UFG
2	And I'm Telling You I'm Not Going	Donna Giles	Ore
3	The Feeling	Tin Tin Out	Deep Distraxion
4	Girls & Boys	The Hed Boys	Deconstruction
5	I Like	Shanice	Motown

indy albums
1. **Snivilisation** — Orbital — Internal Dance
2. **Mars Audiac Quintet** — Stereolab — Duophonic
3. **Burn My Eyes** — Machine Head — Roadrunner
4. **Drums Are Dangerous** — Drum Club — Butterfly
5. **Pandemonium** — Killing Joke — Butterfly

dance singles
1. **Eighteen Strings** — Tinman — ffrr
2. **Everything Is Gonna Be Alright** — Sounds Of Blackness — A&M
3. **Two Fatt Guitars** — Direckt — UFG
4. **Do It** — Tony Di Bart — Cleveland City Blues
5. **The Feeling** — Tin Tin Out — Deep Distraction

uk singles
1. **Love Is All Around** — Wet Wet Wet — Precious Organisation
2. **Crazy For You** — Let Loose — Mercury
3. **Compliments On Your Kiss** — Red Dragon — Mango
4. **7 Seconds** — Youssou N'Dour/Neneh Cherry — Columbia
5. **Searching** — China Black — Wild Card
6. **I Swear** — All-4-One — Atlantic
7. **What's Up** — DJ Miko — Systematic
8. **Regulate** — Warren G/Nate Dogg — Interscope
9. **Eighteen Strings** — Tinman — FFRR
10. **Live Forever** — Oasis — Creation

us singles
1. **Stay (I Missed You)** — Lisa Loeb & Nine Stories — RCA
2. **I'll Make Love To You** — Boyz II Men — Motown
3. **Fantastic Voyage** — Coolio — Tommy Boy
4. **Wild Night** — John Mellencamp/Me'Shell — Mercury
5. **I Swear** — All-4-One — Atlantic
6. **Can You Feel The Love Tonight** — Elton John — Hollywood
7. **Funkdafied** — Da Brat — So So Def
8. **Don't Turn Around** — Ace Of Base — Arista
9. **Any Time, Any Place** — Janet Jackson — Virgin
10. **When Can I See You** — Babyface — Epic

us albums
1. **The Lion King** — Soundtrack — Walt Disney
2. **Forrest Gump** — Soundtrack — Epic Soundtrax
3. **The Sign** — Ace Of Base — Arista
4. **Regulate** — Warren G/Nate Dogg — Violator
5. **Purple** — Stone Temple Pilots — Atlantic
6. **August & Everything After** — Counting Crows — Geffen
7. **Voodoo Lounge** — The Rolling Stones — Virgin
8. **Superunknown** — Soundgarden — A&M
9. **Candlebox** — Candlebox — Maverick
10. **Not A Moment Too Soon** — Tim McGraw — Curb
11. **Smash** — Offspring — Epitaph
12. **All-4-One** — All-4-One — Blitzz
13. **Dookie** — Green Day — Reprise
14. **It Takes A Thief** — Coolio — Tommy Boy
15. **We Come Strapped** — MC Eiht/CMW — Epic Street
16. **Reality Bites** — Soundtrack — RCA
17. **Who I Am** — Alan Jackson — Arista
18. **Chant** — Benedictine Monks — Angel
19. **She** — Harry Connick Jr. — Columbia
20. **Funkdafied** — Da Brat — So So Def

uk virgin Crunchie albums
1. **End Of Part One – Their Greatest Hits** — Wet Wet Wet — Precious Organisation
2. **The Glory Of Gershwin** — Larry Adler/Various — Mercury
3. **The Best Of The Eagles** — The Eagles — Elektra
4. **Voodoo Lounge** — The Rolling Stones — Virgin
5. **Swagger** — Gun — A&M
6. **Seal** — Seal — ZTT
7. **Greatest Hits** — Whitesnake — EMI
8. **God Shuffled His Feet** — Crash Test Dummies — RCA
9. **Parklife** — Blur — Food
10. **The Division Bell** — Pink Floyd — EMI
11. **Everybody Else Is Doing It...** — The Cranberries — Island
12. **The Very Best Of** — Electric Light Orchestra — Dino
13. **Our Town – Greatest Hits** — Deacon Blue — Columbia
14. **Turn It Upside Down** — Spin Doctors — Epic
15. **Live! Live! Live!** — Bryan Adams — A&M
16. **Nevermind** — Nirvana — Geffen
17. **Eddi Reader** — Eddi Reader — Blanco Y Negro
18. **Debut** — Bjork — One Little Indian
19. **Permanent Shade Of Blue** — Roachford — Columbia
20. **Superunknown** — Soundgarden — A&M

indy albums
1. **Snivilisation** — Orbital — Internal Dance
2. **Mars Audiac Quintet** — Stereolab — Duophonic
3. **Burn My Eyes** — Machine Head — Roadrunner
4. **Drums Are Dangerous** — Drum Club — Butterfly
5. **Pandemonium** — Killing Joke — Butterfly

dance singles
1. **On Ya Way** — Helicopter — Helicopter
2. **Trippin On Sunshine** — Pizzaman — Cowboy/Loaded
3. **Everything Is Gonna Be Alright** — Sounds of Blackness — A&M
4. **Eighteen Strings** — Tinman — ffrr
5. **Bring it Back 2 Luv** — Project/Gerideau — Fruittree

uk singles
1. **Love Is All Around** — Wet Wet Wet — Precious Organisation
2. **Compliments On Your Kiss** — Red Dragon — Mango
3. **Crazy For You** — Let Loose — Mercury
4. **7 Seconds** — Youssou N'Dour/Neneh Cherry — Columbia
5. **Searching** — China Black — Wild Card
6. **I'll Make Love To You** — Boyz II Men — Motown
7. **I Swear** — All-4-One — Atlantic
8. **What's Up** — DJ Miko — Systematic
9. **Regulate** — Warren G/Nate Dogg — Death Row
10. **Parklife** — Blur — Food

us singles
1. **I'll Make Love To You** — Boyz II Men — Motown
2. **Stay (I Missed You)** — Lisa Loeb & Nine Stories — RCA
3. **Fantastic Voyage** — Coolio — Tommy Boy
4. **Wild Night** — John Mellencamp/Me'Shell — Mercury
5. **I Swear** — All-4-One — Atlantic
6. **Can You Feel The Love Tonight** — Elton John — Hollywood
7. **Don't Turn Around** — Ace Of Base — Arista
8. **Funkdafied** — Da Brat — So So Def
9. **When Can I See You** — Babyface — Epic
10. **Stroke You Up** — Changing Faces — Spoiled Rotten

us albums
1. **The Lion King** — Soundtrack — Walt Disney
2. **Forrest Gump** — Soundtrack — Epic Soundtrax
3. **The Sign** — Ace Of Base — Arista
4. **Purple** — Stone Temple Pilots — Atlantic
5. **Regulate** — Warren G/Nate Dogg — Violator
6. **August & Everything After** — Counting Crows — Geffen
7. **Candlebox** — Candlebox — Maverick
8. **Dookie** — Green Day — Reprise
9. **Voodoo Lounge** — The Rolling Stones — Virgin
10. **Superunknown** — Soundgarden — A&M
11. **Smash** — Offspring — Epitaph
12. **Not A Moment Too Soon** — Tim McGraw — Curb
13. **All-4-One** — All-4-One — Atlantic
14. **It Takes A Thief** — Coolio — Tommy Boy
15. **Reality Bites** — Soundtrack — RCA
16. **She** — Harry Connick Jr. — Columbia
17. **We Come Strapped** — MC Eiht/CMW — Epic Street
18. **Who I Am** — Alan Jackson — Arista
19. **Chant** — Benedictine Monks — Angel
20. **Age Ain't Nothing But...** — Aaliyah — Blackground

uk virgin Crunchie albums
1. **Come** — Symbol/Prince — Warner Bros
2. **End Of Part One – Their Greatest Hits** — Wet Wet Wet — Precious Organisation
3. **Sleeps With Angels** — Neil Young/Crazy Horse — Reprise
4. **The Glory Of Gershwin** — Larry Adler/Various — Mercury
5. **Seal** — Seal — ZTT
6. **The Best Of The Eagles** — The Eagles — Elektra
7. **Voodoo Lounge** — The Rolling Stones — Virgin
8. **Greatest Hits** — Whitesnake — EMI
9. **Parklife** — Blur — Food
10. **God Shuffled His Feet** — Crash Test Dummies — RCA
11. **The Division Bell** — Pink Floyd — EMI
12. **Swagger** — Gun — A&M
13. **Everybody Else Is Doing It...** — The Cranberries — Island
14. **Stoned & Dethroned** — Jesus And Mary Chain — Blanco Y Negro
15. **Our Town – Greatest Hits** — Deacon Blue — Columbia
16. **The Very Best Of** — Electric Light Orchestra — Dino
17. **Nevermind** — Nirvana — Geffen
18. **Eddi Reader** — Eddi Reader — Blanco Y Negro
19. **Superunknown** — Soundgarden — A&M
20. **Debut** — Bjork — One Little Indian

RECORD COMPANIES

● **4AD LTD,**
15-19 Alma Road,
London SW18 1AA.
081-870-9724

A&M RECORDS,
136-140 New Kings Road,
London SW6 4LE.
071-705 4343

ACE RECORDS LTD,
48-50 Steele Road,
London NW10 7AS.
081-453-1311

ACID JAZZ RECORDS,
11 Greek Street,
London W1V 5LE.
071-437 3444

ALLEGRO,
Pickwick House, The Waterfront,
Elstree Road, Elstree,
Hertfordshire WD6 3BS.
081-207-6207

ALTERNATIVE TENTACLES,
64 Mountgrove Road,
London N5 2LT.
071-354-5455

ALVA RECORDS,
17 West Nicolson Street,
Edinburgh EH8 9DA.
031-668-2374

AMERICAN RECORDINGS,
Lamb House, Church Street,
London W4 2PD.
081-995-3266

ANXIOUS RECORDS,
Devonshire House, 2-4 The
Broadway, London N8 9SN.
081-341-4322

APPLE CORPS LTD,
6 Stratton Street,
London W1X 5FD.
071-499-1543

ARIOLA,
Cavendish House, 423 New Kings
Road, London SW6 4RN.
071-973-8040

ARTLOS RECORDS,
P O Box 132, London W3 8XQ.
081-887-0321

ATLANTIC RECORDS,
83 Baker Street,
London W1M 1AJ.
071-486-6271

AWESOME RECORDS LTD,
59 Moore Park Road,
London SW6 2HH.
071-731-0022

● **BMG ARISTA**
RECORDS (UK) LTD,
Cavendish House, 423 New Kings
Road, London SW6 4RN.
071-973-8040

BMG RECORDS UK LTD,
Bedford House, 69-79 Fulham
High Street, London SW6 3JW.
071-973-0011

BACKS RECORDING CO LTD,
St Mary's Works, St Mary's Plain,
Norwich, Norfolk NR3 3AF.
0603-626221

BEGGARS BANQUET
RECORDS,
17-19 Alma Road,
London SW18 1AA.
081-870-9912

BIG CAT,
P O Box 3074,
London W4 4ZN.
081-995-8464

BIG LIFE RECORDS,
15 Little Portland Street,
London W1N 5DE.
071-323-3888

BLAST FIRST,
21 Wren Street,
London WC1 0HX.
071-278-0916

● **CASTLE**
COMMUNICATIONS PLC,
Unit A29 Barwell Business Park,
Leatherhead Road, Chessington,
Surrey KT9 2NY.
081-974-1021

CHAPTER 22,
Unit 114 The Custard Factory,
Gibb Street, Digbeth,
Birmingham.
021-693-5454

CHARLY RECORDS LTD,
156-166 Ilderton Road,
London SE15 1NT.
071-639-8603

CHEREE RECORDS,
P O Box 653,
London E11 2NX.
081-530-8381

CHERRY RED RECORDS,
Bishop's Park House,
25-29 Fulham High Street,
London SW6 3JH.
071-371-5844

CHINA RECORDS LTD,
27 Queensdale Place,
London W11 4SQ.
071-602-5031

CHRYSALIS GROUP PLC,
The Chrysalis Building, 13 Bramley
Road, London W10 6SP.
071-221-2213

CIRCA,
Kendal House, 553-579 Harrow
Road, London W10 4RH.
081-964-6000

CLAWFIST,
231 Portobello Road,
London W11 1LT.
071-792-3566

CLEVELAND CITY RECORDS,
13B Cleveland Street,
Wolverhampton WV1 3HH.
0902-771186

COOKING VINYL,
3 Park Mews,
213 Kilburn Lane,
London W10 4BQ.
081-960-6000

COOLTEMPO RECORDS,
The Chrysalis Building,
Bramley Road,
London W10 6SP.
071-221-2213

COWBOY RECORDS,
245 Old Marylebone Road,
London NW1 5QT.
071-724-6177

CREATION RECORDS LTD,
10 Westgate Street,
London E8 3RN.
081-986-7145

● **DAMAGED GOODS,**
P O Box 671,
London E17 6NF.
081-807-0618

DEAD DEAD GOOD RECORDS,
2 Witton Walk, Northwich,
Cheshire CW9 5AT.
0606-44559

DECONSTRUCTION RECORDS,
Bedford House,
69-79 Fulham High Street,
London SW6 3JW.
071-384-2298

DEDICATED RECORDS,
37 Uxbridge Street,
London W8 7TQ.
071-221-6677

DEMON RECORDS LTD,
Canal House, Stars Estate,
Transport Avenue, Brentford,
Middlesex TW8 9HF.
081-847-2481

DOVETAIL RECORDS,
2 York Parade, Great West Road,
Brentford, Middlesex TW8 9AA.
081-568-6565

● **EMI RECORDS,**
20 Manchester Square,
London W1A 1ES.
071-486-4488

EARACHE,
P O Box 144,
Nottingham NG3 4GE.
0602-506400

EAST WEST RECORDS,
The Electric Lighting Station,
46 Kensington Court,
London W8 5DP.
071-938-2181

ELEMENTAL RECORDS,
64 Mountgrove Road,
London N5 2LT.
071-354-5455

ENSIGN RECORDS LTD,
The Chrysalis Building,
Bramley Road,
London W10 6SP.
071-221-2213

ESSENTIAL,
29 Barwell Business Park,
Leatherhead Road, Chessington,
Surrey KT9 2NY.
081-974-1021

● **FFRR RECORDS,**
P O Box 1422, Chancellor's
House, Chancellor's Road,
London W6 9RS.
081-741-1234

F-BEAT,
Canal House, Stars Estate,
Transport Avenue, Brentford,
Middlesex TW8 0QP.
081-847-2481

FICTION RECORDS LTD,
Charlotte House,
97 Charlotte Street,
London W1P 1LB.
071-323-5555

FIRE RECORDS,
21a Maury Road,
London N16 7BP.
081-806-9922

FOOD RECORDS,
1st Floor, 172a Arlington Road,
Camden, London NW1 7HL.
071-284-2554

FOURTH & BROADWAY,
22 St Peter's Square,
London W6 9NW.
081-741-1511

● **GEE STREET,**
22 St Peter's Square,
London W6 9NW.
081-741-1511

GO! DISCS,
72 Black Lion Lane,
Hammersmith,
London W6 9BE.
081-748-7973

GREENSLEEVES RECORDS LTD,
Unit 14 Metro Centre,
St John's Road, Isleworth,
Middlesex TW7 6NJ.
081-758-0564

GUERILLA,
Unit 32, Pall Mall Deposit, 124-128
Barlby Road, London W10 6BL.
081-964-1199

GUERNICA,
15-19 Alma Road,
London SW18 1AA.
081-870-9724

● **HEAVENLY RECORDS,**
72 Wardour Street,
London W1V 3HP.
071-437 3350

HIT LABEL,
The Chrysalis Building, 13 Bramley
Road, London W10 6SP.
071-221-2213

HUT,
Kendal House, 553-579 Harrow
Road, London W10 4RH.
081-964-6000

● **IRS RECORDS LTD,**
20 Manchester Square,
London W1A 1ES.
071-486-4488

INFONET,
2nd Floor, 8 Westgate Street,
London E8 3RN.
081-986-7145

INTER-MODO,
P O Box 483, Sheffield,
Yorkshire, S1 2BY.
0742-725804

ISLAND RECORDS LTD,
22 St Peter's Square,
London W6 9NW.
081-741-1511

● **JET STAR PHONOGRAPHICS,**
155 Acton Lane, Park Royal,
London NW10 7NJ.
081-961-5518.

JUNGLE RECORDS,
Old Dairy Mews, 62 Chalk Farm
Road, London NW1 8AN.
071-267-0171

JUNIOR BOYS OWN,
The Saga Centre, 326 Kensal
Road, London W10 5BZ.
081-960-4495

● **KITCHENWARE RECORDS,**
The Stables, St Thomas Street,
Newcastle Upon Tyne,
Tyne & Wear NE1 4LE.
091-232-4895

● **LEMON RECORDS,**
172 Arlington Square,
London NW1 7HL.
071-284-0727

& RECORD LABELS

LONDON RECORDS,
P O Box 1422, Chancellors House,
Chancellor's Road,
London W6 9QB.
081-741-1234

● **M&G RECORDS LTD,**
Queens Studios,
117-121 Salusbury Road,
London NW6 6RG.
071-625-7993

MCA RECORDS LTD,
139 Piccadilly, London W1V 0AX
071-957-8600

MAGNET,
Electric Lighting Station,
46 Kensington Court,
London W8 5DP.
071-938-2181

MUSHROOM RECORDS,
555 Kings Road,
London SW6 2EB.
071-371-7383

MUSIC FOR NATIONS,
333 Latimer Road,
London W10 6RA
081-964-9544

MUSIDISC UK,
32 Queensdale Road,
London W11 4SB.
071-602-1124

MUTE RECORDS,
429 Harrow Road,
London W10 4RE.
081-969-8866

● **NATION RECORDS LTD,**
19 All Saints Road,
London W11 1HE.
071-792-8167

NUDE RECORDS,
6 Warren Mews,
London W1P 5DJ.
071-388-5300

● **OLD GOLD RECORDS,**
Pickwick House, The Waterfront,
Elstree Road, Elstree,
Hertsfordshire WD6 3BS.
081-207-6207

ONE LITTLE INDIAN RECORDS,
250 York Road,
London SW11 3SJ.
071-924-1661

OSCAR RECORDS,
2 Harwood Terrace,
London SW6 2AB.
071-384-1599

OVAL RECORDS,
326 Brixton Road,
London SW9 7AA.
071-622-0111

● **PAISLEY PARK RECORDS,**
The Warner Building,
28a Kensington Church Street,
London W8 4EP.
071-937-8844

PANDEPHONIUM,
The Saga Centre, 326 Kensal Road,
London W10 5BZ.
081-968-8459.

PAPERHOUSE RECORDS,
21a Maury Road,
London N16 7BP.
081-806-9922

PHONOGRAM,
72 Chancellor's House,
Chancellor's Road,
London W6 9RS
081-741-1212

PICKWICK GROUP PLC,
Pickwick House, The Waterfront,
Elstree Road, Elstree,
Hertfordshire WD6 3BS.
081-207-6207

PINNACLE RECORDS,
Electron House, Cray Avenue,
St Mary Cray, Orpington,
Kent BR5 3RJ
0689-870622

PLANET DOG,
Unit 8-9, Millmead Business
Centre, Millmead Road,
London N17 9QU.
081-808-8161

PLINK PLONK,
The Music House,
60 Farringdon Road,
London EC1R 3BP.
071-490-0385

POLYDOR RECORDS,
1 Sussex Place,
London W6 9XS.
081-846-8090

POLYGRAM UK LTD,
1 Sussex Place,
London W6 9XS.
081-846-8515

POSITIVA,
20 Manchester Square,
London W1A 1ES.
071-486-4488

PROFILE,
White Swan House, Bennett
Street, London W4 2AH.
081-995-6229

PULSE 8 RECORDS LTD,
245 Old Marylebone Road,
London NW1 5QT.
071-224-9405

PWL INTERNATIONAL LTD,
4-7 The Vineyard, Sanctuary
Street, London SE1 1QL.
071-403-0007

● **RCA,**
Bedford House,
69-79 Fulham High Street,
London SW6 3JW.
071-973-0011

RAPTURE RECORDINGS,
P O Box 2553,
London N8 9DT.
071-267-6222

REACT MUSIC LTD,
138b West Hill,
London SW15 2UE.
081-780-0305

REVOLVER MUSIC LTD,
152 Goldthorne Hill, Penn,
Wolverhampton,
West Midlands WV2 3JA.
0902-345345

RHINO RECORDS LTD,
The Chilterns, France Hill Drive,
Camberley, Surrey GU15 3QA.
0276-686077

RHYTHM KING RECORDS,
Queens Studios,
117-121 Salusbury Road,
London NW6 6RG.
071-372-3959

RISING HIGH,
7 Westbourne Grove Mews,
London, W11 2RU.
071-221-1580

ROADRUNNER RECORDS,
Tech West, Centre 10,
Warple Way, London, W3 0UL.
081-749-2984

ROBS RECORDS,
11 Whitworth Street West,
Manchester M1 5WG.
061-237-5957

ROCKET RECORD CO LTD,
Singes House,
32 Galena Road,
London W6 0LT.
081-741-9933

ROUGH TRADE RECORDINGS,
66 Golbourne Road,
London W10 5PS.
081-960-9888

**ROUGHNECK RECORDING
COMPANY,**
21a Maury Road,
London N16 7BP.
081-806-9922

RTM,
98 St Pancras Way,
London NW1 9NF.
071-284-1155

● **SETANTA RECORDS,**
130 London Road.
London SE1 9LF.
071-703-0971

SILVERTONE RECORDS,
Zomba House,
165-167 Willesden High Road,
London NW10 2SG.
081-459-8899

SNAP RECORDS,
38 Dalberg Road,
London SW2 1AN.
071-738-6112

SOME BIZARRE,
The Convent, 8-10 Bourdon Street,
London, W1X 9HX.
071-495-2260

SONY MUSIC ENTERTAINMENT,
10 Great Marlborough Street,
London, W1V 2LP
071-911-8200

SOUTHERN RECORDS,
P O Box 59, London N22 1AR.
081-888-8949

SUBURBAN BASE RECORDS,
3 Old Mill Parade, Victoria Road,
Romford, Essex RM1 2HU.
0708-727029

● **TALKIN' LOUD RECORDS,**
Chancellor's House,
72 Chancellor's Road,
Hammersmith,
London W6 9RS.
081-741-1212

TELSTAR RECORDS PLC,
Prospect Studio, Barnes High
Street, London SW13 9LE.
081-878-7888

TEN RECORDS,
Kendal House,
553-579 Harrow Road,
London W10 4RH.
081-964-6000

**THAT'S ENTERTAINMENT
RECORDS,**
107 Kentish Town Road,
London NW1 8PD.
071-485-9593

THIS WAY UP,
10 Kendrick Mews,
London SW7 3HG.
071-584-9944

TOO PURE,
P O Box 1944,
London NW10 5PJ.
071-609-2415

TOPIC RECORDS,
50 Stroud Green Road,
London N4 3EF.
071-263-1240

**TRANSATLANTIC
RECORDS LTD,**
52 Red Lion Street,
London WC1R 4PF.
071-242-9397

TROJAN RECORDINGS LTD,
Twyman House,
31-39 Camden Road,
London NW1 9LF.
071-267-6899

● **ULTIMATE,**
271 Royal College Street,
London NW1 9LU.
071-482-0115

● **VINYL SOLUTION,**
231 Portobello Road,
London W11 1LT.
071-792-9791

VIRGIN RECORDS LTD,
Kensal House,
553-579 Harrow Road,
London W10 4RH.
081-964-6000.

● **WEA RECORDS LTD,**
The Warner Building, 28a
Kensington Church Street,
London W8 4EP.
071-937-8844

WARNER MUSIC (UK) LTD,
The Warner Building,
28a Kensington Church Street,
London W8 4EP.
071-937-8844

WARP RECORDS,
Studio 2, 1 Brown Street,
Sheffield, Yorkshire S1 2BS.
0742-757586

WIIIJA,
130 Talbot Road,
London W11 1JA.
071-609-7408

WORKERS PLAYTIME,
64 Mountgrove Road,
London N5 2LT.
071-354-5455

● **XL RECORDING,**
15-19 Alma Road,
London SW18 1AA.
081-870-9912

● **ZTT RECORDS LTD,**
The Blue Building,
42-46 St Lukes Mews,
London W11 1DG.
071-221-5101

ZOMBA RECORDS LTD,
Zomba House,
165-167 Willesden High Road,
London NW10 2SG.
081-459-8899

Music Publishers

● **ALL BOYS MUSIC,**
4-7 The Vineyard, Sanctuary
Street, London SE1 1QL.
071-403-0007

ANXIOUS MUSIC,
Devonshire House,
2-4 The Broadway, Crouch End,
London N8 9SN.
081-341-4322

ARIWA SOUNDS,
34 Whitehorse Lane,
London SE25 6RE.
081-653-7744

ATMOSPHERE MUSIC LTD,
65 Maltings Place, Bagleys Lane,
London SW6 3AR.
071-371-5888

ATOMIC SONGS,
32 Neal Street, London WC2H 9PS.
071-240-0616

● **BBC ENTERPRISES LTD,**
Woodlands, 80 Wood Lane,
London W12 0TT.
081-743-5588

BMG MUSIC PUBLISHING LTD,
Bedford House, 69-79 Fulham
High Street, London SW6 3JW.
071-973-0980

BTW MUSIC,
125 Myddleton Road,
Wood Green, London N22 4NG.
081-888-6655

BASEHEAD MUSIC,
1st Floor, 21 Denmark Street,
London WC2H 8NE.
071-379-0106

BEETHOVEN ST. MUSIC,
60 Beethoven Street,
London W10 4LG.
081-964-0464

BELSIZE MUSIC LTD,
29 Manor House,
Marylebone Road,
London NW1 5NP.
071-724-6295

BIG LIFE MUSIC LTD,
15 Little Portland Street,
London W1N 5DE.
071-323-3888

BOCU MUSIC LTD,
1 Wyndham Yard,
London W1H 1AR.
071-402-7433

**BOOSEY & HAWKES
MUSIC PUBLISHERS LTD,**
295 Regent Street,
London W1R 8JH.
071-580-2060

BROTHERS ORGANISATION,
74 The Archway,
Station Approach,
Ranelagh Gardens,
London SW6 3UH
071-610-6183

● **CAMBELL CONNELLY &
CO LTD,**
8-9 Frith Street, London W1V 5TZ.
071-434-0066

CARLIN MUSIC CORPORATION,
Iron Bridge House,
3 Bridge Approach, Chalk Farm,
London NW1 8BD.
071-734-3251

**CATALYST (MUSIC
PUBLISHING) LTD,**
171 Southgate Road,
London N1 3LE.
071-704-8541

CAVELL MUSIC LTD,
26 Goodge Street,
London W1P 1FG.
071-580-4740

CAVENDISH MUSIC CO LTD,
295 Regent Street,
London W1R 8JH.
071-580-2060

CELTIC MUSIC,
24 Mercer Row, Louth,
Lincolnshire LN11 9JJ.
0423-888979

CHARISMA MUSIC PUBLISHING,
24 Ives Street,
London SW3 2ND.
071-581-0261

CHARLY PUBLISHING LTD,
156-166 Ilderton Road,
London SE15 1NT.
071-732-5647

CHARMING MUSIC LTD,
56-60 Islington Park Street,
London N1 1PX.
071-354-3414

**CHELSEA MUSIC
PUBLISHING CO LTD,**
70 Gloucester Place,
London W1H 4AJ.
071-224-0066

CHRYSALIS MUSIC LTD,
The Chrysalis Building,
Bramley Road, London W10 6SP.
071-221-2213

CITYBEAT,
17-19 Alma Road,
London SW18 1AA.
081-870-9912

COOKING VINYL,
Unit 3, Park Mews, 213 Kilburn
Lane, London W10 4BQ.
081-960-6000

CORNUCOPIA MUSIC LTD,
29 North End Road, Golders
Green, London NW11 7RJ.
081-455-4707

CRAMER MUSIC LTD,
23 Garrick Street,
London WC2E 9AX.
071-240-1612

● **DE WOLFE MUSIC LTD,**
80-88 Wardour Street,
London W1V 3LF.
071-439-8481

DEAD DEAD GOOD MUSIC LTD,
2 Witton Walk, Northwich,
Cheshire CW9 5AT.
0606-44559

DEJAMUS LTD,
Suite 11, Accurist House,
44 Baker Street,
London W1M 1DH.
071-486-5838

DEMON MUSIC LTD,
Canal House, Stars Estate,
Transport Avenue, Brentford,
Middlesex TW8 9HF.
081-847-2481

● **EG MUSIC PUBLISHERS LTD,**
63a Kings Road,
London SW3 4NT.
071-730-2162

EMI MUSIC PUBLISHING LTD,
127 Charing Cross Road,
London WC2H 0EA.
071-434-2131

EATON MUSIC LTD,
8 West Eaton Place, Belgravia,
London SW1X 8LS.
071-235-9046

KASSNER MUSIC LTD,
Exmouth House, 11 Pine Street,
London EC1R 0JH.
071-837-5020

EMPIRE MUSIC LTD,
Unit 1, Pembridge Studios,
27a Pembridge Villas,
London W11 3EP.
071-229-2020

● **FFRR RECORDS,**
P O Box 1422, Chancellors House,
Chancellors Road,
London W6 9SG.
081-741-1234

FABER MUSIC LTD,
3 Queen Square,
London WC1N 3AU.
071-278-7436

FRESH AIR LTD,
3rd Floor, 9 Carnaby Street,
London W1V 1PG.
071-437-1958

● **GLOBAL MUSIC LTD,**
171 Southgate Road,
London N1 3LE.
071-704-8541

GO! DISCS MUSIC LTD,
72 Black Lion Lane,
Hammersmith, London W6 9BE.
081-748-7973

GREENSLEEVES RECORDS LTD,
Unit 14, Metro Centre,
St Johns Road, Isleworth,
Middlesex TW7 6NJ.
081-758-0564

GRIN,
138b West Hill,
London SW15 2UE.
081-780-0305

● **HABANA PUBLISHING LTD,**
78 Stanley Gardens,
London, W3 7SN.
081-741234

HALLIN MUSIC LIMITED,
8 Wendall Road, London W12 9RT.
081-746-1727

HALYCON MUSIC LTD,
11 Howitt Road, London NW3 4LT.
071-586-0288

**HANDLE GROUP OF
COMPANIES LTD,**
Handle House, 1 Albion Place,
Galena Road, London W6 0QT.
081-846-9111

HEART & SOUL MUSIC,
41 Blackhorse Road,
London E17 7AS.
081-521-2040

HEAVEN MUSIC,
P O Box 92, Gloucester,
Gloucestershire GL4 8HW.
0452-812442

● **ISLAND MUSIC LTD,**
47 British Grove,
London, W4 2NL
081-846-9141

● **JIGSAW MUSIC LTD,**
115 Old Lodge Lane, Purley,
Surrey, CR8 4DP.
081-668-3457

JOSEF WEINBERGER LTD,
12-14 Mortimer Street,
London W1N 7RD.
071-580-2827

● **KPM MUSIC LTD,**
127 Charing Cross Road,
London WC2H 0EA.
071-412-9111

KITCHENWARE RECORDS,
The Stables, St Thomas Street,
Newcastle Upon Tyne,
Tyne & Wear NE1 4LE.
091-232-4895

● **LONDON MUSIC,**
P O Box 1422, Chancellors House,
Chancellors Road,
London W6 9SG.
081-741-1234

● **MCA MUSIC LTD,**
Unit 9, 77 Fulham Palace Road,
London, W6 8JA.
081-741-8686

MJM,
2 Harwood Terrace,
London, SW6 2AB.
071-384-1599

MAD HAT MUSIC,
16 Hyde Park Place,
Bayswater Road,
London W2 2LP.
071-402-5083

MASTERSONG MUSIC (UK),
47 Kelburn Close, Chandlers Ford,
Eastleigh, Hampshire SO53 2PW.
0703-267449

**MAWSON & WAREHAM
MUSIC LTD,**
Midgy Hall, Sharperton, Morpeth,
Northumberland NE65 7AS.
0669-40252

MEMORY LAND MUSIC LTD,
22 Denmark Street,
London WC2H 8NA.
071-240-5439

MINDER MUSIC LTD,
22 Bristol Gardens,
London W9 2JQ.
071-289-7281

MIX MUSIC,
27 Newton Street, Holborn,
London WC2B 5EL.
071-242-0415

MOMENTUM MUSIC LTD,
17-19 Alma Road,
London SW18 1AA.
081-871-2121

MORRISON LEAHY MUSIC LTD,
1 Star Street, London W2 1QD.
071-258-0093

**MULTIMEDIA MUSIC
COMPANY LTD,**
7 The Woodlands, Hither Green,
London SE13 6TZ.
081-698-0534

● **NEGUS-FANCY CO LTD,**
78 Portland Road,
London W11 4LQ
071-727-2063

NERVOUS MUSIC PUBLISHING,
7-11 Minerva Road,
London NW10 6HJ.
081-963-0352

NEW AGE MUSIC,
91-94 Saffron Hill,
London EC1N 8JP.
071-404-3333

NOEL GAY ARTISTS,
6th Floor, 76 Oxford Street,
London W1N 0AT.
071-836-3941

NOVELLO & CO LTD,
8-9 Frith Street,
London,W1V 5TZ.
071-483-2161

● **OBELISK MUSIC,**
32 Ellerdale Road,
London NW3 6BB.
071-435-5255

OPAL MUSIC,
330 Harrow Road,
London W9 2HP.
071-286-9532

● **PASSION RECORDS,**
81 Crabtree Lane,
London SW6 6LW.
071-381-8315

PEERMUSIC (UK) LTD,
8-14 Verulam Street,
London WC1X 8LZ
071-404-7200

PERFECT SONGS,
The Blue Building,
42-46 St Luke's Mews,
London W11 1DG.
071-221-5101

PERFECTO MUSIC LTD,
The Chrysalis Building,
Bramley Road, London W10 6SP.
071-221-2213

POLYGRAM INTERNATIONAL,
8 St. James' Square,
London SW1Y 4JU.
071-747-4000

PRODUCTION LEAGUE,
4 Auckland Court,
London SE27 9PE.
081-761-0178.

● **RAK RECORDING STUDIOS,**
42-48 Charlbert Street,
London NW8 7BU.
071-586-2012

REALLY USEFUL GROUP LTD,
22 Tower Street,
London WC2H 9NS.
071-240-0880

RED BUS RECORDING STUDIOS,
34 Salisbury Street,
London NW8 8QE.
071-402-9111

RHYTHM KING MUSIC,
Queens Studios,
121 Salisbury Road,
Queens Park,
London NW6 6RG.
071-372-5474

**ROCKMASTERS
MANAGEMENT LTD,**
Brunswick Studios, 7 Westbourne
Grove Mews, London W11 2RU.
071-727-8636

**ROCKSONG MUSIC
PUBLISHING LTD,**
152 Goldthorn Hill, Penn,
Wolverhampton,
West Midlands WV2 3JA.
0902-345345

RONDOR MUSIC (LONDON) LTD,
Rondor House, 10a Parsons
Green, London SW6 4TW.
071-731-4161

ROUGH TRADE PUBLISHING,
81 Wallingford Road, Goring,
Reading, Berkshire RG8 0HL.
0491-873612

RYKOMUSIC LTD,
Unit 3, Linen House,
253 Kilburn Lane,
London W10 4BQ.
081-964-3031

● **S&J MUSIC LTD,**
5 Paddington Street,
London W1M 3LA.
071-935-1588

SBK SONGS,
127 Charing Cross Road,
London WC2H 0EA.
071-434-2131

SCHAUER & MAY LTD,
67 Belsize Lane,
London NW3 5AX.
071-794-8038

SCHOTT & CO LTD,
48 Great Marlborough Street,
London W1V 2BN.
071-437-1246

SHAPIRO BERNSTEIN & CO LTD,
8-9 Frith Street,
London W1V 5TZ.
071-434-0066

SONY MUSIC PUBLISHING,
10 Great Marlborough Street,
London W1V 2LP.
071-911-8200

SURVIVAL RECORDS,
P O Box 888, Maidenhead,
Berkshire SL6 2YQ.
0628-788700

● **TKO PUBLISHING LTD,**
P O Box 130, Hove,
Sussex BN3 6QU.
0273-550088

TELSTAR RECORDS PLC,
Prospect Studio,
Barnes High Street,
London SW13 9LE.
081-878-7888

**TONY HALL GROUP
OF COMPANIES,**
3rd Floor, 9 Carnaby Street,
London W1V 1PG.
071-437-1958

● **UNITED MUSIC
PUBLISHERS LTD,**
42 Rivington Street,
London EC2A 3BN.
071-729-4700

**UNIVERSAL EDITION
(LONDON) LTD,**
48 Great Marlborough Street,
London W1V 2BN.
071-437-1246

● **VALENTINE MUSIC GROUP,**
7 Garrick Street,
London WC2E 9AR.
071-240-1628

● **WARNER CHAPPELL
MUSIC LTD,**
129 Park Street,
London W1Y 3FA.
071-629-7600

WOLF MUSIC,
83 Brixton Water Lane,
London SW2 1PH.
071-733-8088

● **ZOMBA MUSIC
PUBLISHERS LTD,**
Zomba House,
165-167 Willesden High Road,
London NW10 3SG.
081-459-8899

Artist management

● **AIR LTD,**
Air House, 17 Clyde Terrace,
Spennymoor, County Durham
DL16 7SE.
0388-814632

ACHIEVEMENT MANAGEMENT,
Unit 3, 9-12 St Anne's Court,
Soho, London W1V 3AX.
071-515-2951

ADDICTIVE MANAGEMENT,
4 Birchfields Road,
Manchester M13 0XR.
061-225-5140

ADRIAN BOSS PROMOTIONS,
363-365 Harrow Road,
London W9 3NA.
081-964-0112

**ALAN ROBINSON
MANAGEMENT,**
Suite 3 Foundry Studios,
207 Putney Bridge Road,
London SW15 2WY.
081-870-5425

ALLIED MANAGEMENT,
76 Tottenham Court Road,
London W1P 9PA.
071-493-3852

**ARTIST MANAGEMENT
SERVICES,**
363-365 Harrow Road,
London W9 3NA.
081-968-5354

ASGARD,
125 Parkway,
London NW1 7PS.
071-387-5090

AVALON PROMOTIONS,
25 Litchfield Street,
London WC2H 9NJ.
071-497-2656

● **BIG LIFE MANAGEMENT LTD,**
15 Little Portland Street,
London W1N 5DE.
071-323-3888

BIGTIME MANAGEMENT,
42 Effingham Road,
London SE12 8NU.
071-403-0007

BLACK MAGIC MANAGEMENT,
296 Earls Court Road,
London SW5 9BA.
071-373-3849

BRIGHT MUSIC LTD,
Chelsea Walk, 2 Harwood Terrace,
London SW6 2AB.
071-384-1599

BRILLIANT ARTISTS,
130 London Road,
London SE1 6LF.
071-620-1383

BRILLIANT MANAGEMENT,
20 Stamford Brook Avenue,
London W6 0YD.
081-846-9469

● **CMO MANAGEMENT
(INTERNATIONAL) LTD,**
Unit 32, Ransomes Dock,
35-37 Park Gate Road,
London SW11 4NP.
071-228-4000

CSA MANAGEMENT,
101 Chamberlayne Road,
London NW10 3ND.
081-960-8466

CHAKRA,
Avondale Coach House,
London Road East,
Bathford,
Bath BA1 7RB.
0225-858028

● **DBM,**
172a Arlington Road,
Camden, London NW1 7HL.
071-284-2554

DAMAGE MANAGEMENT,
16 Lambton Place,
London W11 2SH.
071-229-2992

DANGEROUS MANAGEMENT,
696 Wimbourne Road,
Bournemouth, BH9 2EG.
0202-517896

**DAVID JAYMES
ASSOCIATES LTD,**
P O Box 2902, London W11 2NF.
071-727-0576

**DECONSTRUCTION
MANAGEMENT,**
4th Floor, Bedford House,
69-79 Fulham High Street,
London SW6 3JW.
071-384-2298

DIVINE MANAGEMENT,
37 Bowness Crescent,
London SW15 3QN.
081-546-4590

● **ECCENTRIC DIRECTIONS,**
294 Holloway Road,
London N7 4AH.
071-609-1575

**ECLIPSE ARTIST
MANAGEMENT,**
3 Armstrong Avenue,
Stoke, Coventry,
West Midlands CV3 1BL.
0203-451231

EG MANAGEMENT LTD,
63a King's Road,
London SW3 4NT
071-730-2162

EMKAY ENTERTAINMENTS,
3-5 Slateford Road,
Edinburgh, EH11 1PA.
031-337-1707

ETERNAL MANAGEMENT,
55 Lark Lane,
Aigburth,
Liverpool L17 8UW.
051-728-8400

● **FICTION RECORDS LTD,**
97 Charlotte Street,
London W1P 1LB.
071-323-5555

**FIFTY/FIFTY ONE
MANAGEMENT LTD,**
126 Ashleigh Road,
Mortlake,
London SW14 8PX.
081-876-4433

FORWARD AGENCY BOOKING,
132 Liverpool Road,
London, N1 1LA.
071-609-9900

● **GAILFORCE MANAGEMENT,**
30 Ives Street, London SW3 2ND.
071-581-0261

● **HALL OR NOTHING,**
8 Poplar Mews, Uxbridge Road,
London W12 7JS.
081-740-6288

**HANDLE GROUP
OF COMPANIES,**
Handle House, 1 Albion Place,
Galena Road, Hammersmith,
London W6 0QT.
081-846-9111

HEAVENLY RECORDS,
72 Wardour Street,
London W1V 3HP.
071-437-3350

HIT & RUN MANAGEMENT,
30 Ives Street,
London SW3 2ND.
071-581-0261

HUGE & JOLLY MANAGEMENT,
56-60 Islington Park Street,
London N1 1PX.
071-354-3414

● **ICM ARTISTS (LONDON) LTD,**
Oxford House, 76 Oxford Street,
London W1R 1RB.
071-323-3223

INTER-MODO,
P O Box 483, Sheffield, S1 2BY.
0742-725804

● **JACK BRUCE MANAGEMENT,**
Mayfield, Alphamstone, Bures,
Suffolk CO8 5HW.
0787-269402

JEFF HANLON MANAGEMENT,
1 York Street, London W1H 1PZ.
071-487-2558

JOHN HENRY ENTERPRISES,
The John Henry Building, 16-24
Brewery Road, London N7 9NH.
071-609-9181

JOHN REID ENTERPRISES LTD,
Singes House, 32 Galena Road,
London W6 0LT.
081-741-9933

● **KITCHENWARE RECORDS,**
The Stables, St Thomas Street,
Newcastle Upon Tyne,
Tyne & Wear NE1 4LE.
091-232-4895

● **LJD LTD,**
53 Keyes House, Dolphin Square,
London SW1V 3NA.
071-828-7132

LEGENDARY ARTISTS LTD,
6 Pembridge Road,
London W11 3HL.
071-221-1522

**LEIGHTON-POPE
ORGANISATION,**
8 Glenthorne Mews, 115a
Glenthorne Road, London W6 0LJ.
081-741-4453

LIFETIME MANAGEMENT,
18 St George's Road, St
Margaret's, Twickenham,
Middlesex TW1 1QR.
081-892-4810

LONDON ARTISTS,
P O Box 1077, Slough,
Berkshire SL2 4DB.
0753-655432

LONDON MANAGEMENT LTD,
2-4 Noel Street,
London W1V 3RB.
071-287-9000

**LYSTER, PRYOR &
TODD LTD,**
4 Yeoman's Row,
London SW3A 2AH.
071-589-1111

● **MJM,**
2 Harwood Terrace,
London SW6 2AB
071-384-1599

MAD HAT MUSIC,
16 Hyde Park Place,
Bayswater Road,
London W2 2LP.
071-402-5803

MANAGEMENT WORKS,
Singe House,
32 Galena Road,
London W6 0LT.
081-741-9933

**MANNA ENTERTAINMENTS
& MANAGEMENT LTD,**
3rd Floor,
9 Carnaby Street,
London W1V 1PG.
071-437-1958

MARSHALL ARTS LTD,
Leeder House,
6 Erkskine Road,
London NW3 3AJ.
071-586-3831

MATRIX MANAGEMENT,
12 Bergham Mews,
Plythe Road,
London W14 0HN.
071-603-7275

METRO MANAGEMENT,
155d Holland Park Avenue,
London W11 4AU.
071-371-6211

**MIKE MALLEY
ENTERTAINMENTS,**
10 Holly Park Gardens,
Finchley, London N3 3NJ.
081-346-4109

MISMANAGEMENT,
754 Fulham Road,
London SW6 5SH.
071-731-7074

MIX MANAGEMENT,
27 Newton Street,
Holborn, London WC2B 5EL.
071-242-0415

MUSIC FACTORY
MASTERMIXES,
Hawthorne House,
5-7 Fitzwilliam Street,
Parkgate, Rotherham,
Yorkshire S62 6EP.
0709-710022

● NEW CRAZY GANG,
The Parson's Nose,
11 Archbishops Place,
London SW2 2AH.
081-671-5926
NOEL GAY ARTISTS,
6th Floor, 76 Oxford Street,
London W1N 0AT.
071-836-3941
NORTHERN MUSIC,
Cheapside Chambers,
43 Cheapside, Bradford,
Yorkshire BD1 4HP.
0274-306361

● ON,
19 All Saints Road,
London W11 1HE.
071-229-7661
OUR MANAGEMENT,
14a Longbeach Road,
Battersea, London SW11 5ST.
071-350-1195

● PAN MANAGEMENT,
21a Noel Street,
London W1V 3PD.
071-434-2345
PWL MANGEMENT LTD,
4-7 The Vineyard,
Sanctuary Street,
London SE1 1QL.
071-403-0007
PET SHOP BOYS
PARTNERSHIP,
Studio 8, 27a Pembridge Villas,
London W11 3EP.
071-221-3355
POLAR UNION LTD,
119-121 Freston Road,
London W11 4BD.
071-243-0011
PRO-BANG MANAGEMENT,
148 Cavendish Mansions,
London EC1R 5EQ.
071-278-7292
PROTOCOL MANAGEMENT,
23a Benwell Road,
Islington, London N7 7BW.
071-607-9495

● REAL LIFE LTD AND
PAUL LILLY LTD,
122 Holland Park Avenue,
London W11 4UA.
071-221-3077

ROBERT REED
ORGANISATION,
17 Greenacres, Duxford,
Cambridgeshire CB2 4RB.
0480-434686
ROCK HARD MANAGEMENT,
19d Pinfold Road,
London SW16 2SL.
081-677-8466
ROCKMASTERS
MANAGEMENT LTD,
Brunswick Studios,
7 Westbourne Grove Mews,
London W11 2RU.
071-727-8636
ROGER DAVIES
MANAGEMENT UK,
37 Limerston Street,
London SW10 0BQ.
071-352-9607
RUNNING DOG
MANAGEMENT LTD,
Minka, Lower Hampton Road,
Sunbury, Middlesex TW16 5PR.
081-941-8180

● SDM LTD,
5 Paddington Street,
London W1M 3LA.
071-935-1588
SOS MANAGEMENT,
81 Harley House,
Marylebone Road,
London NW1 5HT.
071-486-8794
SANCTUARY GROUP PLC,
The Colonnades,
82 Bishop's Bridge Road,
London W2 6BB.
071-243-0640
SELECT MANAGEMENT,
8 Woodnook Way,
Ashgate, Chesterfield,
Derbyshire S42 7PZ.
0246-569873
SERIOUS SPEAKOUT,
42 Old Compton Street,
London W1V 5PB.
071-439-0807
SINCERE MANAGEMENT,
421 Harrow Road,
London W10 4RD.
081-960-4438
SINCLAIR MANAGEMENT,
St Peters House,
Hewitt Street,
Manchester M15 4GB.
061-228-3555
SOLID BOND
PRODUCTION LTD,
Nomis Studios,
45-53 Sinclair Road,
London W14 0NS.
071-602-6351

SOME BIZARRE,
The Convent, 8-10 Bourdon
Street, London W1X 9HX.
071-495-2260
STARGARD ORGANISATION,
302-304 Wellingborough Road,
Northampton,
Northamptonshire NN1 4EP.
0604-34105
SWANYARD MANAGEMENT,
12-27 Swan Yard,
London N1 1SD.
071-354-3737

● TALENT ARTISTS LTD,
4 Mews House, Princes Lane,
London N10 3LU.
081-444-4088
TONY BEARD MANAGEMENT,
145a Ladbroke Grove,
London W10 6HJ.
071-221-8353
TONY HALL GROUP
OF COMPANIES,
3rd Floor,
9 Carnaby Street,
London W1V 1PG.
071-437-1958

● VAGUE MANAGEMENT,
Top Floor,
940 Sauchiehall Street,
Glasgow G3 7TH.
041-339-2263
VALUE ADDED TALENT,
1-2 Purley Place,
London N1 1QA.
071-704-9720

● WAR ZONES,
33 Kersley Road,
London N16 0NT.
071-249-2894
WILD! MANAGEMENT,
Brunswick Studios,
7 Westbourne Grove Mews,
London W11 2RU.
071-727-0608

● XL TALENT,
Studio 7,
27a Pembridge Villas,
London W11 3EP.
071-938-1917

● ZOMBA PRODUCTIONS,
Zomba House,
165-167 Willesden High Road,
Willesden,
London NW10 2SG.
081-459-8899

Music Solicitors

● BURLEY & CO,
6 Portugal Street,
London WC2A 2HH.
071-404-4002

● CLINTONS,
55 Drury Lane,
London WC2B 5SQ.
071-379-6080

● DAVENPORT LYONS,
1 Old Burlington Street,
London W1X 1LA.
071-287-5353

● EATONS,
22 Blades Court,
Deodar Road, Putney,
London SW15 2NU.
081-877-9727

● FRERE, CHOLMELEY
BISCHOFF,
4 John Carpenter Street,
London EC4Y 0NH.
071-615-8000

● HARBOTTLE & LEWIS,
Hanover House,
14 Hanover Square,
London W1R 0BE.
071-629-7633
HART-JACKSON & HALL,
3a Ridley Place,
Newcastle Upon Tyne,
Tyne & Wear NE1 8JQ.
091-232-1987
HEPBURN,
Blenheim House,
Blenheim Grove,
London SE15 4QX.
071-639-9991
HILLS SEARLE,
The Chapel, 26a Munster Road,
London SW6 4EN.
071-371-0555
HOLMAN, FENWICK & WILLAN,
Marlow House,
Lloyd's Avenue,
London EC3N 3AL.
071-488-2300

● KELLY MUSIC LTD,
West Wing House,
Beacon Hill Park,
Churt Road,
Hindhead,
Surrey GU26 6HU.
0428-605771

● LEE & THOMPSON SOLICITORS,
Green Garden House,
St Christopher's Place,
London W1M 5HD.
071-935-4665

● RUSSELLS,
Regency House, 1-4 Warwick
Street, London W1R 5WB.
071-439-8692

● SALAMONS,
5-8 Lower John Street,
Golden Square,
London W1R 3PE.
071-439-0388
SIMKINS PARTNERSHIP,
45-51 Whitfield Street,
London W1P 5RJ.
071-631-1050
STARGARD ORGANISATION
(BAILIFFS),
Conisgold House,
302-304 Wellingborough Road,
Northampton,
Northamptonshire NN1 4EP.
0604-34105

● WILLIAMS & PHILLIPS,
216 Tower Bridge Road,
London SE1 2UP.
071-378-7779
WOOLF SEDDON,
5 Portman Square,
London W1H 9PS.
071-486-9681

● **ALAN JAMES PR,**
1st Floor, 130 London Road,
London SE1 6LF.
071-620-1383

ANGLO PLUGGING,
72 Black Lion Lane,
Hammersmith,
London W6 9BE.
081-748-3297

APPEARING MEDIA PROMOTIONS,
1 Star Street,
London W2 1QD.
071-402-2334

● **BAD MOON,**
19 All Saints Road,
London W11 1HE.
071-221-9612

BEER DAVIS,
50 Margaret Street,
London W1N 7FD.
071-323-3003

BRASSNECK,
Warehouse D, 6th Floor,
Metropolitan Wharf,
Wapping Wall, London E1 9SS.
071-481-2172

● **DISC CONNECT,**
43 Stafford Street, Norwich NR2 3BD.
0603-250020

● **ENCORE SPECIALIST PROMOTIONS,**
81 Crabtree Lane, London SW6 6LW.
071-381-8315

● **FRONTIER PROMOTION,**
115 Old Lodge Lane, Purley,
Surrey. CR8 4DP.
081-668-3457

● **HALL OR NOTHING PR,**
8 Poplar Mews, Uxbridge Road,
London W12 7JS.
081-740-6288

● **JUDY TOTTON PUBLICITY,**
EBC House, 1a Ranelagh
Gardens, London SW6 3PA.
071-371-8158/8159

● **MEL BUSH ORGANISATION,**
5 Stratfield Saye, 20-22 Wellington
Road, Bournemouth, BH8 8JN.
0202-293093

● **NEWS PR AGENCY,**
14-15 D'Arblay Street,
London W1V 3FP.
071-437- 3588

● **POOLE EDWARDS,**
2nd Floor,
44 Charlotte Street,
London W1P 1HA.
071-436-3633

POP PROMOTIONS,
The Saga Centre, 326 Kensal
Road, London W10 5BZ.
081-968-8459

POWER PROMOTIONS,
32 Holmes Road, Kentish Town,
London NW5 3AB.
071-482-0728

● **RAPTURE PROMOTIONS (RTMP),**
P O Box 2553,
London N8 9DT.
071-267-6222

REVOLUTION PROMOTIONS,
172 Arlington Road,
London, NW1 7HL.
071-267-3871

ROCK HARD PR,
19d Pinfold Road,
London SW16 2SL.
081-677-8466

RUSH RELEASE LTD,
74 The Archways,
Station Approach,
Ranelagh Gardens,
London SW6 3UH.
071-610-6227

● **SAVAGE AND BEST,**
172 Arlington Road,
London NW1 7HL.
071-284-1922

SINGLE MINDED PROMOTIONS,
32 Queensdale Road,
Holland Park,
London W11 4SB.
071-602-5200

STATION II STATION,
322 Kentish Town Road,
London NW5 2TH.
071-482-5272

STONE IMMACULATE,
Studio 2, 8 Nursery Road,
London SW9 8BP.
071-737-6359

SUBSTANCE,
Devonshire House,
12 Barley Mow Passage,
London W4 4PH.
081-995-2325

● **TONY BEARD PRESS,**
145a Ladbroke Grove,
London W10 6HJ.
071-221-8353

● **WAYWARD,**
38 Dalberg Road,
London SW2 1AN.
071-978-8611

WOODSTOCK PROMOTIONS,
40 Brightling Road,
Crofton Park,
London SE4 1SQ.
081-690-6777

● **X-RAY AIR PLAY PROMOTIONS,**
12 Vale Court,
South Vale,
Sudbury Hill, Harrow,
Middlesex HA1 3PJ.
081-423-2569

CENTREPOINT TICKETS,
105 Charing Cross Road,
London, WC2 1DT.
071-434-1647

FIRSTCALL,
73-75 Endell Street,
London WC2H 9AJ.
071-836-9001

PREMIER BOX OFFICE,
188 Shaftesbury Avenue,
London WC2H 8JN.
071-240-2245

STAR GREEN BOX OFFICE LTD,
20-21a Argyll Street,
London W1V 1AA.
071-734-8932

TICKETMASTER LTD,
48 Leicester Square,
London WC2H 7LR.
071-344-4000

● **ABBEY ROAD STUDIOS,**
3 Abbey Road, London NW8 9AY.
071-286-1161

AOSIS AUDIO & REWIND,
10a Belmont Street,
London NW1 8HH.
071-485-4810

● **BACKYARD STUDIO,**
Units 4 & 5 Willow Brook,
Crickhowell Road, St Mellons,
Cardiff, Wales CF3 0EF.
0222-777739

BANDWAGON STUDIOS,
c/o Folk House, Westfield Lane,
Mansfield, Nottinghamshire
NG18 1TL.
0623-422962

● **CHOP 'EM OUT,**
Trinity Mews, Cambridge Gardens,
London W10 6JA.
081-960-8128

COPYMASTERS,
13 The Talina Centre, Bagley's
Lane, London SW6 2BW.
071-731-5758

● **DUPLITAPE RECORDING SERVICES,**
37 Shaw Road, Heaton Moor,
Stockport, Cheshire SK4 4AG.
061-442-6910

● **THE EXCHANGE,**
42 Bruges Place,
Randolph Street,
London NW1 0TX.
071-485-0530

● **FAIRVIEW MUSIC,**
Great Gutter Lane, Willerby, Hull,
Humberside, HU10 6DP.
0482-653116

● **GWBB AUDIOVISION,**
42 Lancaster Gate,
London W2 3NA.
071-723-5190

GOLDDUST STUDIOS,
14 Cromwell Avenue,
Bromley, Kent BR2 9AQ.
081-466-7435

● **MAGNETIC IMAGE MASTERING,**
6 Grand Union Centre,
West Row, London W10 5AS.
081-960-7222

MASTER ROOM CO LTD,
59-61 Ridinghouse Street,
London W1P 7PP.
071-637-2223

MAX SOUND (LEEDS) LTD,
6 Stainbeck Lane, Leeds,
Yorkshire LS7 3QY.
0532-370441

MAYKING RECORDS,
250 York Road,
London SW11 3SJ.
071-924-1661

MIRROR IMAGE,
Studio 204, Ducie House,
37 Ducie Street, Piccadilly,
Manchester M1 2JW.
061-442-9045

MUSIC MEDIA MANUFACTURERS LTD,
104 Harmood Street,
London NW1 8DS.
071-916-4450

● **OCTAGON RECORDS & TAPES,**
A18 Stonehills, Shields Road,
Gateshead, NE10 0HW.
091-495-2324

ON-Q PRODUCTIONS,
P O Box 3213, London SW11 3SJ.
081-671-4431

● **PRERECORD LTD,**
The Heritage Complex, Fleck Way,
Stockton, Cleveland TS19 9JZ.
0642-762600

● **RMS STUDIOS,**
43-45 Clifton Road,
London SE25 6PX.
081-653-4965

RTS LTD,
Units M1 & M2, Prescot Trade
Centre, Albany Road, Prescot,
Merseyside L34 2SH.
051-430-9001

REAL RECORDINGS LTD,
The Works, Unit 1,
Britannia Road, Sale,
Cheshire M33 2AA.
061-973-1884

REFLEX AUDIO SYSTEMS,
Unit 5, Cirrus Court, Glebe Road,
Huntingdon, Cambridgeshire
PE18 7DX.
0480-434333

● **SVS TAPE DISTRIBUTORS (UK) LTD,**
Shentonfield Road,
Sharston Industrial Estate,
Manchester M22 4RW.
061-491-6660

SELECTA SOUND,
5 Margaret Road, Romford,
Essex RM2 5SH.
0708-453424

SILVERWORD LTD,
16 Lime Trees Avenue,
Llangattock, Crickhowell,
Wales NP8 1LB.
0873-810142

SOUND CELLAR,
2-4 Trinity Mews, Cambridge
Gardens, London W10 6JA.
081-969-9488

● **TAPE DUPLICATION CO,**
77 Barlow Road, Stannington,
Sheffield, S6 5HR.
0742-330033

TOUCHSTONE,
TPL House, Beccles Business
Park,Copland Way, Beccles,
Suffolk NR34 7TL.
0502-716056

TOWNHOUSE CUTTING ROOMS,
150 Goldhawk Road,
London W12 8HH.
081-743-9313

TRANSFERMATION,
63 Lant Street, London SE1 1QN.
071-417-7021

● **WHITE HOUSE SOUND,**
24a Brookfield Street, Syston,
Leicestershire LE7 2AD.
0533-609401

WHITFIELD RECORDING STUDIOS
31-37 Whitfield Street,
London W1P 5RE.
071-636-3434

● **24-SEVEN,**
21-22 Poland Street,
London W1V 3DD.
071-734-0247

● **APPLAUSE,**
132 Liverpool Road, London N1 1LA.
071-700-0248

AUDIO MEDIA,
Media House, 3 Burrell Road, St Ives,
Huntingdon, Cambridge PE17 4LE.
0480-61244

ARENA,
3rd Floor, Block A, Exmouth House,
Pine Street, London EC1R OJL.
071-837-7270

● **BIG!,**
Mappin House, 4 Winsley Street,
London W1N 7AR.
071-436-1515

THE BIG ISSUE,
Fleet House, 57-61 Clerkenwell Road,
London EC1M 5NP.
071-418-0418

BILLBOARD,
23 Ridgmount Street,
London WC1E 7AH.
071-323-6686

BLUES & SOUL,
153 Praed Street, London W2 1RL.
071-402-6869

● **DAILY MIRROR,**
1 Canada Square,
London, E14 5AP
071-510-3000

DAILY STAR,
Ludgate House,
245 Blackfriars Road,
London SE1 9UX.
071-928-8000

DEADLINE,
36 Leroy Street, London SE1 4SS.
071-232-2840

DJ,
40 Bowling Green Lane,
London, EC1R ONE.
071-415-7113

● **ECHOES,**
7-9 Charlotte Street,
London W1P 1HD.
071-436-4540

● **THE FACE,**
3rd Floor, Block A, Exmouth House,
Pine Street, London EC1R OJL.
071-837-7270

● **GENERATOR,**
4-8 Peartree Street,
London EC1V 3SB.
071-454-7855

G-SPOT,
11 Marshallsea Road, London
Bridge, London SE1 1EP.
071-717-1228

THE GUARDIAN,
119 Farringdon Road,
London EC1R 3ER.
071-278-2332

GUITARIST,
Alexander House, Forehill, Ely,
Cambridgeshire CB7 4AF.
0353-665577

THE GUITAR,
9 Dingwall Avenue, Croydon,
Surrey CR9 2TA.
081-686-2599

● **HERB GARDEN,**
P O Box 66, Leeds LS2 7XH.
0532-371888

HEY - TONI!,
11 Marshallsea Road, London Bridge,
London SE1 1EP.
071-717-1228

HI-FI NEWS,
Link House, 9 Dingwall Avenue,
Croydon, Surrey CR9 2TA.
081-686-2599

HIP HOP CONNECTIONS,
Alexander House, Forehill, Ely,
Cambridgeshire CB7 4AX.
0353-665577

● **I-D,**
Universal House, 251-255 Tottenham
Court Road, London W1P 0AE.
071-813-6170

THE INDEPENDENT,
40 City Road, London EC1Y 2DB.
071-253-1222

● **JAZZ RAG,**
P O Box 944, Birmingham,
West Midlands B16 8UT.
021-454-7020

JOCKEY-SLUT,
Unit 226, Ducie House, Ducie Street,
Manchester M1 2JW.
061-237-3128

● **KERRANG,**
52-55 Carnaby Street,
London W1V 1PF.
071-437-8050

KEYBOARD PLAYER,
27 Russell Road, Enfield,
Middlesex EN1 4TN.
081-367-2938

KEYBOARD REVIEW,
Alexander House, Forehill, Ely,
Cambridgeshire, CB7 4AF.
0353-665577

● **LIGHTING & SOUND
INTERNATIONAL,**
7 Highlight House, St Leonards Road,
Eastbourne, Sussex
BN21 3UH.
0323-642639

LIVE!,
35 High Street, Sandridge, St Albans,
Hertfordshire AL4 9DD.
0727-843995

LOADED,
King's Reach Tower, Stamford Street,
London SE1 9LS.
071-261-7619

● **M8,**
11 Lynendoch Place, Glasgow,
Scotland G3 6AV.
041-353-1118

MAKING MUSIC,
20 Bowling Green Lane, London
EC1R 0BD.
071-251-1900

MEDIA WEEK,
33-39 Bowling Green Lane,
London EC1 0DA.
071-837-1212

MELODY MAKER,
26th Floor, King's Reach Tower,
Stamford Street, London SE1 9LS.
071-261-6229

METAL HAMMER,
19 Bolsover Street,
London W1P 7HJ.
071-631-1433

MIXMAG,
P O Box 89, London W14 8ZW.
071-602-3977.

THE MIX MAGAZINE
Alexander House, Forehill, Ely,
Cambridgeshire CB7 4AF.
0353-665577

MOJO,
4 Winsley Street, London W1N 7AR.
071-436-1515

MUSIC STARS,
Riff Raff Productions,
P O Box 1900, London N5 1EP.
071-226-4695.

MUSIC TECHNOLOGY,
Alexander House, Forehill, Ely,
Cambridgeshire CB7 4AX.
0353-665577

MUSIC WEEK,
245 Blackfriars Road, London SE1 9UR.
071-620-3636

● **NEWS OF THE WORLD,**
1 Virginia Street, London E1 9BD.
071-782-5000

NEW MUSICAL EXPRESS,
25th Floor, King's Reach Tower,
Stamford Street, London SE1 9LS.
071-261-6472

● **THE OBSERVER,**
119 Farringdon Road,
London EC1R 3ER.
071-278-2332

● **Q,**
Mappin House, 4 Winsley Street,
London W1N 7AR.
071-436-1515

● **RADIO TIMES,**
Woodlands, 80 Wood Lane,
London W12 0TT.
081-576-2000

RAW,
52-55 Carnaby Street, London W1V 1PS.
071-437-8050

RIFF RAFF,
P O Box 1900, London N5 1EP.
071-226-4695

● **SELECT,**
Mappin House, 4 Winsley Street,
London W1N 7AR.
071-436-1515

SKY,
Mappin House, 4 Winsley Street,
London W1N 7AR.
071-436-1515

SMASH HITS,
Mappin House, 4 Winsley Street,
London W1N 7AR.
071-436-1515

SOUND ON SOUND,
P O Box 30, St Ives,
Cambridgeshire PE17 4XQ.
0480-461244

STUDIO SOUND,
8th Floor, Ludgate House,
245 Blackfriars Road,
London SE1 9UR.
071-620-3636

THE SUN,
1 Virginia Street, Wapping,
London E1 9BD.
071-782-4031

● **TIME OUT,**
Universal House,
251 Tottenham Court Road,
London W1P 0AE.
071-813-3000

TV TIMES,
10th Floor, King's Reach Tower,
Stamford Street, London SE1 9LS.
071-261-7000

● **UPDATE,**
P O Box 89, Slough,
Berkshire SL1 8NA.
0628-667124

● **VOLUME,**
22 Brook Mews North,
London W2 3BW.
071-706-8122

VOX,
25th Floor, King's Reach Tower,
Stamford Street, London SE1 9LS.
071-261-6312

● **THE WIRE,**
45-46 Poland Street,
London W1V 3DF.
071-439-6422

● **THE ZINE,**
P O Box 288, Shere,
Guildford, Surrey, GU5 9JS.
0483-202041

● **APRS,**
2 Windsor Square, Silver Street,
Reading, Berkshire RG1 2TH.
0734-756218

ASCAP,
Suite 10-11, 52 Haymarket,
London SW1Y 4RP.
071-973-0069

● **BEA (BRITISH
ENTERTAINMENT AGENCIES),**
240 Tolworth Rise South,
Surbiton, Surrey TK5 9NB.
081-330-3070

BPI,
25 Savile Row, London W1X 1AA
071-287-4422

**BLACK MUSIC INDUSTRY
ASSOCIATION,**
146 Manor Park Road,
Harlesden, London NW10 4JP.
081-961-4857

**BRITISH ACADEMY OF
SONGWRITERS COMPOSERS &
AUTHORS (BASCA),**
34 Hanway Street,
London W1P 9DE.
071-436-2261

**BRITISH MUSIC
INFORMATION CENTRE,**
10 Stratford Place,
London W1N 9AE.
071-499-8567

● **GUILD INTERNATIONAL
SONGWRITERS COMPOSERS,**
12 Trewartha Road,
Penzance, Cornwall TR20 9ST.

● **IEAM (INSTITUTE OF
ENTERTAINMENT & ARTS
MANAGEMENT),**
3 Trinity Road,
Scarborough,
Yorkshire YO11 2TD.
0723-367449

**INCORPORATED SOCIETY
OF MUSICIANS,**
10 Stratford Place,
London W1N 9AE.
071-629-4413

● **MCPS,**
Elgar House, 41 Streatham High
Road, London SW16 1ER.
081-769-4400

**MUSIC PUBLISHERS
ASSOCATION,**
3rd Floor, Strandgate, 18-20 York
Buildings, London WC2B 6QX.
071-839-7779

**MUSIC RETAILERS
ASSOCIATION,**
P O Box 249, London W4 5EX.
081-994-7592

MUSICIANS BENEVOLENT FUND,
16 Ogle Street, London W1P 7LG.
071-636-4481

MUSICIANS UNION,
60-62 Clapham Road,
London SW9 0JJ.
071-582-5566

● **PERFORMING RIGHTS
SOCIETY LTD,**
29-33 Berners Street,
London W1P 4AA.
071-580-5544

**PHONOGRAPHIC
PERFORMANCE LTD,**
Ganton House,
14-22 Ganton Street,
London W1V 1LB.
071-437-0311

● **BATH MOLES,**
14 George Street, Avon BA1 2EN.
0225-333423

BIRMINGHAM ASTON UNIVERSITY,
Aston Triangle, West Mids B4 7ES
021-359-6531

BIRMINGHAM EDWARDS
No.8, Lower Severn Street,
West Midlands B1 1LR.
021-643-5835

BIRMINGHAM NEC,
P O Box 3348,
Birmingham B40 1NS
021-780-4133

BIRMINGHAM QUE CLUB,
Central Hall, Corporation Street,
Birmingham B4 6QB.
021-212-0550

BOURNEMOUTH INTERNATIONAL CENTRE.
Exeter Road, Dorset BH2 5BH.
0202-552122

BOURNEMOUTH MR SMITH'S,
49 Poole Hill, Dorset, BH2 5PW.
0202-291617.

BRADFORD ST GEORGE'S HALL,
Bridge Street, Yorkshire BD1 1JS.
0274-752000

BRIGHTON CENTRE,
Kings Road, East Sussex BN1 2GR.
0273-203131

BRIGHTON DOME COMPLEX,
29 New Road,
East Sussex BN1 1UG.
0273-700747

BRIGHTON THE EVENT,
Kings West Centre, West Street,
East Sussex BN1 2RE.
0273-732627

BRIGHTON UNIVERSITY OF SUSSEX,
Mandela Hall, Falmer House,
Falmer, East Sussex BN1 9QF.
0273-643816

BRISTOL BIERKELLER,
The Pithay, All Saints Street,
Avon BS1 2NA.
0272-268514

BRISTOL COLSTON HALL,
Colston Street, Avon BS1 5AR.
0272-223693

BRISTOL FLEECE & FIRKIN,
12 St Thomas Street,
Avon BS1 6JJ.
0272-277150

BUCKLEY TIVOLI,
Brunswick Road, Clywdd,
North Wales CH7 2EF.
0244-550782

● **CAMBRIDGE ARTS THEATRE,**
6 St Edward's Passage,
Cambridgeshire CB2 3PL.
0223-355246

CAMBRIDGE CORN EXCHANGE,
3 Parson's Court, Wheeler Street,
Cambridgeshire CB2 3QE.
0223-463204

CAMBRIDGE JUNCTION,
Clifton Road,
Cambridgeshire CB1 4GX.
0223-412600

CARDIFF ST DAVID'S HALL,
The Hayes, South Glamorgan,
Wales CF1 2SH.
0222-342611

CARDIFF UNIVERSITY,
Main Hall, Park Place, South
Glamorgan, Wales CF1 3QN.
0222-396421

CARLISLE SANDS CENTRE,
The Sands, Cumbria CA1 1JQ.
0228-810208

CHELMSFORD ARMY & NAVY,
Army & Navy Roundabout,
Parkway, Essex CM2 7PU.
0245-262424

CHESTER TELFORD'S WAREHOUSE,
Tower Wharf, Chester CH1 3EZ.
0244-390090

COLCHESTER ARTS CENTRE,
Church Street, Essex CO1 1NF.
0206-577301

COLCHESTER ESSEX UNIVERSITY,
Wivenhoe Park, Essex CO4 3SQ.
0206-863211

CORNWALL COLISEUM,
Cornish Leisure World, Carlyon Bay,
St Austell, Cornwall PL25 3RG.
0726-814261

COVENTRY UNIVERSITY,
Priory Street,
West Midlands CV1 5FJ.
0203-221167

COVENTRY WARWICK UNIVERSITY,
Arts Centre Hall, Gibbet Hill Road,
West Midlands CV4 7AL.
0203-524524

CRAWLEY THE HAWTH,
Hawth Avenue,
West Sussex RH10 6YZ.
0293-552941

● **DERBY ASSEMBLY ROOMS,**
Market Place,
Derbyshire DE1 3AH.
0332-255443

DERBY THE WHEREHOUSE,
110a Friargate,
Derbyshire DE1 1EX.
0332-381169

DUNDEE FAT SAM'S,
31 South Ward Road, Tayside,
Scotland DD1 1PU.
0382-26836

● **EAST GRINSTEAD DORSET ARMS,**
101 Club, 58 High Street,
West Sussex RH19 3DE.
0342-316363

EDINBURGH ASSEMBLY ROOMS,
54 George Street, Lothian,
Scotland EH2 2LR.
031-220-4348

EXETER CAVERN CLUB,
83-84 Queen Street, Devon EX4 3RP.
0392-495370

● **FOLKESTONE LEAS CLIFF HALL,**
The Leas, Kent CT20 2DZ.
0303-254695

● **GLASGOW ARENA,**
15 Oswald Street, Glasgow G1 4PA.
041-248-1632

GLASGOW BARROWLANDS,
244 Gallow Gate, Glasgow,
Strathclyde, Scotland G4 OTT.
041-552-4601

GLASGOW KING TUT'S WAH WAH HUT,
272a St Vincent Street,
Strathclyde, Scotland G2 5RL.
041-248-5158

GUILFORD CIVIC HALL,
London Road, Surrey
GU1 2AA.
0483-444720

● **HARLOW SQUARE,**
4th Avenue, Harlow,
Essex CN20 1DW.
0279-417029

HATFIELD FORUM,
Lemsford Road,
Hertfordshire AL10 0EB.
0707-263117

HULL ADELPHI,
89 De Grey Street, Beverley Road,
Humberside HU5 2RU.
0482-48216

HULL CITY HALL,
Queen Victoria Square,
Humberside HU1 3NA.
0482-20123

HULL TOWER BALLROOM,
52 Anlaby Road,
Humberside HU1 2PD.
0482-446777.

● **LEEDS DUCHESS OF YORK,**
Vicar Lane, Yorkshire LS1 6QA.
0532-453929

LEEDS METROPOLITAN UNIVERSITY,
Caverley Street, Yorkshire LS1 3HE.
0532-430171

LEEDS TOWN & COUNTRY CLUB,
55 Cookridge Street,
Yorkshire LS2 3AW.
0532-800100

LEICESTER DE MONTFORT HALL.
Granville Road,
Leicestershire LE1 7RU.
0533-544444

LEICESTER PRINCESS CHARLOTTE,
8 Oxford Street,
Leicestershire LE1 5XZ.
0533-553956.

LICHFIELD ARTS CENTRE,
Bird Street,
Staffordshire WS13 6PR.
0543-262223

LIVERPOOL KRAZY HOUSE,
Wood Street, Merseyside.
051-708-5016

LIVERPOOL THE PICKET,
24 Hardman Street,
Merseyside L1 9AX.
051-709-3995

LIVERPOOL ROYAL COURT,
1 Roe Street,
Merseyside L1 1HH.
051-709-1808

● **MANCHESTER ACADEMY,**
Oxford Road,
Greater Manchester M13 9PR.
061-275-2959

MANCHESTER APOLLO,
Stockport Road,
Greater Manchester M12 6AP.
061-273-6921

MANCHESTER BAND ON THE WALL,
25 Swan Street,
Greater Manchester M4 5JQ.
061-832-6625

MANCHESTER BOARDWALK,
Little Peter Street,
Greater Manchester M15 4PS.
061-228-3555

MANCHESTER HACIENDA,
11-13 Whitworth Street West,
Greater Manchester M1 5WG.
061-236-5051

MANCHESTER UMIST,
Sackville Street,
Greater Manchester M60 1QD.
061-200-3271

MANCHESTER UNIVERSITY UNION,
Oxford Road,
Greater Manchester M13 9PR.
061-275-2959

MANCHESTER WITCHWOOD,
152 Old Street,
Ashton-Under-Lyne, Thameside,
Greater Manchester OL6 7SF.
061-344-0321

MIDDLESBROUGH TOWN HALL,
Albert Road,
Cleveland TS1 1EL.
0642-263848

MILTON KEYNES NATIONAL BOWL,
Watling Street,
Buckinghamshire.
0908-234466

● **NEWCASTLE MAYFAIR SUITE,**
Newgate Street,
Tyne & Wear NE1 5XA.
091-232-3109

NEWCASTLE RIVERSIDE,
57-59 Melbourne Street,
Tyne & Wear NE1 2JQ.
091-261-4386

NEWCASTLE UNIVERSITY,
Kings Walk,
Tyne & Wear WE1 8QB.
091-232-8402

NEWPORT CENTRE,
Kingsway, Gwent,
Wales NP9 1UH.
0633-841522

NORTHAMPTON ROADMENDER CENTRE,
1 Lady's Lane,
Northamptonshire NN1 3AH.
0604-604222

NORTHAMPTON SLURPS, FRIDGE TWO,
36 Bridge Street,
Northamptonshire NN1 2AN.
0604-22331

NORWICH OVAL ROCKHOUSE,
Dereham Road, Norfolk NR5 8TD.
0603-748244

NORWICH UNIVERSITY OF EAST ANGLIA (UEA),
University Complex,
Norfolk NR4 7TG.
0603-56161

NORWICH THE WATERFRONT,
139 King Street, Norfolk NR1 1QH.
0603-632717

NOTTINGHAM ROCK CITY,
8 Talbot Street,
Nottinghamshire NG1 5GG.
0602-412544

NOTTINGHAM ROYAL CONCERT HALL.
South Sherwood Street,
Nottinghamshire NG1 5ND.
0602-483505

NOTTINGHAM UNIVERSITY,
Social Committee, Portland
Building, University Park,
Nottinghamshire NG7 2RD.
0602-505912

● **OXFORD APOLLO THEATRE,**
George Street,
Oxfordshire OX1 2AG.
0865-243041

OXFORD JERICHO TAVERN,
56 Walton Street,
Oxfordshire OX2 6AE.
0865-54502

● POOLE ARTS CENTRE,
Wessex Hall, Kingland Road,
Dorset BH15 1UG.
0202-670521
PORTSMOUTH PYRAMIDS CENTRE,
Clarence Esplanade, Southsea,
Hampshire PO5 3ST.
0705-877895
PORTSMOUTH WEDGEWOOD ROOMS,
147b Albert Road, Southsea,
Hampshire PO4 0JW.
0705-863911
● READING UNIVERSITY,
Whiteknights Park, Reading,
Berkshire RG6 2AZ.
0734-860222

● SALISBURY ARTS CENTRE,
Bedwin Street,
Wiltshire SP1 3UT.
0722-321744
SHEFFIELD ARENA,
Broughton Lane,
South Yorkshire S9 2DS.
0742-562002
SHEFFIELD CITY HALL,
Bakers Pool,
South Yorkshire S1 2JA.
0742-722885
SHEFFIELD LEADMILL,
6-7 Leadmill Road,
South Yorkshire S1 4SF.
0742-754500

SHEFFIELD UNIVERSITY AND OCTAGON,
Western Bank,
South Yorkshire S10 2TG.
0742-753300
SOUTHAMPTON JOINERS ARMS,
St Mary's Street,
Hampshire SO1 1NS.
0703-225612
SOUTHAMPTON MAYFLOWER THEATRE,
Commercial Road,
Hampshire SO15 1GE.
0703-330083

ST HELEN'S CITADEL,
Waterloo Street,
Merseyside WA10 1PX.
0744-735436
STOKE WHEATSHEAF,
Church Street, Stoke On Trent,
Staffordshire ST4 IBU.
0782-44438
●TUNBRIDGE WELLS ASSEMBLY HALL,
Crescent Road,
Kent TN1 1RS.
0892-526121
TUNBRIDGE WELLS THE FORUM,
The Common, Kent.
0892-530411

● UXBRIDGE BRUNEL UNIVERSITY,
Kingston Lane,
Middlesex UB8 3PH.
0895-239125
● WHITLEY BAY ICE RINK,
Hill Heads Road, Hill Heads,
Tyne & Wear NE25 8HP.
091-252-6240
WINDSOR OLD TROUT,
River Street, Berkshire SL4 1HL.
0753-869897
WOLVERHAMPTON CIVIC HALL AND WULFREN HALL,
North Street,
West Midlands WV1 1RQ.
0902-312029

● 100 CLUB,
100 Oxford Street, W1N 9FB.
071-636-0933
● ACADEMY,
211 Stockwell Road,
Brixton, SW9 9SL.
071-924-9999
ALEXANDRA PALACE,
Alexandra Park,
Wood Green, N22 4AY.
081-365-2121
AMERSHAM ARMS,
The Gig, 388 New Cross Road,
New Cross, SE14 6TY.
081-694-8992
ARENA,
Limeharbour,
Isle Of Dogs, E14 9TH.
071-538-8880
ASTORIA,
157 Charing Cross Road,
WC2H 0EN.
071-434-0403
● BARBICAN CENTRE,
Barbican Complex, EC2Y 8DS.
071-638-4141
BASS CLEF,
35 Coronet Street, N1 6NU.
071-729-2476
BLOOMSBURY THEATRE,
15 Gordon Street,
Euston, WC1 0AH.
071-383-5976
BORDERLINE,
Orange Yard, Manette Street,
W1V 5LB.
071-734-2095
BOTTOM LINE,
Shepherd's Bush Green,
W12 8QE.
081-746-0255
BULL & GATE,
389 Kentish Town Road,
Kentish Town, NW5 2TG.
071-485-5358

● CAMDEN PALACE,
1a Camden Road, Camden, NW1.
071-387-0428
● DOME,
178 Junction Road, Tufnell Park,
N19 5QQ.
071-281-2195
DOMINION THEATRE,
Tottenham Court Road, W1P 0AG.
071-580-1889
DUBLIN CASTLE,
94 Parkway, Camden, NW1 7AN.
071-485-1773
● EARLS COURT EXHIBITION CENTRE,
Warwick Road, SW5 9TA.
071-385-1200
ELECTRIC BALLROOM,
184 Camden High Street, NW1 8QP.
071-485-9006
EQUINOX,
Leicester Square, WC2H 7NH.
071-437-1446
● THE FALCON,
234 Royal College Street,
NW5 9LT.
071-485-3834
THE FORUM,
9-17 Highgate Road,
Kentish Town, NW5 1JY.
071-284-2200
THE FRIDGE,
Town Hall Parade, Brixton Hill,
SW2 1RJ.
071-326-5100
● THE GARAGE,
20-22 Highbury Corner, N5 1RD.
071-607-1818
GEORGE CANNING,
95 Effra Road, SW2 1DS.
071-738-4959
THE GRAND,
St John's Hill,
Clapham Junction, SW11 2RS.
071-738-9000

● HACKNEY EMPIRE,
291 Mare Street, Hackney, E8 1EJ.
081-986-0171
HALF MOON,
10 Half Moon Lane, Herne Hill,
SE24 9HU.
071-274-2733
HALF MOON,
93 Lower Richmond Road,
Putney, SW15 1EU.
081-780-9383
THE HIPPODROME,
Hippodrome Corner, Leicester
Square, WC2 7JH.
071-437-4837
● INSTITUTE OF CONTEMPORARY ART (ICA),
The Mall, SW1Y 5AH.
071-930-0493
● JAZZ CAFE,
5 Parkway, Camden, NW1 7PG.
071-916-6000
● KING'S HEAD,
4 Fulham High Street, SW6 3LQ.
071-736-1413
● LA2,
165 Charing Cross Road, WC2.
071-434-0403
LABATT'S APOLLO,
Queen Caroline Street,
Hammersmith, W6 9QH.
081-741-4868
LE PALAIS,
242 Shepherd's Bush Road,
W6 7NL.
081-748-2812
● MARQUEE,
105 Charing Cross Road,
WC2H 0DT.
071-437-6603
MEAN FIDDLER AND ACOUSTIC ROOM,
24-28a High Street,
Harlesden, NW10 4LX.
081-961-5490

● THE ORANGE,
North End Crescent, North End
Road, West Kensington, W14 8TG.
071-371-4317
● POWERHAUS,
1 Liverpool Road, Islington, N1 0RP.
071-837-3218
● QUEEN MARY COLLEGE,
327 Mile End Road, E1 4NS.
071-975-5555
●THE ROBEY,
240 Seven Sisters Road,
Finsbury Park, N4 2HX.
071-263-4581
ROCK GARDEN,
The Piazza,
Covent Garden, WC2E 8HA.
071-240-3961
RONNIE SCOTT'S,
47 Frith Street, W1V 6HT.
071-439-0747
ROYAL ALBERT HALL,
Kensington Gore, SW7 2AP.
071-589-3203
ROYAL FESTIVAL HALL,
Belvedere Road, SE1 8XX.
071-928-8800
ROYAL STANDARD,
1 Blackhorse Lane,
Walthamstow, E17 6DS.
081-527-1966
● SAMUEL BECKETT,
175 High Street,
Stoke Newington, N16 0LH.
071-254-2266
SHEPHERD'S BUSH EMPIRE,
Shepherd's Bush Green, W12.
081-740-7474
SUBTERANIA,
12 Acklam Road,
Ladbroke Grove, W10.
081-960-4590
THE SWAN,
1 Fulham Broadway, SW6 1AA.
071-385-1840

THE TORRINGTON,
4 Lodge Lane,
North Finchley, N12 8JR.
081-445-4710
● UNIVERSITY OF GREENWICH,
Thomas Street, SE18 6HU.
081-855-0618
UNIVERSITY OF LONDON UNION (ULU),
Malet Street, WC1H 7DY.
071-580-9551
UNIVERSITY OF NORTH LONDON,
Holloway Road, N7 8DB.
071-607-2789
UNIVERSITY OF WESTMINSTER,
104-108 Bolsover Street,
W1P 7HF.
071-636-6271
UNDERWORLD,
174 Camden High Street,
Camden, NW1 0NE.
071-482-1932
● THE VENUE,
2a Clifton Rise,
New Cross, SE14 6JP.
081-692-4077
THE VOX CLUB,
9 Brighton Terrace,
Brixton, SW9 8DJ.
071-737-2095
● WATER RATS,
Splash Club, 328 Gray's Inn Road,
King's Cross, WC1X 8BZ.
071-278-3879
THE WEAVERS,
98 Newington Green Road,
N1 4RG.
071-226-6911
WEMBLEY STADIUM AND ARENA,
Empire Way, Middlesex HA9 0DW.
081-902-8833

RECORDING

● **2001,**
19 Ash Street, Ash,
Surrey GU12 6LA.
0252-336505

● **ABBEY ROAD STUDIOS,**
3 Abbey Road, London NW8 9AY.
071-286-1161

AIR STUDIOS (LYNDHURST) LTD,
Lyndhurst Hall, Lyndhurst Road,
Hampstead, London NW3 5NG.
071-794-0660

ALASKA STREET STUDIOS,
127-129 Alaska Street, Waterloo,
London SE5 1 8XE.
071-928-7440

ANGEL RECORDING STUDIOS,
311 Upper Street, London N1 2TU.
071-354-2525

AOSIS,
10a Belmont Street,
London NW1 8HH.
071-485-4810

ARIWA SOUND STUDIO,
34 Whitehorse Lane,
London SE25 6RE.
081-653-7744

AXIS RECORDING STUDIO,
3 Brown Street, Sheffield,
Yorkshire S1 2BS.
0742-750283

● **BTW RECORDING STUDIOS,**
125 Myddleton Road, Wood
Green, London N22 4NG.
081-888-6655

BACKTRACK STUDIO,
Acacia Cottage, Princess Road,
Thornton Heath, Croydon,
Surrey CR0 2QS.
081-683-2492

BACKYARD STUDIO,
Units 5, Willowbrook, Crickhowell
Road, St Mellons, Cardiff CF3 0EF.
0222-777739

BATTERY STUDIOS,
1 Maybury Gardens,
London NW10 2SG.
081-459-8899

BILLIARD ROOM RECORDING STUDIO,
4 Welburn Drive, West Park,
Leeds, Yorkshire LS16 5QD.
0532-786671

BLACK BARN STUDIOS,
3 Dunsborough Cottages, The
Green, Ripley, Surrey GU23 6AL.
0483-222600

BLACKWING RECORDING STUDIOS,
All Hallows Church, 1 Pepper
Street, London SE1 0EP.
071-261-0118

BLISS RECORDING STUDIO,
Higher Penwartha Farm,
Blowinghouse, Perranporth, Truro,
Cornwall TR6 0BA.
0872-572757

BRITANNIA ROW STUDIOS,
35 Britannia Row, Islington,
London N1 8QH.
071-226-3377

THE BUNKER,
111 Power Road, Chiswick,
London W4 5PY.
081-995-2723

● **CABIN STUDIOS,**
82 London Road, Coventry,
Warwickshire CV1 2JT.
0203-220749

CASTLE SOUND STUDIOS LTD,
The Old School Park View,
Pencaitland EH34 5DT.
0875-340143

CAVA EAST,
Albion Business Centre,
78 Albion Road,
Edinburgh, EH7 5QZ.
031-659-6673

CHANNEL 1 RECORDING,
6 Jubilee Road, Reading,
Berkshire RG6 1NX.
0734-267362

CHARLOTTE STREET STUDIOS,
63 Charlotte Street, London W1P 1LA.
071-636-4840

CHISWICK REACH RECORDING,
Lamb House, Church Street,
Chiswick, London W4 2PD.
081-995-6504

THE CHURCH STUDIOS,
145h Crouch Hill, London N8 9QH.
081-340-9779

CLOCK HOUSE STUDIOS,
The Clock House, Keele,
Staffordshire ST5 5BG.
0782-583301

COACH HOUSE RECORDING STUDIOS,
7 Richmond Hill Avenue, Clifton,
Bristol, Avon BS8 1BG.
0272-238444

CUTTING ROOMS,
Abraham Moss Centre, Crescent
Road, Manchester M8 6UF.
061-740-9438

CYBERZONE DIGITAL,
14 Wenlock Court, New North
Road, London N1 7QR.
071-253-8865

● **DE WOLFE MUSIC LTD,**
80-88 Wardour Street,
London W1V 3LF.
071-439-8481

● **E-ZEE STUDIOS,**
14-18 Market Road,
London N7 9PW.
071-609-0246

EARTH,
163 Gerrard Street, Birmingham,
West Mids B19 2AP.
021-554-7424

EASY STREET STUDIOS,
45 Blythe Street, Bethnal Green,
London E2 7AW.
071-739-8887

EDEN STUDIOS LTD,
20-24 Beaumont Road,
Chiswick, London W4 5AP.
081-995-5432

ELEPHANT RECORDING STUDIOS,
Basement N, Metropolitan Wharf,
Wapping Wall, London E1.
071-481-8615

● **FX STUDIOS,**
Chantry Mews,
Upper High Street,
Sevenoaks, Kent TN13 1NZ.
0732-460515

FAB RECORDING STUDIOS,
15 Knoll Street, Salford,
Manchester M7 2EQ.
061-792-0203

FAIR DEAL RECORDING STUDIOS,
1 Gledwood Drive, Hayes,
Middlesex UB4 0AG.
0753-890400

FALCONER STUDIOS,
17 Ferdinand Street,
London NW1 8EU.
071-267-7777

FON STUDIOS LTD,
3 Brown Street, Sheffield,
Yorkshire S1 2BS.
0742-754644

● **GOLDDUST STUDIOS,**
14 Cromwell Avenue, Bromley,
Kent BR2 9AQ.
081-466-7435

GRAPEVINE STUDIOS,
25 Vine Street, Brighton,
Sussex BN1 4AG.
0273-698555

GREENHOUSE RECORDING STUDIOS,
34-38 Provost Street,
London N1 7NJ.
071-253-7101

GWBB AUDIOVISION,
42 Lancaster Gate,
London W2 3NA.
071-723-5190

● **HEAR NO EVIL,**
17 Baron's Court Road,
West Kensington,
London W14 9DP.
071-385-8244

HI-LEVEL RECORDING,
Level Four, British India House,
Carliol Square, Newcastle,
Tyne & Wear NE1 6UF.
091-261-5869

THE HIT FACTORY,
31-37 Whitfield Streeet,
London W1P 5RE.
071-636-3434

THE HOUSE IN THE WOODS,
The Yews, Hextalls Lane, Whitehill,
Bletchingley, Surrey, RH1 4QU.
0883-343027

HUMAN LEAGUE STUDIO,
3 Brown Street, Sheffield,
Yorkshire S1 2BS.
0742-730300

● **ISLAND STUDIO - THE FALLOUT SHELTER,**
47 British Grove, London W4.
081-741-1511

ISLINGTON MUSIC WORKSHOP LTD,
44 Peartree Street,
London EC1V 3SB.
071-608-0231

● **JACOBS STUDIOS,**
Ridgway House, Runwick Lane,
Near Farnham, Surrey GU10 5EE.
0252-715546

JIGSAW STUDIOS,
115 Old Lodge Lane, Purley,
Surrey CR8 4DP.
081-668-3457

JOHN MOUNTFORD STUDIOS LTD,
Park Farm, Hethersett, Norwich,
Norfolk NR9 3DL.
0603-811855

● **KD STUDIOS,**
78 Church Path,
Fletcher Road,
London W4 5BJ.
081-994-3142

KOH-SAN,
Avondale Coach House,
London Road, East Bathford,
Bath, Avon BA1 7RB.
0225-858028

KONK STUDIOS,
84-86 Tottenham Lane, Hornsey,
London N8 7EE.
081-340-7873

● **LILLIE YARD STUDIOS,**
6 Lillie Yard, 19 Lillie Road,
London SW6 1UB.
071-385-9299

LOGICOM SOUND & VISION,
1 Portland Drive, Willen,
Milton Keynes,
Buckinghamshire MK15 9JW.
0908-663848

● **MAISON ROUGE STUDIOS,**
2 Wansdown Place,
Fulham Broadway,
London SW6 1DN.
071-381-2001

MANOR STUDIOS,
The Manor, Shipton On Cherwell,
Oxfordshire OX5 1JL.
0865-377551

MATRIX STUDIOS,
35 Little Russell Streeet,
London WC1A 2HH.
071-580-9956

METROPOLIS STUDIOS,
The Power House,
70 Chiswick High Road,
London W4 1SY.
081-742-1111

MILL RECORDING STUDIOS,
Mill Lane, Cookham,
Berkshire SL6 9QT.
0628-810788

MOLES STUDIO,
14 George Street, Bath,
Avon BA1 2EN.
0225-333448

MOLINAIRE,
34 Foubert's Place,
London W1V 2BH.
071-439-2244

MPF,
Bon Marche Buiding, Ferndale
Road, London SW9 8EJ.
071-737-7152

STUDIOS

MUSHROOM RECORDING STUDIOS,
18 West Mall, Clifton,
Avon BS8 2BQ.
0272-735994

● **NARK MIDI SUITE,**
Flat 20, Whiteoak Court, Whiteoak
Road, Fallowfield, Manchester
B14 6UA. 061-225-0633

NETWORK MUSIC & MEDIA,
22a Forest Road West,
Nottingham NG7 4EQ.
0602-784714

NOMIS STUDIOS,
45-53 Sinclair Road,
London W14 0NS.
071-602-6351

NOVA STUDIOS,
27-31 Bryanston Street,
London W1H 7AB.
071-493-7403

● **OLYMPIC STUDIOS,**
117 Church Road, Barnes,
London SW13 9HL.
081-748-7961

● **PWL,**
4-7 The Vineyard,
Sanctuary Street,
London SE1 1QL.
071-403-0007

PARR STREET STUDIOS,
33-45 Parr Street, Liverpool,
Merseyside L1 4JN.
051-707-1050

PINK MUSEUM,
1 Hesketh Street, Liverpool,
Merseyside L17 8XJ.
051-727-7557

PRIORITY,
246 West Street, Sheffield,
Yorkshire S1 4EU.
0742-761117

PROTOCOL STUDIOS,
23a Benwell Road,
London N7 7BW.
071-607-9495

● **Q BROADCAST LTD,**
148 Melton Road, Queniborough,
Leicestershire LE7 8FP.
0533-608813

● **RAK RECORDING STUDIOS,**
42-48 Charlbert Street,
London NW8 7BU.
071-586-2012

RAVEN RECORDING,
Swaysland, Tanner's Green,
Garvestone, Norwich,
Norfolk NR9 4QR.
0362-850326

RED BUS RECORDING STUDIOS LTD,
34 Salisbury Street,
London NW8 8QE.
071-402-9111

REVIVAL STUDIOS,
17-19 Motherwell Road,
Carfin, ML1 4EB.
0698-275581

REVOLUTION STUDIOS,
11 Church Road, Cheadle,
Cheshire SK8 7JD.
061-485-8942

REVOLVER STUDIOS,
152 Goldthorn Hill,
Penn,
West Midlands WV2 3JA.
0902-345345

RICH BITCH STUDIOPLEX,
505 Bristol Road,
Selly Oak,
Birmingham,
West Midlands B29 6AU.
021-471-1339

RIDGE FARM STUDIOS,
Rusper Road, Capel,
Surrey RH5 5HG.
0306-711202

RIVERSIDE STUDIO COMPLEX,
7 Lower Mill Road,
Busby,
Glasgow, G76 8BJ.
041-644-5572

ROCKFIELD STUDIOS,
Amberley Court,
Rockfield Road,
Monmouth,
Gwent NP5 4ET.
0600-712449

ROOSTER RECORDING STUDIOS,
117 Sinclair Road,
London W14 0NP.
071-602-2881

ROUNDHOUSE RECORDING STUDIOS,
100 Chalk Farm Road,
London NW1 8EH.
071-485-0131

● **SARM EAST,**
9-13 Osborn Street,
London E1 6TD.
071-247-1311

SARM WEST,
8-10 Basing Street,
London W11 1ET.
071-229-1229

SELECT SOUND,
1 Stevenage Road,
Knebworth,
Hertfordshire SG3 6AN.
0438-814433

SHAW SOUND,
Basement,
346 North End Road,
London SW6 1NB.
071-385-1816

SOUND ADVICE,
Unit C104, Faircharm Trading
Estate, 8-12 Creekside,
London SE8 3DX.
081-694-9484

THE SOUND HOUSE,
Forth House, Forth Street,
Edinburgh, EH1 3LF.
031-557-1557

SOUNDSPACE STUDIO COMPEX,
West Wharf Road,
Cardiff CF1 5DD.
0222-373707

SOUTHERN STUDIOS,
10 Myddleton Road,
London N22 4NS.
081-888-8949

SPIRIT RECORDING STUDIOS,
10 Tariff Street,
Manchester M1 2FF.
061-228-3072

STEAMROOM STUDIOS,
Poplar Baths,
East India Dock Road,
London E14 0EH.
071-987-2738

ST. MARKS STUDIO
Bridge Park, Brentfield,
Harrow road,
London NW10 0RG.
081-963-1526

STRAWBERRY HILLS STUDIOS,
2 New King's Road,
London SW6 4SA.
071-736-1234

STRONGROOM,
120 Curtain Road,
London EC2A 3PJ.
071-729-6165

STUDIO 125,
125 Junction Road,
Burgess Hill,
Sussex RH15 0JL.
0444-871818

SULTAN SOUND,
51 Loveridge Road,
London NW6 2DU.
071-624-1816

SURREY SOUND STUDIOS,
70 Kingston Road, Leatherhead,
Surrey, KT22 7BW.
0372-379444

SWALLOW STUDIOS,
Congleton Road, Smallwood,
Sandbach, Cheshire CW11 0UT.
0477-500201

SWANYARD RECORDINGS STUDIOS,
12-27 Swan Yard,
London N1 1SD.
071-354-3737

● **TARAN STUDIOS,**
Unit M3, Cardiff Workshops,
Lewis Road, Cardiff, CF1 5EJ.
0222-484298

TEESBEAT RECORDING STUDIOS,
74-76 Dovecott Street, Stockton
On Tees, Cleveland TS18 1BZ.
0642-602839

TONE DEAF LTD,
The Lane, Gangsdown Hill,
Wallingford, Oxfordshire OX9 6QE.
0491-641942

TOUCHWOOD STUDIOS,
6 Hyde Park Terrace, Leeds,
Yorkshire LS6 1BJ.
0532-787180

TOWNHOUSE STUDIOS,
150 Goldhawk Road,
London W12 8HH.
081-743-9313

TOWNHOUSE THREE,
115 Thessaly Road, Battersea,
London SW8 4EJ.
071-720-5066

● **VON'S RECORDING STUDIOS,**
505-507 Liverpool Road,
London N7 8NS.
071-609-9450

● **WESTAR RECORDING STUDIOS,**
1 Priory Way, Southall,
Middlesex UB2 5EH.
081-571-4679

WOOL HALL STUDIOS,
Castle Corner, Beckington,
Near Bath, Somerset BA3 6TA.
0373-830731

● **YMCA RECORDING STUDIO,**
East Street, Leicester,
Leicestershire LE1 6EY.
0533-556507

● **ZIPPER NEW AGE PRODUCTIONS,**
7 Oakleigh Park South,
London N20 9JS.
081-446-3098

REHEARSAL STUDIOS

● **A&R STUDIOS,**
Unit 1 Horseshoe Close,
Off Oxgate Lane, Cricklewood,
London NW2 7JJ.
081-450-0869

ALASKA STREET STUDIOS,
127-129 Alaska Street, Waterloo,
London SE1 8XE.
071-928-7440

AUTOMATIC REHEARSALS,
Bombay Wharf, 59 St Mary
Church Street, London SE16 4JE.
071-252-2206

● **B M R S,**
48 The Wicker, Sheffield,
Yorkshire S3 8JB.
0742-769676

**BACKSTREET REHEARSAL
STUDIOS,**
313 Holloway Road,
London N7 9SU.
071-609-1313

BAK 2 BAK MUSIC,
Unit 4b, 11-13 Benwell Road,
Holloway, London N7 7BL.
071-607-4347

BANDWAGON STUDIOS,
Westfield Lane, Mansfield,
Nottingham NG18 1TL.
0623-422962

BASEMENT STUDIOS,
 Park House, 15-19 Greenhill
Crescent, Watford,
Hertfordshire WD1 8QU.
0923-220169

BERKELEY 2,
 54 Washington Street,
Glasgow G3 8AZ.
041-248-7290

BLISS REHEARSALS,
Higher Penwortha Farm,
Blowinghouse, Perranporth,
Cornwall TR6 0BA.
0872-572757

BLUESTONE STUDIOS,
Hebron, Whitland,
Dyfed SA34 0YP.
0994-419425

**THE BRILL BUILDING
RECORDING & REHEARSAL
COMPLEX,**
7 Oxbourne Street,
Glasgow G1 5QQ.
041-552-6677

● **CHANNEL STUDIOS,**
Channel C Business Centre,
Canning Road,
London E15 3ND.
081-503-1665

**COURTYARD RECORDING
STUDIOS,**
Unit 2, Gorsey Mount Street,
Stockport, Cheshire SK1 3BU.
061-477-6531

CRASH REHEARSAL STUDIOS,
Imperial Warehouse,
11 Davies Street, Liverpool,
Merseyside L1 6HB.
051-236-0989

● **DAMAJIVE STUDIOS,**
Unit 5b Station Approach, Hitchin,
Hertfordshire SG4 9UW.
0462-457264

THE DEPOT,
Unit L, Albion Yard, Balfe Street,
King's Cross, London N1.
071-226-1356

● **E-ZEE STUDIOS,**
14-18 Market Road,
London N7 9PW.
071-609-0246

**ENGLISH FOLK DANCE &
SONG SOCIETY,**
Cecil Sharp House,
2 Regents Park Road,
London NW1 7AY.
071-485-2206

● **THE GREENHOUSE,**
Unit 16, Brighton Road Industrial
Estate, Heaton Norris, Stockport,
Cheshire SK4 2BE.
061-431-4127

GUITAR CENTRE,
126 Meadfield Road, Langley,
Slough, Berkshire SL3 8JF.
0753-542720

● **INTERGALACTIC ART**
31 Markam Street,
London SE17 1DX.
071-701-9323

● **JOHN HENRY ENTERPRISES,**
16-24 Brewery Road,
London N7 9NH.
071-609-9181

JUMBO STUDIOS,
387-389 Chapter Road,
Willesden, London NW2 5NQ.
081-459-7256

● **LA ROCKA,**
Cross Lane, Hornsey,
London N8 7SA.
081-348-2822

● **MAPLE STUDIOS,**
Unit 39-45, Grainger Road
Industrial Estate, Southend-on-
Sea, Essex SS2 5DD.
0702-613066

MUSIC CITY,
122 New Cross Road,
London SE14 5BA.
071-277-9657

MUSIC COMPLEX LTD,
Unit 5, Bessemer Park Trading
Estate, 250 Milkwood Road,
London SE24 0HG.
071-924-0166

THE MUSIC ROOM,
116-118 New Cross Road,
London SE14 5BA.
071-252-8271

THE MUSIC STUDIOS,
29 Marylebone Lane,
London W1M 5FH.
071-486-0025

● **NOMIS STUUDIOS,**
45-53 Sinclair Road,
London W14 0NS.
071-602-6351

● **THE PLAYGROUND,**
Unit J, 44 St Paul's Crescent,
Camden, London NW1 9TN.
071-485-7412

PORKY PIG PA HIRE,
Fiddington Farm Estate,
Fiddington, Tewkesbury,
Gloucestershire GL20 7DJ.
0684-290181

THE PREMISES,
201-203 Hackney Road,
London E2 8JL.
071-729-7593

● **QUAY SOUND STUDIOS,**
11-15 High Bridge Wharf,
Eastney Street, London SE10.
081-853-2950

● **RED TAPE STUDIOS,**
50 Shoreham Street, Sheffield,
Yorkshire S1 4SP.
0742-761151

RICH BITCH STUDIOPLEX,
505 Bristol Road, Bournbrook,
Birmingham,
West Midlands B29 6AU.
021-414-1139

RITZ REHEARSAL STUDIOS,
110-112 Disraeli Road, London
SW15 2DX.
081-870-1335

RIVERSIDE STUDIO COMPLEX,
7 Lower Mill Road, Clarkston,
Glasgow, Scotland G76 8BJ.
041-644-5572

ROGUE STUDIOS,
Unit RA 4, Bermondsey Trading
Estate, Rotherhithe New Road,
London SE16 3LL.
071-231-3257

● **THE SCOUNDREL ROOMS,**
Beehive Mill, Jersey Street,
Manchester M4 6JG.
061-228-0357

SHOW ME STUDIOS,
Block C, Imperial Works,
Perran Street, Kentish Town,
London NW5 3ED.
071-267-4555

SOUND ADVICE,
Unit C102, Faircharm Trading
Estate, 8-12 Creekside,
London SE8 3DX.
081-694-9484

**SOUNDSPACE STUDIO
COMPLEX,**
West Wharf Road,
Cardiff CF1 5DD.
0222-373707

THE SOUND STATION,
37 Commercial Street,
Birmingham,
West Midlands B1 1RS.
021-643-5952

STANBRIDGE STUDIOS,
A23 Brighton Road, Near
Handcross, Sussex RH17 6BB.
0444-400432

SUNDAY SCHOOL STUDIOS,
Rotary Street,
London SE1 6LG.
071-928-1960

SURVIVAL STUDIOS,
Unit B18, Acton Business Centre,
School Road,
Acton,
London NW10 6TD.
081-961-1977

SWALLOW STUDIOS,
Congleton Road,
Smallwood, Sandbach,
Cheshire CW11 0UT.
0477-500201

SYNC CITY,
Millmead Business Centre,
Mill Mead Road,
Tottenham,
London N17 0QU.
081-808-0472

● **TERMINAL STUDIOS,**
4-10 Lamb Walk,
London SE1 3TT.
071-403-3050

TRACKSIDE,
24 Wallis Avenue,
Southend-on-Sea,
Essex SS2 6HS.
0702-333453

● **WAREHOUSE STUDIOS,**
Unit A01, Tower Bridge Business
Complex, Clements Road,
London SE16 4DG.
071-237-9570

THE WARREN,
Warren Road,
Orpington,
Kent BR1 0BS.
0689-836817

WATERSHED STUDIOS,
Unit F4, Cumberland Business
Centre, Northumberland Road,
Portsmouth, Hampshire PO5 1DS.
0705-839224

WESTAR STUDIOS,
1 Priory Way,
Southall,
Middlesex UB2 5EH.
081-571-4679

**WOOD WHARF REHEARSAL
STUDIOS,**
28-30 Wood Wharf,
Horseferry Place,
Greenwich,
London SE10 9BT.
081-853-4766

PA Hire

● **AB ACOUSTICS,**
Unit 4 Ely Industrial Estate,
Rhondda,
Mid Glamorgan CF40 1RA.
0443-440404

AUDIO & ACOUSTICS LTD,
United House, North Road,
London N7 9DP.
071-700-2900

AUDIO CONTROL,
26 Church Lane, Dore,
Sheffield,
Yorkshire S17 3GS.
0742-369772

AUDIO LEISURE HIRE,
28a Raglan Road, Bromley,
Kent BR2 9NW.
081-466-7359

AUDIOTECH,
54 St James Road, Bridlington,
Yorkshire YO15 3PQ.
0262-672780

● **COMPOST PA,**
11 Page Moss Parade, Huyton,
Merseyside L36 2PA.
051-489-3384

CONCERT SOUND LTD,
Unit 4, Shakespeare Industrial
Estate, Shakespeare Street,
Watford, Hertfordshire WD2 5HD.
0923-240854

● **ESS PA HIRE,**
Unit 14 Bleak Hill Way, Hermitage
Lane Industrial Estate, Mansfield,
Nottinghamshire NG18 5EZ.
0623-647291

ENCORE GROUP,
Audio House, Penny Road,
Park Royal, London NW10 7RW.
081-965-2044

ENTEC SOUND & LIGHT,
517 Yeading Lane, Northolt,
Middlesex UB5 6LN.
081-842-4004

● **GEARHOUSE LTD,**
17 Penn Street, Birmingham,
West Midlands B4 7RJ.
021-333-3390

● **HARDWARE HOUSE,**
West Works, Chalgrove Road,
London E9 6PB.
081-986-6111

● **JHE AUDIO,**
16-24 Brewery Road,
London N7 9NH.
071-609-9181

● **THE MUSIC ROOM,**
116-118 New Cross Road,
London SE14
071-252-8271

● **PW ENTERPRISES LTD,**
Unit 11, Chelsea Fields Industrial
Estate, 278 Western Road,
Merton, London SW19 2QA.
081-646-6131

PANDORA PRODUCTIONS,
Unit 38, Hallmark Trading Centre,
Fourth Way, Wembley,
Middlesex HA9 OLB.
081-795-2432

PORKY PIG PA HIRE,
Fiddington Farm Estate,
Fiddington, Tewkesbury,
Gloucestershire GL20 7DJ.
0684-290181

PRO AUDIO SYSTEMS LTD,
Unit M7, Enterprise 5, Five Lane
Ends, Idle, Bradford,
Yorkshire BD20 8BW.
0274-777200

● **SOUND COMPANY,**
2-4 Foulden Terrace, Foulden
Road, London N16 7UT.
071-923-4121

SOUNDPLANT,
Unit 38, Hallmark Trading Centre,
Fourth Way, Wembley,
Middlesex HA9 OLB.
081-795-2432

STAGE AUDIO SERVICES,
Unit 4, Talbot Street, Brierley Hill,
West Midlands DY5 3EA.
0384-263629

STAGE NORTH,
Unit 4- 5 Woodham Road,
Aycliffe Industrial Estate,
County Durham DL5 6HT.
0325-314946

STAGE TWO LTD,
Unit J, Penfold Trading Estate,
Imperial Way, Watford,
Hertfordshire WD2 4YY.
0923-230789

STAR HIRE,
Milton Road, Thurleigh,
Bedfordshire MK44 2DG.
0234-772233

● **TEN OUT OF TEN
PRODUCTIONS LTD,**
Unit 14, Forest Hill
Business Centre,
Clyde Vale,
London SE23 3JF.
081-291-6885

TERMINAL STUDIO HIRE,
4-10 Lamb Walk,
London SE1 3TT.
071-403-3050

**TOURCO CONCERT
PRODUCTIONS,**
Unit 4, Kent House,
Kent Street, Birmingham,
West Midlands B5 6QF.
021-622-1894

TOURTECH,
26 St Andrew's Street,
Northampton NN1 2HY.
0604-30322

● **THE WAREHOUSE SOUND
SERVICES LTD,**
23 Water Street, Leith,
Edinburgh EH6 6SU.
031-555-6900

WILLPOWER PA SYSTEMS LTD,
Unit 4, Acorn Production Centre,
105 Blundell Street,
London N7 9BN.
071-609-9870

WING SOUND & LIGHT,
442 Upper Elmers End Road,
Eden Park, Beckingham,
Kent BR3 3HQ.
081-688-0440

● **YORKSHIRE AUDIO,**
537 Dewsbury Road,
Leeds,
Yorkshire LS11 5LE.
0532-770952

Instrument Hire

● **ADVANCED SOUNDS LTD,**
259 Queensway,
West Wickham,
Kent BR4 9DX.
081-462-6261

ASTRA MUSIC,
Fairview Farm, Fiddling Lane,
Monks Horton, Ashford,
Kent TN25 6AP.
0303-812715

AUDIO HIRE,
2 Langler Road,
Kensal Rise,
London NW10 5TL.
081-960-4466

● **BABEL SYSTEMS,**
7 Goldhawk Mews,
London W12 8PA.
081-749-8222

● **CHANDLER GUITARS,**
300-302 Sandycombe Road,
Richmond,
Surrey TW9 3NG.
081-940-5874

CHILTERN PIANO COMPANY,
127 Station Road, Amersham,
Buckinghamshire HP7 0AH.
0494-727077

CHRISTOFORI PIANOFORTE LTD,
29 Marylebone Lane,
London W1M 5FH.
071-486-0025

● **DRUMHIRE,**
Unit 14, Triangle Business Centre,
Enterprise Way, Salter Street,
London NW10 6UE.
081-960-0221

● **EMPIRE DRUMS,**
Arch 64, Ewer Street,
London SE1 0NR.
071-928-1286

● **FX RENTALS LTD,**
Unit 3, Park Mews,
213 Kilburn Lane,
London W10 4BQ.
081-964-2288

● **GP PA CO,**
Unit D, 51 Brunswick Road,
Edinburgh,
Scotland EH7 5PD.
031-661-0022

GIGSOUNDS LTD,
20 Rushey Green,
London SE6 4JF.
081-690-8622

GUITAR CENTRE,
126 Meadfield Road,
Langley, Slough,
Berkshire SL3 8JF.
0753-542720

● **IMPACT PERCUSSION,**
120-122 Bermondsey Street,
London SE1 3TX.
071-403-5900

● **JOHN HENRY ENTERPRISES,**
The John Henry Building,
16-24 Brewery Road,
London N7 9NH.
071-609-9181

● **LOUDMOUTH SOUND
SERVICES,**
14-18 Station Street, Mansfield,
Woodhouse, Nottingham
NG19 8AB.
0623-653000

● **MX HIRE,**
Old Snow Hill, Birmingham,
West Midlands B4 6HX.
021-212-0102

MAPLE EQUIPMENT HIRE,
Unit 39-45, Grainger Road
Industrial Estate,
Southend On Sea,
Essex SS2 5DD.
0702-613066

MUSIC CONTROL,
Chapel Mews,
68 Crewe Road, Alfager,
Stoke on Trent, ST7 2HA.
0270-883779

● **OCTAVE CLASSICS,**
414 Essex Road, London N1 3PJ.
071-226-5759

● **PETER WEBBER HIRE,**
110-112 Disraeli Road,
London SW15 2DX.
081-870-1335

PORKY PIG PA HIRE,
Fiddington Farm Estate,
Fiddington, Tewkesbury,
Gloucestershire GL20 7DJ.
0684-290181

● **SENSIBLE MUSIC LTD,**
Unit 10, Acorn Production Centre,
105 Bludell Street,
London N7 9BN.
071-700-6655

STUDIO HIRE,
8 Daleham Mews,
London NW3 5DB.
071-431-0212

● **TERMINAL STUDIO HIRE,**
4-10 Lamb Walk,
London SE1 3TT.
071-403-3050

● **VINTAGE & RARE CLASSICS,**
68 Kenway Road,
London SW5 0RA.
071-370-7835

● **WORLD OF SOUND
SYSTEMS,**
144 Fleet Road, Hampstead,
London NW3 2QX.
071-482-4090

alexander

Phil Alexander is the editor of *Kerrang!*, the world's heavy metal bible. Despite the constant passage of time, he remains 15 years old, talks about "Satan", "hate" and "doughnuts" a lot, and has a deep appreciation of very load guitars. His ambition is to eat a steak killed and cooked by US guitar guru Ted Nugent. Then again…

blakebrough

Once an aspiring media brat, **Lisa Blakebrough** is now turning her back on full time employment within the publishing industry in order to return to study. Her favourite phrase, however, remains "Me plus one on the guest list, please."

Tom Doyle is a London-based writer for *Q*, *Smash Hits* and others who blathered on about Paul Weller in this book, as well as lovingly compiling The Critics' A-Z, which he really hopes "you dig".

doyle

Nick Duerden is a freelance music journalist who has had his considered and considerable opinions printed in far too many magazines to mention. And as a result of this book, he's a bloody walking encyclopedia on all matters rock and, indeed, its dancing partner, roll. *Pop Quiz* beckons, inevitably…

duerden

Jim Irvin spent the '80s fronting moody pop combo Furniture, who once started a near-riot in pre-revolution Romania by simply performing their chart-shagging single *Brilliant Mind*. The group kind of petered out and Jim kind of petered in to music journalism, contributing to *Melody Maker*, *Time Out* and *The Guardian* under the name Jim Arundel, eventually becoming *The Maker*'s reviews editor. In May 1994 he was appointed Features Editor of *Mojo* magazine.

irvin

Since last year's Virgin Yearbook, **Cliff Jones** has abandoned his eagerly awaited debut album, *The Psychedelic Soul Banjo Of Cliff Jones*, in favour of an all-new band he's called Elvis Beatle. He is currently listening to a lot of British folk records, dressing in hessian sacking and boring his few remaining friends with finger-in-the-ear renditions of *John Barleycorn Must Die* and *Mr Fox Came-a-Courting*.

jones

In his spare time he still scrapes a living writing for *The Face*, *Mojo*, *Country Music International*, *The Observer* etc, and is currently writing a biography of Iggy Pop.

Graeme Kay. Throat infection, no beer for a year. Better photo than last time. Severe hair cut dispensed with for something altogether more casual and alluring. Nicky and Josh doing just fine. Weather great. Wish you were here.

Jenny Kirby lives in West London, likes loud music, cooking and golf. Ambitions are to win the Football Fantasy League, and own a 1966 convertible Mustang.

Paul Lester is the only titian-haired features editor currently working for *Melody Maker* who used to ride a big, blue motorbike. Fact.

Caitlin Moran has now retired from being a teenage prodigy, and spends her time knitting and waiting to be 20. In the last *Virgin Yearbook* she asked for kittens for her birthday. She now has two kitten-fur coats and a pair of slippers. Thank-you for your support.

Andrew Mueller was born in 1968 in Wagga Wagga, Australia, and doesn't care who knows it. He is a freelance journalist based in London, where he writes about music or travel or almost anything else for *Melody Maker*, *Time Out*, *The Independent*, *Deadline* and anybody else who'll have him. His ambition is to fly his helicopter around the world.

Peter Paphides was born three days before man first landed on the moon and has quietly been upstaging major world events ever since. Between 1986 and 1991 he edited his own fanzine, *Perturbed*. In 1992 he got himself a philosophy degree. Then he did some stuff for *Melody Maker*. Then he became *Time Out*'s music editor. He's ace!

Sylvia Patterson is a freelance journalist specialising in making a complete gonzo of herself by writing about music, sex and alcohol (and sometimes all three at the same time) for *NME*, *Sky*, *FHM* and *Details Magazine USA*.

She has taken to dressing like a Nazi stormtrooper and no-one knows why. Least of all herself.

Andy Pemberton is the Deputy Editor of *Mixmag*, the world's leading dance music magazine. He's also written for *Select*, *Hip Hop Connection*, *The Daily Telegraph*, *i-D* and once made a fleeting appearence on the music programme *Raw Soup*, where he looked like "a complete prat."

Chris Roberts' compilation, *Idle Worship*, was published recently and has been described as "the most original music book ever". He has written for *Melody Maker* and countless others for several years and has just been appointed deputy editor of *Ikon* magazine. After two records with Catwalk, he is about to release his magnus opus, *Breathing Down The Neck Of Reason*, by Scalaland. His favourite record of all time is *What Love Has Joined Together* by Smokey Robinson and The Miracles, and when it comes to TV, he's very much a *NYPD Blue* man.

David Sinclair is chief rock critic for *The Times* and a contributor to *Rolling Stone* and *Q* magazine. He edits the Global Music Pulse column in Billboard, broadcasts weekly on BBC Greater London Radio and is author of *Rock On CD* (Kyle Cathie, £10.99, few copies available!).

Paul Trynka describes 1994 as "My blues year", having spent much of it tracking down blues singers in Mississippi, Chicago and New Orleans for a book to be published in 1995. Prior to his blue period, he edited and contributed to various magazines, while, according to his detractors, his career as a musician had more than a little to do with the sad demise of Factory records…

A former male model for the Grattan Catalogue, **Jon Wilde** now divides his time between novel-writing, freelance journalism and fishing for freshwater salmon. The highlight of his career to date is being compared by Dennis Potter to "the young Brian Clough when he was knocking in goals for Middlesbrough."

wilde

tryr

sinclair

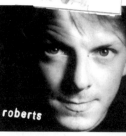
roberts

pemberton

patterson

kay

kirby

lester

moran

mueller — mr. blond

paphides